NEW
TRENDS
& ISSUES
IN TEACHING
JAPANESE
LANGUAGE
& CULTURE

NEW TRENDS & ISSUES IN TEACHING JAPANESE LANGUAGE & CULTURE

edited by
HARUKO M. COOK
KYOKO HIJIRIDA
MILDRED TAHARA

SECOND LANGUAGE TEACHING & CURRICULUM CENTER
University of Hawai'i at Mānoa

The contents of this Technical Report were developed under a grant from the Department of Education (CFDA 84.229, P229A60007). However, the contents do not necessarily represent the policy of the Department of Education, and one should not assume endorsement by the Federal Government.

ISBN 0–8248–2067–3

∞™ The paper used in this publication meets the minimum requirements of the American National Standard for Information Sciences–Permanence of Paper for Printed Library Materials.

ANSI Z39.48–1984

Book design by Deborah Masterson

Distributed by
University of Hawai'i Press
Order Department
2840 Kolowalu Street
Honolulu, HI 96822

ABOUT THE NATIONAL FOREIGN LANGUAGE RESOURCE CENTER

THE SECOND LANGUAGE TEACHING AND CURRICULUM CENTER of the University of Hawai'i is a unit of the College of Languages, Linguistics, and Literature. Under a grant from the US Department of Education, the Center has since 1990 served as a National Foreign Language Resource Center (NFLRC). The general direction of the Resource Center is set by a national advisory board. The Center conducts research, develops materials, and trains language professionals with the goal of improving foreign language instruction in the United States. The Center publishes research reports and teaching materials; it also sponsors a summer intensive teacher training institute. For additional information about Center programs, write:

Dr. Richard Schmidt, Director
National Foreign Language Resource Center
1859 East-West Road #106
University of Hawai'i
Honolulu, HI 96822

or visit our Web site: http://www.lll.hawaii.edu/nflrc

NFLRC ADVISORY BOARD

CONTENTS

Haruko M. Cook, Kyoko Hijirida, and Mildred Tahara
University of Hawai'i

PREFACE

This Technical Report includes nine papers, eight of which were presented at the Association of Teachers of Japanese (ATJ) Thursday Seminar held in Honolulu, Hawai'i in 1996 in conjunction with the Association for Asian Studies. These papers are representative of the several important issues that studies in the teaching of Japanese as a foreign language at the university level are currently addressing:

- Literature and literature teaching

- Technology in language classroom

- Orthography

- Testing

- Grammatical vs. pragmatic approaches to language teaching

Japanese literature courses are part of Japanese language programs in many colleges and universities in the United States. One of the challenging questions is how do such courses teach American students Japanese literature that is often written in a different set of cultural and historical frames of reference from those of the West. The focus of Nobuko Miyama Ochner's paper is on the different perceptions of values of students who read Japanese literature in translation. Ochner surveys students' reactions to Enchi Fumiko's *The waiting years* (*Onnazaka*, 1949–1957) which describes a long-suffering neglected wife and her ultimate revenge. Ochner concludes that the instructor must endeavor to show the students the specific historical and cultural conditions surrounding the protagonist in order that they truly understand her response to them.

One of the effective ways to teach Japanese literature is to utilize new vision technology in classroom. Visionary images take students to a specific time and place depicted in the Japanese literary work while they are in the classroom. Elaine Gerbert focuses on the role played by film and other new vision technologies which have opened up new possibilities for literary expression. Among the works she refers to as being rich in visual effects are Uno Kōji's novella, *Love of mountains* (*Yamagoi*, 1968, [original work published in 1918]), Satō's *Gloom in the country* (*Den'en no yūutsu*, 1993 [original work published in 1918]) and Tanizaki Junichirō's *The carbuncle with a human face* (*Jinmensō*, 1968 [original work published in 1918]).

The computer is a technological tool that transcends geographical and cultural boundaries and allows students to experience direct contact with people using the same technology in different countries. A new trend in the field of teaching Japanese as a foreign language is utilization of this technology. Its adaptation is already seen at many colleges and universities in the United Sates and will certainly be necessary for effective language teaching in the 21st century. Yukie Aida discusses how advanced technology, via electronic networking activities, can be integrated into Japanese language programs. Activities such as the use of personal computers, e-mail, electronic discussion and conferencing, and reading authentic materials enhance both language skills and motivation. Software and hardware requirements, their benefits and related issues are also discussed.

In learning Japanese, orthography — in particular, *kanji* (Chinese characters) — presents a great challenge for many learners of Japanese whose native language does not use *kanji*. How and when to introduce *kanji* has been a controversy. And yet there has been little scientific research on the cognitive effects on learning *kanji*. In order to develop an effective instructional strategy for teaching *kanji*, instructors of Japanese need to understand the cognitive processes underlying *kanji* learning. Hideko Shimizu reports and compares the results of recent psycholinguistic research on word identification in English orthography and that in Japanese *kanji*. She points out that these research results indicate that various levels of information, including orthographic, phonological, and semantic, are involved in processing *kanji*. She concludes that *kanji* identification skills will improve when learners are intensively exposed to the characters visually in a meaningful way.

Another problem surrounding learning *kanji* is whether or not students should be exposed to *kanji* at the beginning level. Taking the position of the primacy of spoken language and authenticity of material, some scholars (e.g., Unger, Lorish, Noda, & Wada, 1993) claim that *kanji* as well as *kana* (Japanese syllabic characters) should not be introduced at the beginning level and that romanized texts initially reduce the burden of learning Japanese. Do different approaches to *kanji* teaching influence students' belief systems on how to learn *kanji*? If so, what effects do these approaches have on students? So far there has been no scientific research on this issue; Yoko Okita's study is the first of this kind. Her study focuses on students at the University of Hawai'i at Mānoa (many of them are Japanese Americans with past Japanese learning experience) from 1994 to 1996 when the basic Japanese textbook was switched from *Japanese: the Spoken Language* (Jorden & Noda, 1987–1988) to *Situational Functional Japanese* (Tsukuba Language Group, 1992). These two textbook series represent opposite poles in Japanese pedagogy. The former takes the position of the primacy of spoken language and uses romanization whereas the latter uses *kana* and *kanji* from the beginning. Detailed statistics are provided, and Okita concludes that students' beliefs about *kanji* learning did not differ regardless of the textbook used and that beginning students require instruction on how to learn *kanji*.

The number of students enrolled in college-level Japanese language courses in the United States as of 1995 is 44,723, which ranks Japanese fourth after Spanish, French and German (MLA Newsletter, October, 1996). In fact, Japanese is the most commonly taught Asian language in the United States. As the number of students who study Japanese increases dramatically, more students enter the Japanese language program at the college level with prior training. Placement of such incoming students at an appropriate level of the Japanese class has become an increasing burden in many departments and units which offer Japanese courses. Thus, there is an urgent need to develop an effective measurement tool for placement in all Japanese language programs. Yukiko Hatasa and Yasu-Hiko Tohsaku found that SPOT (Simple Performance-Oriented Test), which was developed by Tsukuba University, is a time-saving measurement of over all language proficiency and a highly efficient and reliable test method. The authors discuss the designing principles, development process, and administration procedure as well as the interpretation of test scores for placement purposes. They also explore the possibility of SPOT as a standardized test or a proficiency test based on the conceptual validity of indirect tests and their response process.

The *cloze* procedure, which is similar to that employed by SPOT, has been studied extensively by researchers in the field of ESL. Based on the results of these studies, the cloze procedure and has been considered as a reliable measure of the inter-sentential components of language. Thus, it has been applied to testing ESL students' reading proficiency (e.g., Oller, 1979; Hinofotis, 1987). However, this procedure has not been investigated much in Japanese. Sayoko Yamashita's study is the first systematic research on the cloze test applied to Japanese. She compares native Japanese first-graders and learners of Japanese as a second language with respect to their performance on a reading comprehension cloze test. Statistical analysis indicates that while in some areas the groups performed similarly, in other areas they show significant differences. Although the cloze test used in this study has limitations, the study indicates that first and second language development are different and further provides some evidence that classroom learning improves JSL performance.

Situation-driven versus *structure-driven* language instruction has been a long-standing issue in foreign language methodology. In recent years, the current theoretical trend strongly favors situation-driven or pragmatically-oriented methodology in the second and/or foreign language teaching. In Japanese, a number of textbooks have incorporated the situational and pragmatical orientation (e.g., *Situational and Functional Japanese*, Tsukuba Language Group, 1992). The last two papers of this volume take contrastive positions with respect to this issue. Naoya Fujita's paper is a challenge to the currently favored trend of situation-driven methodology. He reexamines this old issue with the fresh insight that one approach is not necessarily superior to the other, but rather the issue of situation-driven versus structure-driven language instruction is a language-specific issue. The distance between the target language and the learner's language is the crucial point in his argument. He argues that the structure-driven approach is more suitable in teaching Japanese to native speakers of English, for it can fill the crosslinguistic conceptual gaps created by the different grammatical patterns of the two languages. He concludes that the structure-driven approach takes precedence in teaching Japanese to English speaking learners, although he acknowledges that both strategies are important and necessary in developing language proficiency. Andrew Cohen's paper was presented not at the ATJ Seminar but at the Brownbag Seminar of the ESL Department of the University of Hawai'i at Mānoa. In contrast to Fujita's position, he presents his arguments from the perspective of development of pragmatic ability. His paper is a report of his own language learning experience in one of the accelerated Japanese language classes at the University of Hawai'i. His description of the class in which he was enrolled indicates that the class was more structure-driven than situation-driven. He concludes that this approach, which requires long hours of study gives students a lot of linguistic information about the Japanese language, but pragmatic ability does not develop and retention level is low. The fact that there are diverging views such as those expressed by Fujita and Cohen is perhaps healthy for the discipline.

It is our sincere hope that the issues brought up in this volume will stimulate discussion and improve the language teaching profession.

REFERENCES

Enchi, F. (1957). Onnazaka. (N. M. Ochner, Trans.).Tokyo: Kadokawa Shoten.

Hinofotis, F. B. (1987). Cloze testing: An overview. In M. Long & J. Richards, (Eds.) Methodology in TESOL: A book of readings (pp. 412–417). Rowley, Mass: Newbury House.

Jorden, E., & Noda, M. (1987–1988). Japanese: The spoken language (Parts 1 and 2). New Haven, CT: Yale University Press.

MLA Newsletter. (1996, October). New York: Modern Language Association of America.

Oller, J. W., Jr. (1979). Language tests at school: A pragmatic approach. London: Longman.

Satō, H. (1993). Gloom in the country. In F. B. Tenny (Trans.) The sick rose, a pastoral elegy, or gloom in the country. Honolulu: University of Hawai'i Press. (Original work published in 1918)

Tanizaki J. (1968). Jinmensō [The carbuncle with a human face]. In Tanizaki Jun'ichirō zenshū [The collected works of Tanizaki Jun'ichirō] (Vol. 5, pp. 283–305). Tokyo: Chūō Kōronsha. (Original work published in 1918)

Tsukuba Language Group. (1992). Situational functional Japanese (Vols. 1–3, Note and Drill). Tokyo: Bonjinsha.

Unger, J. M., Lorish, F. C., Noda, M., and Wada, Y. (1993). A framework for introductory Japanese language curricula in American high schools and colleges. Washington DC: National Foreign Language Center.

Uno K. (1968). Yamagoi [Love of Mountains]. In Uno Kōji zenshū [The collected works of Uno Kōji] (Vol. 3, pp. 330–411). Tokyo: Chūō Kōronsha. (Original work published in 1922)

Nobuko Miyama Ochner
University of Hawai'i at Mānoa

BEYOND STEREOTYPE: TEACHING JAPANESE CULTURE THROUGH LITERATURE

INTRODUCTION

In my twelve years of teaching Japanese literature in English translation to American college students, I have encountered instances of different perceptions of values. Among the many aspects involved in the topic, the value system concerning strength and power is one of the most intriguing and troubling. Some students seem to equate a person's power over others with his or her personal strength. One of the possible explanations for such a view is that it is culturally influenced. The term *culture* is used here to refer to the way a group of people think or behave, based on their shared values. I must add that what follows is not a controlled experiment with statistical analyses or a definitive answer to the topic under discussion. Rather, it is a description of a challenging problem that I faced in my dialogue with my students, coupled with some research and reflections. Through my discussion, I wish to raise the question: can we, as teachers and interpreters of Japanese culture to American undergraduate students, "teach" culture through literature beyond stereotype? My aim, therefore, is to engage in a fruitful dialogue with colleagues to see if a similar situation exists elsewhere, and, if so, what pedagogical implications it might have.

Enchi Fumiko's[1] novel entitled *Onnazaka* (published over the period 1949–1957 and put into book form in 1957), translated into English by John Bester as *The waiting years* (1971), is perhaps one of the best examples in which this difference in values plays a key role in determining the students' interpretations of the work. That is to say, what the novel means hinges, to a significant extent, on the reader's perception of the relationship between a person's power over others and his or her strength of character.

THE AUTHOR

Enchi Fumiko (1905–1986), daughter of the philologist Ueda Kazutoshi (1867–1937), began her literary career as a playwright in the 1920s during the ascendancy of the Proletarian literary movement. However, there was a long period of silence due to marriage, childbirth, two major surgeries, and her father's death. She regained her voice in the post-World War II era, mainly through writing fiction. Many of her works focus on unhappy marriages, female psychology, and sexuality.

---

[1] In this paper, Japanese names are given in the regular Japanese order: surname (e.g., Enchi) first and given name (e.g., Fumiko) second, except for the names of those who prefer to use the Western order in their publications.

Ochner, N. (1997). Beyond stereotype: Teaching Japanese culture through literature. In H. M. Cook, K. Hijirida, & M. Tahara (Eds.), *New trends and issues in teaching Japanese language and culture* (Technical Report #15, pp. 1–14). Honolulu: University of Hawai'i, Second Language Teaching and Curriculum Center.

Among traditional Japanese literature, she was attracted to the Kabuki theater of the Edo Period (1600–1868) and the eleventh-century masterpiece *Genji monogatari* (*The tale of Genji*) by Murasaki Shikibu. In fact, Enchi even translated *Genji* into modern Japanese, publishing it in ten volumes between 1972 and 1973 (Murasaki, 1972–1973). Among the modern writers, she particularly admired the writings of the novelist Tanizaki Jun'ichirō (1886–1965). A number of Enchi Fumiko's works have been translated into English, including two book-length works, *The waiting years* [*Onnazaka*] (Enchi, 1971) and *Masks* [*Onnamen*] (Enchi, 1983), as well as such short stories as "Enchantress" [*Yō*] (Enchi, 1958), "Skeletons of men" [*Otoko no hone*] (Enchi, 1988), "A bond for two lifetimes: Gleanings" [*Nise no enishi: Shūi*] (Enchi, 1983), "Blind man's buff" [*Mekura oni*] (Enchi, 1986), and "Boxcar of chrysanthemums" [*Kikuguruma*] (Enchi, 1982).

THE NOVEL

The novel *Onnazaka*, published in several installments between 1949 and 1957 and the winner of the 1957 Noma Literary Prize, is one of the best known works by Enchi Fumiko. Yet it is somewhat atypical among her works, in that the treatment of female sexuality is more subdued than in other works by Enchi, such as *Onnamen* or "Nise no Enishi: Shūi." *Onnazaka* realistically treats the marriage of Shirakawa Tomo, who is modeled after the author's maternal grandmother (Fuke, 1989, pp. 64–65).

On the surface, the novel contains the dominant male and submissive female figures — representing the stereotypical relationship between husband and wife in the traditional Japanese family before World War II. The marital relationship between the heroine Shirakawa Tomo and her husband Yukitomo is one based on the Confucian model in which the husband is the "ruler" (*teishu kanpaku*, the term used in Lebra [1984, p. 129 and *passim*]) and the wife obeys him in every way. The narrative time span of the novel is approximately thirty years, from the mid-1880s (mid-Meiji) to the late 1910s (early Taishō). (Tomo's marriage is about fifteen years longer than the narrative time, since she married at age fifteen, and she is thirty years old at the outset of the novel.) She makes her way to Tokyo by order of her husband, the powerful chief secretary to the governor of a prefecture, to select a young inexperienced girl to be his concubine. The custom of acquiring concubines was not especially uncommon in that era; however, to have one's wife select her rival is considered unusual, judging from the reactions of those involved: the male geisha who is asked to help with the selection feels "disgust" at the lack of sensitivity of the husband (Enchi, 1971, p. 20); Shirakawa's steward thinks "the master's a queer one. . ." (Enchi, 1971, p. 32); Shirakawa's subordinate official is "astonished" to learn of the arrangement (Enchi, 1971, p. 33). Ostensibly, such an assignment shows the husband's trust in the wife, yet it is obvious that he is insensitive and selfish in his actions. Despite her distaste for the task, Tomo stoically carries out her assignment, because of her belief in Confucian ethics which taught the wife's absolute obedience to her husband. Tomo's choice, a beautiful fifteen-year-old girl, pleases her husband so much that Tomo feels insecure about her position as the wife. She considers divorce but decides against it, mainly for the sake of her two children. In the event she would one day need it, she keeps the remainder of the large sum of money given to her by her husband when she went to Tokyo. Being a scrupulously honest person by nature, she is troubled by such a secret. The bulk of the novel treats chronologically the various problems Tomo must face, caused primarily by her philandering husband, Yukitomo. For example, in time he acquires another concubine, keeping both concubines in his household as his personal maids, but legally registering them as his adopted daughters (an example of incest). Moreover, after his retirement from his government office, he comes to have liaisons with his daughter-in-law (another example of incest).

For all his licentious activities and incestuous relationships, no one reproaches him or rebels against him. Tomo accommodates her husband's wishes in practically everything — from choosing an ideal girl for her husband's first concubine, enduring the pain and shame of his taking immoral pleasure in an illicit relationship with his son's wife, to managing in an impeccable manner the household and his extensive real estate holdings. Whatever emotional distress she feels, she keeps in check through the nearly forty years of her marriage. This action of suppressing her emotions, to ensure that the family name is unsullied, requires tremendous self-control, and it is made possible only through the exercise of her powerful will. In her effort to maintain composure in painful situations, she gradually assumes the expressionless face of the No mask. Only on her deathbed, when she is in a semi-coma and no longer in full control of her rational faculties, does she give vent to any anger or resentment that she has repressed for decades: she wants her husband to "dump" her body into the sea when she dies. This action would be a symbolic divorce, since they would not be sharing the same grave in the afterlife; this would also be a concrete physical manifestation of the way her husband has treated her in life. The effect of Tomo's words on her husband is "enough to split his arrogant ego in two" (Enchi, 1971, p. 203).

READERS' RESPONSES

The novel The waiting years was read in a semester-long undergraduate course on modern Japanese fiction in English translation, a course which was open to all students regardless of their majors. Seven novels were read and discussed in their entirety; these works dealt mostly with human relationships in marriage and family in the modern period in Japan (i.e., since 1868), with the exception of one novel focusing directly on World War II, which had a profound and devastating effect on the Japanese people. The course was designated as a "writing intensive" course, which meant that the students were required to write a minimum of sixteen pages during the semester and to use writing to learn the subject matter of the course. Each student was required to keep a reading journal, in which he or she wrote seven times per semester (one for each novel). Also required were two short papers on assigned topics and a term paper (draft and revision required) on the topic of the student's choice dealing with the works read in the course. The reading journal proved to be particularly valuable in eliciting the student's unprompted responses, that is, in finding what the student considered important or interesting.

The students' responses to the novel have been mixed. Most students, as I would expect, recognize the inner strength of the outwardly submissive wife, in contrast to the relative inner weakness of the powerful and dominant husband. The author Enchi underscores the relative strength of the couple specifically on two occasions. First is the recollected scene from their early years of marriage, in which Tomo shows presence of mind and inner strength in throwing out a snake which has crept into their bedroom, before Yukitomo can even react. This example of Tomo's show of "strength that was a fraction greater than his own" (Enchi, 1971, p. 16) causes her husband to gradually lose his desire for her, leading eventually to his acquisition of meek and naive concubines. On the second occasion, Yukitomo returns from a ball at the Rokumeikan, an architectural symbol of the Meiji government's policy of Westernization, where he has chanced upon his former enemy now flourishing. Feeling threatened by the approaching new age and the end of his era, he wishes for comfort and support from his wife. Yukitomo "wanted to place his daunted spirit in Tomo's protective arms... The wound could only be soothed, the blood only staunched, by a woman stronger and more resilient of will than himself" (Enchi, 1971, p. 78). It is clear that the author is portraying the wife as being inwardly stronger than her husband.

In fact, the author's own afterword to the Japanese edition of the novel *Onnazaka* states that she conceived of the story as a struggle between the husband and wife:

> The heroine, Tomo, depicted in this novel has not received intellectual training, but she is prompted not by instinct but always by ethical code and ideas. The ties of the "household" and "husband" that bind her are unrelenting, but by handling those constraints (*kizuna o tadotte*) she advances forward and develops into a strong person. I wanted to portray the struggle between a man, who lived his life, clinging to much of the feudalistic thinking and complacently occupying his seat as "husband, the ruler" (*teishu kanpaku*), and his wife, who had within her the budding intellect. (Enchi, 1957, p. 191; English translation by N. M. Ochner)

Despite the author's unambiguous portrayal of the wife's strength, some students have commented in their writing that the wife is weak, or the husband is strong. Two examples follow.

The first student response is written by a female student estimated to be in her early twenties; she appears to fit the profile of regular undergraduate students at the University of Hawai'i at Mānoa. Below is an excerpt from the student reading journal, a free writing assigned as a part of the writing intensive component of the course:

> It seems that Enchi wrote from the heart and conveyed a realistic insight into Tomo. The story was too upsetting to me, which caused me not to enjoy the book. I disliked the acceptance of mistresses and concubine by Tomo. The weakness and lack of self-esteem in Tomo made me so angry. (student journal, Spring 1995)

The student is clearly equating Tomo's lack of outward protest, of not standing up to her husband, with her "weakness and lack of self-esteem." In other words, Tomo's apparent powerlessness against her husband is seen as her weakness. ("Lack of self-esteem" is an expression often used in contemporary popularized discourse of psychology; many personal problems are explained in such terms in the United States.)

Another example of student response comes from a short analytical paper comparing two novels, *The waiting years* by Enchi Fumiko and *The wild geese* [*Gan*] (Mori, 1959) by Mori Ōgai (1862–1922). The writer of the paper is a male student estimated to be in his thirties, with a US mainland background. An excerpt from the paper is as follows:

> The actions of Suezo [the money lender and unfaithful husband in *The wild geese*] and Shirakawa [Yukitomo], of course, differ only in degree. Suezo, being at heart a weakling — or, if one prefers, pretentiously moral — must sneak about and plot childishly to achieve his aims. Shirakawa, on the other hand, is an extremely strong and powerful individual with no sympathy for weakness. He knows what he wants and takes it. (student paper, Spring 1995)

To this student, Shirakawa Yukitomo is "an extremely strong and powerful individual." Clearly, the student equates Yukitomo's power, as the head of the household and a high-ranking official, with his personal strength. In addition, the student apparently thinks that being strong means being ruthless and amoral, as well as having power.

These responses seem to indicate types of perception influenced by cultural stereotypes. A stereotype is defined as "a standardized mental picture held in common by members of a group and representing an oversimplified opinion, affective attitude, or uncritical judgment (as of a person, a race, an issue, or an event)" (Gove, 1971); in this case the stereotypes are the dominant male and the submissive female in Japan. These student responses also indicate different standards of personal conduct, a different system of values, from the one Enchi envisioned, and these value systems seem to be culturally defined. (At this point, let me reiterate that the responses cited above are only a portion of the student responses rather than being representative. However, they forced me to confront a cultural "Other," that is, to consider assumptions different from my own, hence a challenge in teaching Japanese literature and culture in the United States. The present study is somewhat analogous to what may be termed "error-analysis" in second language teaching research, since this may be a case of the students' "native" culture interfering with their comprehension of the "target" culture.)

PLACING IN CONTEXT

In our reading process, Terry Eagleton reminds us, "we always interpret literary works to some extent in the light of our own concerns…" (Eagleton, 1983, p. 12).

He also adds that "[a]ll literary works... are 'rewritten,' if only unconsciously, by the societies which read them," but that process may be "one reason why certain works of literature seem to retain their value across the centuries" (Eagleton, 1983, p. 12). Richard Beach categorizes theoretical perspectives on the examination of reading process in his 1993 study of the students' reading in English literature courses as follows: a) textual, b) experiential, c) psychological, d) social, and e) cultural. Beach states that these perspectives are moving from the specific to the global in this sequence, somewhat paralleling the historical development of criticism in the twentieth century. Recent concerns among literary critics appear to be moving toward social and cultural perspectives. Cultural theorists, for example, "focus on how readers' cultural roles, attitudes, and values, as well as the larger cultural, historical context, shape responses," in other words, "how readers create meaning" (Beach, 1993, p. 9). These views seem to justify an approach to understanding the students' responses to literary works in terms of cultural contexts.

My next step, therefore, was to determine, if possible, whether these student responses were isolated cases or a part of a larger phenomenon. Stereotypes are held in common by a group of people, usually the general public rather than specialists in a field — this is the distinction between the "latent" (general public's) and the "manifest" (specialists') attitudes referred to by Edward Said in his discussion of Orientalism (Said, 1979, p. 206); therefore, checking book reviews in the United States seemed to offer a glimpse into the opinions of the so-called general American readers regarding the marital relationship in Enchi's novel.

My search of the reviews of *The waiting years* uncovered an interesting fact: the attention reviewers paid to the English translations of *Onnazaka* (*The waiting years*) and another novel by Enchi titled *Onnamen* (*Masks*) differed significantly. According to *Book Review Index*, *The waiting years* (published in 1971) received six reviews in 23 years, between 1972 and 1994; whereas *Masks*, translated by Juliet Winters Carpenter (published in 1983) garnered 11 reviews in three years, between 1983 and 1985. The difference may be due to the presence or absence of Enchi's prior publication record in the United States — in other words, whether she was a known writer to the reviewers. However, it may also be because *The waiting years* describes a situation fitting the stereotype of the seemingly dominant male and submissive female, and hence lacking in surprise; whereas *Masks* depicts a powerful female who manipulates males, a clearly atypical and hence an "intriguing" (*Booklist*, 1983, p. 1187) Japanese work from the Western perspective. The influence of feminism in the 1980s in the United States may also have played a part in this phenomenon. It is, of course, impossible to be certain of precise reasons for reviewers' choices.

As for the book reviews of *The waiting years*, I examined the six available reviews but found no specific reference to Tomo's strength. They refer to Tomo's endurance, "resigned shame," and "hidden passion" (*Booklist*, 1972, p. 487), or to Tomo as "a woman with much bitterness walled up inside her icy exterior" (Burk, 1972), or to Tomo as "a woman trapped within a traditional marriage" (*Quill & Quire*, 1980, p. 40), or to Tomo as the suppressed wife who "silently bears this humiliation... until her final minutes of life" when "she makes a quiet, defiant and final gesture of indignation against her husband" (Blewitt, 1981, p. 45), or, again, to Tomo as the "oppressed... quiet and attractive wife" who "silently suffers" (Sakurai, 1981, p. 728), and to the novel as a depiction of "the heartrending social predicament faced by Japanese women at that time" (Ms., 1994, p. 74).

Because the book reviews were too few to be a sufficient basis, I turned to the reference works and critical commentaries on the novel and the writer. This shift in my study, to include the opinions of specialists, made it more problematic simply to connect the results to broader cultural assumptions. Needless to say, specialists are more knowledgeable and less likely to be influenced by stereotypes than non-specialists. Nevertheless, in the hope of finding some pattern, I included sources available to me in my research. Twenty-seven sources were consulted; out of these, eleven were written by Japanese in the Japanese language; sixteen were written in English by critics in the United States, Japan, and Europe.

These sources were divided into three groups: (a) those containing no evaluative comments on the character of Tomo, hence not useful to the given topic, (b) those containing no references to Tomo's strength, except the term "endurance," or *nintai*, and (c) those referring to Tomo's strength. (The interpretation of "endurance" is a point that may raise questions, since an ability to endure hardship can be a type of strength. However, in Tomo's case, my reading of the novel emphasizes her strength of will in choosing to stand her ground and reprove her husband's immorality by her exemplary moral action. The name Tomo is written in the character which is the first element in the compound *rinri* 'ethical code', a rather unusual character for a woman's name, obviously chosen by Enchi for its symbolic significance. Therefore, the term "endurance" alone seems inadequate to describe Tomo.)

Category one, for those with no comment on Tomo's character, has three sources, all brief accounts in reference works (Nakamura, 1969; Hisamatsu, 1976; *Kōdansha encyclopedia of Japan*, 1983).

Category two, those with no reference to Tomo's strength, includes 11 sources (six Japanese, four American, and one European). The six Japanese sources are from the 1950s through the 1970s, five written by men, one by a woman; the four American sources are from the 1980s and the 1990s, two by women and two by men; the European source is from the 1990s, written by a woman (see Table 1).

Table 1: Category two

decade	Japanese	American	European
1950s	2	0	0
1960s	2	0	0
1970s	2	0	0
1980s	0	2	0
1990s	0	2	1

The comments range in focus from Tomo's personality traits to her situation. For example, Kamei Katsuichirō notes Tomo's "tenacity and pathos" (cited in Rieger, 1986, p. 89); Takami Jun sees in Tomo "a prototype of the woman in the Meiji era and a type of universal image of woman" (Takami, 1973, p. 187); Shibukawa Gyō notes Tomo's sad heart and perseverance (Shibukawa, 1960, p.139); Mishima Yukio describes the novel as "a typical representation of the sensibilities and will of the Japanese woman" (Mishima, 1966, pp. 147–148); Etō Jun regards Tomo as the example of "Enchi's first 'fixing' of the type of woman who endures the weight of 'women's secrets,' without changing facials expressions, just like Nō masks" (Etō, 1971, p. 419). Takenishi Hiroko comments on Tomo's "enduring the humiliation of living with her husband's concubines" (Takenishi, 1977, p. 237). Yoko McClain states that "the stoic heroine endures long years of humiliation by her husband" (McClain, 1980, p. 32); Van C. Gessel compares Tomo to the "long suffering" Lady Aoi in *The tale of Genji* (Gessel, 1988, p. 310); Yumiko Hulvey describes the novel as "the story of a woman oppressed by patriarchal society" and notes Tomo's "stoicism," but states that "the focal point of the novel is the psychological damage inflicted upon women in a polygynous household" (Hulvey, 1994, pp. 51–52); Sachiko Schierbeck also notes "the plight of women who had no alternative but to accept the demeaning roles that the patriarchal family system had assigned to them" (Schierbeck, 1994, p. 113). Thus, the last two women critics seem to regard Tomo and the other female characters as victims of the "patriarchal" system. Hence, they seem to regard Tomo as a relatively "weak" character.

Interestingly, Wayne Pounds finds, in his comparison of Tomo and Mieko, the heroine of *Masks*, that "Mieko's 'shamanistic' vengeance seems preferable to Tomo's stoicism, since it is an active rather than a passive response to the injustice of which she is a victim" (Pounds, 1990, p. 170). Pounds' valorization of activeness in contrast to passivity seems revealing as another case of culturally influenced evaluation, at least in part, because the "active" Mieko manipulates others and even sacrifices her daughter's life in fulfilling her wish (i.e., self-fulfillment), while the "passive" Tomo suppresses her emotions to keep the family together (i.e., self-abnegation). The anthropologist George DeVos tells us that the "Japanese ethical ideal of the self-sacrificing role of woman" as seen in plays and novels is "considered very moving by the Japanese." (DeVos, 1986, pp. 96–97). In other words, self-sacrifice or self-abnegation is appreciated more highly in Japanese culture than in American culture, while self-fulfillment seems to be more highly regarded in the United States than in Japan.

To sum up category two, the above-cited critics, who comprise nearly half of the number surveyed, do not refer to Tomo's strength (other than stoic endurance); moreover, some of them regard her as a passive character. In that sense, they partially underscore the first student's response that Tomo is "weak."

The third category, those referring to Tomo's strength, comprises thirteen sources (five Japanese, seven American, and one European). The five Japanese sources range from the 1960s to the 1990s, all written by men; the seven American sources are from the 1980s and the 1990s, three by men and four by women; the European source is from the 1980s, written by a woman (see Table 2).

Table 2: Category three

decade	Japanese	American	European
1950s	0	0	0
1960s	2	0	0
1970s	1	0	0
1980s	1	3	1
1990s	1	4	0

In their descriptions, these critics note Tomo's strength: for example, Komatsu Shinroku refers to Tomo as "a woman who has strong sense of self hidden within" (Komatsu, 1962, p. 537). Senuma Shigeki also points out Tomo's "innate intelligence and tenacious will power" and "stern will" (*reigen na ishi*) (Senuma, 1966, p. 422). Okuno Takeo compares Tomo's character to Lady Rokujō's in *The tale of Genji*, because, like Rokujō who is more than Genji's match in strength of character, Tomo "cannot be overcome" by Yukitomo (Okuno, 1974, pp. 135–136). Yamaguchi Shōji notes how Tomo's strength makes her seem like an elder sister to her husband, causing him to lose his desire for her (Yamaguchi, 1988, p. 153). Uesaka Nobuo notes Tomo's "struggle" (*tatakai*, which also means "fight," "combat," or "battle") against her husband, thus suggesting that Tomo's personality is anything but weak or submissive (Uesaka, 1993, p. 133).

Similar descriptions are given by American and European critics: Alfred Marks and Barry Bort label Tomo as "a strong, capable, and long-suffering wife" (Marks and Bort, 1984, p. 116). This description is also echoed by Reiko Nemoto (Nemoto, 1989, p. 500). Naoko Alisa Rieger regards Tomo as "an introspective, sensible, reserved and strong-minded woman," who wages in her mind a "fierce fight against the male principle" (Rieger, 1986, pp. 169, 170). Victoria Vernon notes "both the strength and the vulnerability of a woman raised in the Tokugawa mold" (Vernon, 1988, p. 160). However, Vernon is somewhat of an exceptional case, because, despite her reference to Tomo's strength, she focuses on Tomo's situation of being trapped in the oppressive family system (Vernon, 1988, pp. 160–163). Claire Mamola comments on how Tomo's "iron will" enables her to fulfill her responsibilities to the family (Mamola, 1989, p. 27). Juliet Winters Carpenter notes that, despite Tomo's "compliant and meek" appearance, her "unspoken protests" against her husband increase in time until she has her "revenge" on her deathbed (Carpenter, 1990, p. 352). John Lewell notes the "battle of wills" between the couple and comments on Tomo's "unshakable determination to show not the slightest trace of resentment" (Lewell, 1993, p. 75). As seen above, these critics refer to Tomo's strength, perseverance, and resilience.

CONCLUSION

The above survey of the specialists' views of strength in relation to power in *The waiting years* indicates that the opinions are split more or less evenly along both the gender and nationality lines, as well as chronological spread. Even though the survey appears numerically inconclusive, nonetheless, a number of observations may be made. One potentially meaningful fact is that more women critics than men in the United States and Europe refer to the "patriarchal" system, such as that of the family or society of Meiji Japan. The references to the patriarchal system, which imply woman's powerlessness within it, are accompanied by no reference to Tomo's strength; this seems to indicate that for those critics being powerless means being weak. Another revealing point is that an American critic and a reviewer find the manipulative and self-absorbed woman "active," "intriguing," and "preferable" to the stoic woman who puts others' interest before her own. The same type of disregard for others that Yukitomo shows is considered "strength" by the second student. Such assessment points out cultural differences between the United States and Japan. Thus, even with the inherent limitations noted above, the survey was helpful in shedding additional light on the topic.

Considering the topic from another perspective, the point may simply be a difference in emphasis: a focus on Tomo's situation may show her as a "passive" figure of stoic resignation and endurance; whereas a focus on Tomo's thoughts and emotions may emphasize her strength and will power. Returning to the two student responses, the first response that sees Tomo's "weakness" seems to be based on Tomo's doing nothing about her husband's blatant philandering, that is, her lack of action to change the situation. In this connection, it is interesting to note that, according to the anthropologist Takie Sugiyama Lebra in her study of "compensative justice and moral investment among Japanese, Chinese, and Koreans," the Japanese "place more importance than do the other groups on the 'human' consequence, instead of an external outcome, of perseverance" (Lebra, 1986, p. 49), and that the "Japanese tend to seek compensation for moral or immoral action in the inner state of feeling," such as feeling good for having been kind (Lebra, 1986, p. 58). It is possible that, in pointing out Tomo's "weakness," that is, inability to produce a favorable outcome, the student was working from her own non-Japanese value system. Needless to say, a person's value system is an inseparable part of one's culture in which one is embedded. It is historical and culture-specific. It may be called one's *positionality* (cf. Miyoshi, 1991, p. 123 and *passim*).

I believe that one of the basic endeavors of teachers of another culture is to try to show the students the specific historical and cultural conditions that shaped the protagonist's world as well as the characters' responses (both external and internal) to these conditions; simultaneously we need to remain alert to the students', as well as our own, respective cultural positions vis-a-vis the work. As basic as it may be, my encounter with different cultural "positions" of some students made me keenly aware of how challenging it can be at times to succeed in it.

Acknowledgment

The author is grateful to Kathy Phillips for providing valuable comments on an earlier draft of this paper.

REFERENCES

Beach, R. (1993). *A teacher's introduction to reader-response theories*. Urbana: National Council of Teachers of English.

Book Review Index. (1972–1994). Detroit: Gale Research.

Blewitt, C. G. (1981). Review of *The waiting years*. *Best Sellers, 41* (2), 45.

Burk, A. M. (1972). Review of *The waiting years*. *Library Journal, 97* (7), 1345.

Carpenter, J. W. (1990). Enchi Fumiko: 'A writer of tales'. *Japan Quarterly, 32* (3), 343–355.

DeVos, G. (1986). The relation of guilt toward parents to achievement and arranged marriage among the Japanese. In T. S. Lebra & W. P. Lebra (Eds.), *Japanese culture and behavior*. (Rev. ed.) (pp. 80–101). Honolulu: University of Hawai'i Press.

Eagleton, T. (1983). *Literary theory: An introduction*. Minneapolis: University of Minnesota Press.

Enchi, F. (1957). *Onnazaka*. Tokyo: Kadokawa Shoten. (Original serial publication 1949–1957)

Enchi, F. (1958). Enchantress. (J. Bester, Trans.). *Japan Quarterly, 5* (3), 339–357. (Original work, *Yō*, published 1956)

Enchi, F. (1971). *The waiting years*. (J. Bester, Trans.). Tokyo, New York: Kodansha International. (Original work, *Onnazaka*, published serially 1949–1957)

Enchi, F. (1982). Boxcar of chrysanthemums. (Y. Tanaka & E. Hanson, Trans.). In Y. Tanaka & E. Hanson (Eds.), *This kind of woman: Tenstories by Japanese women writers 1960–1976* (pp. 69–86). New York: Putnam. (Original work, *Kikuguruma*, published 1967)

Enchi, F. (1983). A bond for two lifetimes: Gleanings. (P. Birnbaum, Trans.). In P. Birnbaum (Ed.), *Rabbits, crabs, etc.* (pp. 25–47). Honolulu: University of Hawai'i Press. (Original work, *Nise no enishi: shūi*, published 1957)

Enchi, F. (1983). *Masks.* (J. W. Carpenter, Trans.). New York: Knopf. (Original work, *Onnamen*, published 1958)

Enchi, F. (1986). Blind man's buff. (B. Cary, Trans.). In M. Ueda (Ed.), *The mother of dreams and other short stories: Portrayals of women in modern Japanese fiction* (pp. 165–177). Tokyo, New York: Kodansha International. (Original work, *Mekura oni*, published 1962)

Enchi, F. (1988). Skeletons of men. (S. Matisoff, Trans.). *Japan Quarterly, 35* (4), 417–426. (Original work, *Otoko no hone*, published 1956)

Etō, J. (1971). Kaisetsu [Commentary]. In *Enchi Fumiko shū* (Enchi Fumiko's works] (pp. 408–419). Tokyo: Shinchōsha.

Fuke, M. (1989). *Haha, Enchi Fumiko* [My mother, Enchi Fumiko]. Tokyo: Shinchōsha.

Gessel, V. C. (1988). The 'medium' of fiction: Fumiko Enchi as narrator. *World Literature Today, 62* (3). 380–385.

Gove, P. B. (Ed.). (1971). *Webster's third new international dictionary of the English language, unabridged.* Springfield, MA: G. & C. Merriam.

Hisamatsu, S. (1976). *Biographical dictionary of Japanese literature.* Tokyo: Kōdansha International.

Hulvey, S. Y. (1994). Enchi Fumiko. In C. I. Mulhern (Ed.), *Japanese women writers: A bio-critical sourcebook* (pp. 40–60). Westport, CT & London: Greenwood Press.

Komatsu, S. (1962). Kaisetsu [Commentary]. In F. Enchi & A.Kōda (Eds.) *Shōwa bungaku zenshū* [Collected works of Shōwa literature], (Vol. 15, pp. 537–543). Tokyo: Kadokawa Shoten.

Kōdansha encyclopedia of Japan (Vol. 2). (1983). Tokyo: Kōdansha

Lebra, T. S. (1986). Compensative justice and moral investment among Japanese, Chinese, and Koreans. In T. S. Lebra & W. P. Lebra (Eds.), *Japanese culture and behavior*, (Rev. ed.) (pp. 49–61). Honolulu: University of Hawai'i Press. (First ed. 1974)

Lebra, T. S. (1984). *Japanese women: constraint and fulfillment.* Honolulu: University of Hawai'i Press.

Lewell, J. (1993). *Modern Japanese novelists: A biographical dictionary.* New York: Kōdansha International.

Mamola, C. Z. (1989). *Japanese women writers in English translation: An annotated bibliography* (Vol. 1). New York: Garland Publishing.

Marks, A. H. & B. D. Bort (Eds.), (1984). *Guide to Japanese prose.* (2nd ed.) Boston: G. K. Hall.

McClain, Y. (1980). Eroticism and the writings of Enchi Fumiko. *Journal of the Association of Teachers of Japanese, 15* (1), 32–46.

Mishima, Y. (1966). Enchi Fumiko. In *Mishima Yukio hyōron zenshū* [Complete critical writings by Mishima Yukio] (pp. 145–154). Tokyo: Shinchōsha. (First published in 1964 in *Gendai no bungaku*. Tokyo: Kawade Shobō)

Miyoshi, M. (1991). *Off center: Power and culture relations between Japan and the United States*. Cambridge: Harvard University Press.

Mori, Ō. (1959). *The wild geese*. (K. Ochiai & S. Goldstein, Trans.). Tokyo: Rutland & Tuttle. (Original work, *Gan*, published 1911–1913).

Murasaki, S. (1972–1973). *Genji monogatari* [The tale of Genji] (Vol. 1–10). (Enchi, F., Trans.). Tokyo: Shinchōsha. (Original work written in 11th century)

Nakamura, M. (1969). *Contemporary Japanese fiction, 1926–1968*. Tokyo: Kokusai Bunka Shinkōkai.

Nemoto, R. (1989). Fumiko Enchi. In F. N. Magill (Ed.), *Encyclopedia of world authors* (Vol. 2, pp. 499–500). Pasadena: SalemPress.

Okuno, T. (1974). *Joryū sakka ron* [On women writers]. Tokyo: Daisan Bunmei sha.

Pounds, W. (1990). Enchi Fumiko and the hidden energy of the supernatural. *Journal of the Association of Teachers of Japanese, 24* (2), 167–183.

Masks [Reveiw]. (1983). *The Booklist, 79* (18), 1187.

The waiting years [Reveiw]. (1972). *The Booklist, 68* (12), 487–488.

The waiting years [Reveiw]. (1980). *Quill and Quire, 46* (November), 47.

The waiting years] [Reveiw]. (1994). *Ms., 4* (May), 74.

Rieger, N. A. (1986). *Enchi Fumiko's literature: The portrait of women in Enchi Fumiko's selected works*. Hamburg: Gesellschaft für Natur- und Völkerkunde Ostasiens.

Said, E. W. (1979). *Orientalism*. New York: Vintage Books.

Sakurai, E. (1981). Review of *The waiting years. World Literature Today, 55* (4), 728.

Schierbeck, S. (1994). *Japanese women novelists in the 20th century: 104 biographies 1900–1993*. Copenhagen: Museum Tusculanum Press.

Senuma, S. (1966). Sakuhin kaisetsu [Commentary on the works]. In S. Itō, K. Kamei, M. Nakamura, K. Hirano, & K. Yamamoto (Eds.), *Enchi Fumiko, Kōda Aya shū* (Works of Enchi Fumiko and Kōda Aya] (pp. 421–427). Nihon gendai bungaku zenshū (Collected works of modern Japanese literature], vol. 96. Tokyo: Kōdansha.

Shibukawa, G. (1960). Onnazaka. In Yoshida Seiichi (Ed.), *Nihon bungaku kanshō jiten: kindaihen* [Dictionary of Japanese literature appreciation: Modern period] (pp. 138–140). Tokyo: Tōkyōdō.

Takami, J. (1973). Onnazaka ni tsuite [On *The waiting years*]. In *Takami Jun zenshū* (Collected works of Takami Jun] (Vol. 16, pp. 187–191). Tokyo: Keisō Shobō. (First published in 1959 in Enchi Fumiko, *Kadokawa Bunko*. Tokyo: Kadokawa Shoten.)

Takenishi, H. (1977). Enchi Fumiko. In *Nihon Kindai Bungakukan (Comp.), Nihon kindai bungaku daijiten* [Dictionary of modern Japanese literature] (Vol. 1, pp. 235–237). Tokyo: Kōdansha.

Uesaka, N. (1993). *Enchi Fumiko: Sono Genji monogatari henshō* [Enchi Fumiko: Reflections of *The tale of Genji* on her works]. Tokyo: Yūbun Shoin.

Vernon, V. V. (1988). *Daughters of the moon: Wish, will, and social constraint in fiction by modern Japanese women*. Berkeley: Institute of East Asian Studies, University of California.

Yamaguchi, S. (1988). Onnazaka. In Y. Inoue, M. Nagai, K. Fukuda, S. Matsunami, S. Miura, Y. Miyoshi, & K. Yamamoto (Eds.), *Nihon bungei kanshō jiten, 1988* [Dictionary for appreciating Japanese literary works, 1988] (Vol. 17, pp. 147–156). Tokyo: Gyōsei.

Elaine Gerbert
University of Kansas

A NEW LOOK: THE INFLUENCE OF VISION TECHNOLOGY ON NARRATIVE IN TAISHŌ

It is no revelation to say that certain technological inventions and innovations, regardless of the time and place they occur, and the cultural changes they engender, are some of the most constant markers, from narrations to narrations, of human history.

Today, writes J. Crary, "a transformation in the nature of visuality" is taking place "probably more profound than the break that separated medieval imagery from renaissance perspective." He mentions computer animation, robotic image recognition, synthetic holography, magnetic resonance imaging, and multispectral sensors as some of the technologies of image production that have effected "a sweeping reconfiguration of relations between observing subject and modes of representation," and are thereby transforming the ways in which individuals and institutions function in society (Crary, 1990, p. 2).

In retrospect, it seems that modern Japan in Meiji Taishō underwent similar shifts in perspective that reordered the ways in which individuals and the society as a whole saw itself. By considering some of the technologies of vision that were instrumental in effecting new relationships between the observing subject and the world, this paper seeks to participate in a larger discourse on vision and visuality in modern Japanese literature, and beyond it, in Japanese culture.

That Meiji Taishō was an age in which new optically constructed spaces emerged, transforming the position of the observer vis-à-vis the world, can hardly be contested. These shifts in modes of viewing were accompanied by fundamental changes in the intellectual frameworks by which ordinary Japanese saw themselves, frameworks that were constantly dismantled, adjusted, and enlarged through challenges posed in the fields of education, media communications, and popular culture (Tanaka, 1993). Public spectacles and exhibitions enabled ordinary Japanese to see the world anew, and to be changed by what they saw. "The most spectacular of spectacles... were the expositions that were organized in the name of industry and nationhood" (Silverberg, 1993, 127). The showcasing of new commodities such as "the nation's first escalator... the gas bathtub, stove, and range" in the Tokyo Taishō Exposition of 1914 conveyed the idea of modernity in all its shining glamour (Silverberg, 1993), while the Taiwan and Korea rooms of the same exposition, and later the addition of the South Pacific room in the Tokyo Peace Exhibition of 1922, brought home to viewers in a concrete tangible way the idea of an imperial Japan and its emerging significance as a colonial and world power.

Gerbert, E. (1997). A new look: The influence of vision technology on narrative in Taishō. In H. M. Cook, K. Hijirida, & M. Tahara (Eds.), *New trends and issues in teaching Japanese language and culture* (Technical Report #15, pp. 15–30). Honolulu: University of Hawai'i, Second Language Teaching and Curriculum Center.

With the establishment of western style department stores and merchandising, commodity display and poster advertising became additional forces determining what urban dwellers should look at and how they should see it. The seductive power of these displays was enhanced by the technologies of illumination, such as electric lighting established in Tokyo in the first fifteen years of the century (gas lamps were replaced with electric lights on the streets of Tokyo between 1912 and 1915) and by the new technologies of display, which included the importation of recently invented plate glass for show windows.[1] Soon neon lights would be included among the ways in which the urban landscape dazzled the eye. In the meantime, new modes of transportation — the train, the trolley, and automobile — introduced new relationships between motion, space, and vision.

New technologies of sight led to the creation of centers where the techniques of seeing were commodified. Asakusa,[2] a site of public exhibition of popular types of amusement during Edo, was one such place for the reception of western culture filtered through the vision mediating devices of dioramas, panoramas, stereoscopes, kinetoscopes, and, eventually, moving pictures.[3] These new optical devices created new positions for the observer, who was now situated inside an enclosed space that was dark and private. Like the impersonal spaces of new urban centers themselves, the darkness of the spaces of the movie theaters offered new opportunities to experience anonymity and freedom from the gaze of the known Other. Fantasies generated by visual images on the screen would be individual and personal. In the words of Crary, "the dark isolated center where the viewer sat came to constitute the single definable point from which the world could be logically deduced and represented (Crary, 1990, p. 6).

---

[1] Show windows, like exhibitions and movies, were important venues for introducing western commodity culture to the Japanese. Noguchi Fujio names Wrigley's chewing gum, Libby's corned beef, Sunmaid raisin, S&W canned fruit, and florist shops with "Say it with Flowers" signs as some of the items on display in Tokyo during Taishō (Kawamoto, 1990, p. 250).

[2] Entertainments located in Asakusa "Rokku," Tokyo's sprawling entertainment district — where Japanese cinema would soon find its first spiritual "hometown", included storyboard men, nozoki karakuri peep boxes, all-female Kabuki theaters, the Chinseikan (World of Amazements Hall) which featured a vaudeville-like mixture of acts; two Edison Kinetoscope boxes introduced into Japan in 1896, the Taiseikan theater which specialized in tamanori or "ball riders," yose halls featuring rakugo performances, and motion pictures theaters (High, 1984, pp. 30–31).

[3] According to Peter B. High the first film showing in Japan took place at the Nanchi Theater in Osaka in 1897 (High, 1984, pp. 24) and the nation's first permanent movie theater was the Denkikan ("Electricity Hall") in Asakusa, which opened in 1903. (High, 1984, p. 32). "By 1908–09, promotion of film had grown by leaps and bounds. In almost every substantial-sized town in the nation, there was furious competition to see who could put up the first movie theater." (High, 1984, pp. 49–50). Movies and movie magazines spread quickly throughout the newly emerging urban centers, and by mid-Taishō the most popular features of the new consumer culture were the three k's of "kuruma, katsudō shashin, kafue" (cars, motion pictures, cafes), (Kawamoto, 1990, p. 80). By 1926 there were 1,056 movie theaters in Japan, showing both Western and Japanese films (Silverberg, 1993, p. 124).

Fittingly, Donald Keene's *Modern Japanese literature*, which gives an overview of fiction from Meiji through Shōwa (Keene, 1956, pp. 34–36), opens with a translated excerpt from Hattori Busho's satirical *Tokyo shin hanjō ki* (A record of new prosperity in Tokyo, 1874), written in *kambun*, in which Hattori describes the western peep shows of Asakusa: viewing parlors several stories tall, wherein viewing machines, placed at intervals several feet apart, allowed the customer to go from one machine to another, peeping through eye pieces attached to the machines like eyes of a giant snake, at the spectacular wonders of countries all over the world. Dioramas[4] were touted as satisfying not only a hunger for entertainment, but, given the determinedly utilitarian positivistic spirit of the times and the impulse to learn and rise in the world *(risshin shusse)*, of popular instruction as well. Hattori underlines their educational value. Whether it be a steel bridge in London, a palace in Paris, a Russian general, an American fire, a warship, a steam engine, or a hot air balloon, the peep show offers the latest curiosities of the world and the customs of every nation. To experience them is like touring the world at a glance, broadening people's knowledge while delighting their eyes, writes Hattori (Keene, 1956, pp. 34).

Forty-three years later, in the essay *Katsudō shashin no genzai to shōrai* (*The present and future of motion pictures*, 1917), Tanizaki Jun'ichirō would praise the educational value of motion pictures, which he called "the art form with the most promising future." He noted the important role that movies played in teaching Japanese about the customs and manners of foreigners and expressed the hope that in the future foreigners would in turn be able to learn about Japan through Japanese films.

This marvelous new technology could transcend the limitations of time and space that bound theatrical performances; it could transport the viewer backward and forward in time at will, and in an instant bring spots separated geographically by miles before the eyes of the observer. Using close up shots, directors could focus the attention of the audience upon fine details and dramatically shrink the distance between actors and audience. Motion pictures were permanent in contrast to the short lives of theatrical productions, which were limited to the times of their performances.

For Tanizaki, movies were also the art form "most in keeping with the democratic temper of the times" (Tanizaki, 1917, pp. 13–14). Movies could be duplicated and shown to mass audiences, including international audiences, and could thus inspire actors to the greatest heights of achievement. Movies were not only less expensive to attend, but in the movie theater the distinction between expensive orchestra

---

[4] Credit for the invention of the diorama is assigned to Louis-Jacques-Mande Daguerre, a French painter, physicist, and inventor of the daguerreotype, who, with his coworker Charles Marie Bruton opened an exhibit in Paris in 1822 that he called the Diorama. Crary sees the diorama, the kaleidoscope (invented in 1815 by David Brewster), and the stereoscope as marking fundamental shifts in the position of the observer. "Unlike the static panorama painting that first appeared in the 1790's, the diorama is based on the incorporation of an immobile observer into a mechanical apparatus and a subjection of a predesigned temporal unfolding of optical experience." (Crary, 1990, p. 112–113).

seats and less expensive balcony seats was minimized as one had a more or less equal view of the details on the screen no matter where one sat.

Tanizaki wrote about film again three years later in the essay, *Tokyo o omou*, (*Thinking of Tokyo*, 1920) (Tanizaki, 1968c). Reminiscing on life in Tokyo in 1918, he recalled that nothing was more pleasurable than to go to the Teikokukan or the Odeon-za, where the silver screen brought the enchanting exoticism of western countries to the Japanese viewer. Yes, the movie theater was a place that helped one to forget the dreary reality of being in Japan!

Literary narrative style reflected these new kinds of visual experience imported from and closely associated with the West. Tayama Katai's *heimen byōsha* 'surface description' (Fowler, 1988, p. 123) and the ideology of *aru ga mama* 'depicting phenomenal reality "just as it is"' (Fujii, 1993, p. 152) would have been unthinkable in the days before photography. And as Stephen Dodd has noted, Satō Haruo's "fascination... with the effect of light — electric light" played a major role in shaping the imagination behind the writing of the story, *Utsukushii machi*, (*Beautiful town*, 1919). (Dodd, 1994, p. 304). There was new interest in the act of seeing. Gazing became the theme of stories; the desire to see became a primary psychological motivation; and seeing was the primary action upon which the plot or meaning of many a work hinged.[5] Seeing was often problematized — made more complicated and interesting — by an optical device. The artists who create a model town in Satō Haruo's *Utsukushii machi*, (*Beautiful town*, 1919), for example, experiment with mirror images under electric lights, and draw their inspiration for the site of their town from the perspectival innovations of Shiba Kōkan, the Edo painter well known for his early experiments with western style perspective, and for his experimentations involving the drawing of objects viewed through a Dutch microscope.[6]

Ironically, the *shishōsetsu* (often translated as I novel), presumably the most private of genres, entailed staging, performing, and presenting the self before a public audience to achieve affirmation and validation of the individual self, and within the context of this national tendency toward exhibitionism, became the most widely recognized and widely practiced narrative genre of the time.

Tanizaki, Satō, Akutagawa, and Uno Kōji who have been traditionally distinguished from literary naturalism through their prioritization of the imagination, were all interested in visual technology and seeing. Experiences with viewing technologies led to new topographies of the imagination in their works, and viewing machines and the optical illusions created through them became important means of stimulating the aesthetic imagination.

---

[5] Gazing, of course, was important in early literature as well (see, for example, Sarra, 1994). What I mean to suggest is that there emerged a more conscious framing of a more sharply focused, and often magnified, image after the introduction of new viewing devices.

[6] Citing Sugano Yō's *Edo no Dōbanga* (Tokyo: Shinchōsensho, 1984), Kawamoto suggests that Shiba Kōkan also drew pictures for *nozoki-megane*, that is, dioramas (Kawamoto, 1990, p. 56).

The reader is situated in the text of Satō Haruo's fantasy, *Supein inu no ie* (*House of a Spanish dog*, 1916), much as a viewer looking through the aperture of a peephole at a marvelous magical world. And marvelous it is as the black Spanish dog inside the house "in a twinkling becomes a middle aged man in glasses and a black suit who stands leaning against the chair by the desk with the still unlit cigarette in his mouth and who slowly turns the pages of one of those large books." (Satō, H., 1962, p. 172)

Like the enclosed diorama or peepshow, the interior space of the unusual cottage transforms reality: brings the distant and exotic near, and freezes time. The narrator surrenders himself to the mood of fantasy enveloping the cottage in the wood, and exhibits a passivity akin to that of the spectator who looks through the peep hole of the peepshow, not to impose his intellectual view of reality, but to be present the moment that the marvelous scene unfolds before the eye.

A similar mood is exhibited by the protagonist of Uno Kōji's novella, *Yamagoi* (*Love of mountains*, 1922). The visual effects introduced into the text recall the experience of gazing through a stereoscope.[7] Like those views, the narrator's views of mountain landscape are framed: by the window of the train that carries him to the mountains of Nagano, and later, by the window of his third floor room in the inn in Suwa.

His room in the inn with its many windows overlooking the mountain landscape in all directions functions as his "viewing machine." When he first enters this room, he surveys the scene outside from each of its windows in turn, testing its views, as though through a viewing apparatus with different adjustments. And with a degree of attention to detail reminiscent of the way in which Victorians diagrammed their dioramas, stereoscopes, and kaleidoscopes (Crary, 1990, pp. 114–115, 128) he draws for his reader a floor plan of the room and situates it within the text.

In the stereoscopic picture separate areas of spatial coherence assembled in separate zones and planes of assemblage give an effect of foreground and distant background, of "both modeled depth and cut out flatness" in an illumined space in which objects emerge with hyper- (at times hallucinatory) clarity. (Crary, 1990, pp. 124–126).

The world outside the transforming "lens" of the protagonist's window is lustrous as if freshly washed and outlined in lines as clear and sharp as stereoscopic cut outs. Scenery in the foreground is set off from mountains in the background, creating "the sense of 'in front of' and 'in back of' that seems to organize the [stereoscopic] image as a sequence of receding planes." (Crary, 1990, p. 125) Crooked cubes push into the sky above a screen-like range of lower mountains. Mountains bedecked with

---

7   Early stereoscopes were devised by Charles Wheatstone and David Brester in the 19th century. The widespread commercial diffusion of the stereoscope throughout North America and Europe occurred after 1850. By 1856, two years after its founding, the London Stereoscopic Company alone had sold over half a million viewers (Crary, 1990, p. 118)

grasses, trees, and entire woods seem to rise up against the blue sky as if they were moving toward his window to pay a formal call.

Seen from within the shadowy enclosed interior of the room, the panorama that he looks out upon possesses a luminous magical quality as a view seen through a stereoscope. As he raises the awning of his window to see the mountains, "two tall mountains rising steeply and with icy sharpness emerge under a blue sky with a glittering radiance that pierces the eye." Its snow covered peaks "gleam like ice" and its mountains seem "not like mountains of ordinary earth and rock but mountains of ice polished at night by an unseen hand as day by day they turn bluer and brighter than a sword" (Uno, 1968a, p. 341).

And here it is the coach of a train emerging from a tunnel that affords the enclosed perspective from which the landscape outside takes on a marvelous animated quality:

> My eyes were drawn to the astonishing Kai Komagadake thrusting its full figure right before us, as Danjūrō would, stepping onto the kabuki stage, hiding the other mountains in its shadow, baring its grotesque shape, showing off the nearly ten thousand feet of its fantastic mass from the bottom, up, while bathing its foothills in the Kamanashi River while its distorted top, draped with snow down to its shoulders, peered over the heads of the other mountains and down at the land of Shinano next door.[8] (Uno, 1968a, p. 339)

Fascination with viewing gadgetry consumes the narrator of Uno's *Yume miru heya* (*The dream viewing room*, 1923), in which the magic lantern (*gentōki*) is evoked as the dearest companion of the first person narrator's childhood.[9] The narrator furnishes the reader with a diagram of the room in which he now, as an adult, seeks and enjoys ocular illusions. At the end of the story he lies down in a futon under the skylight in the ceiling and fantasizes that he is in a magic lantern placed face up toward the night sky, and that the interior of the perfectly square four-and-a-half-mat room, with himself, his books, and his futon, merges into a single picture that is projected onto the night sky through the lens of the square skylight. In this manner he assimilates his being into, and becomes part of, the viewing device which stands

---

[8]   For an English translation of *Yamagoi*, see Uno, 1997.
[9]   According to Satō Tadao, the magic lantern (*gentō*) entered Japan from Holland in the latter half of the 17th century and became popular between the end of the Bakumatsu period and early Meiji (when it was referred to as *utsushi-e* ('magic lantern pictures') in the Kantō; and as *Nishiki-kage-e* ('brocade shadow pictures') in the Kansai). It was customary to move both the magic lantern projector and the glass plates on which scenes were drawn to produce interesting motion effects in the images, which were projected upon a screen of Mino paper. Music and dialogue were added to create a more complete theatrical performance (Satō, T., 1995, p. 4).

as a metaphor for the imagination: namely, the magic lantern that creates illusionary forms and projects them outward.[10]

Uno was fond of describing situations wherein the eye is deluded into seeing something that is not there, and the imagination transforms visual stimuli into imaginary images. In *Yume miru heya* the narrator's heated imagination turns the naked eye into a viewing device capable of producing optical tricks. As he walks down a hill in Ueno at a certain time of the day when the sun is at a given angle to the sidewalk, the roof of the museum down below shimmers in such as way as to produce the sensation that he is looking at the surface of Lake Suwa (an optical illusion that makes him shiver with pleasure), which is associated in his mind with the country geisha he loves. Another way in which he enhances the pleasure of seeing is to use a book of French portraits to trick himself into thinking that he is seeing the geisha Yumeko (*Dream girl*) while full well knowing that he isn't.

Liberated from the physical appearance of external phenomena by experimentations with visual gadgetry, and influenced by readings in European symbolism, writers like Uno Kōji and Satō Haruo explored alternate perceptual realities and in so doing, were drawn to the motifs of dreams and fairy tales.[11]

Indeed, much of the fascination and attraction of their writing is generated by their pursuit of unusual optical illusions. In some stories by Satō, these illusions are experienced in a state of heightened neurasthenia, in which the interaction between the eye and the agitated brain becomes the means by which customary perceptions of outer reality are given a surreal, hallucinatory twist. In the poetic reverie, *Den'en no yūutsu* (*Gloom in the country*), the fevered mind operating upon phenomenal reality transforms ordinary scenery into strange dreamlike sequences. In some passages, descriptions recall the power of film to magically magnify and diminish the size of objects and scenes through techniques of close up, panning, and fade out.

> As he stared closely, the whole street receded from his nose and became even tinier, seeming about to disappear, but then the scene grew rapidly larger. Unchanged but now very large, almost life-size, the street kept growing relentlessly to become almost gigantic, as big as the whole world... He watched vacantly and the scene shrank quietly back to its former miniature scale and returned to its former place about his nose. In a few minutes — or was it seconds — it had gone in one flight, he felt, from the fabled Lilliput to the country of giants and then back to miniature Lilliput. (Satō, H., 1993, p. 76)

Of all the optical devices, however, motion pictures had the most wide sweeping and profound effects upon literary and artistic imaginations of the time. The

---

[10] The magic lantern was frequently invoked as a metaphor for the mind by 19th century British empiricists. who likened the "screen," on which image-traces of past sensations were projected, to memory (Castle, 1988, p. 30).

[11] For a discussion of these and other writers' concerns with illusion and fantasy see Kawamoto Saburō (1990).

enthusiasm for motion pictures held by Satō and Tanizaki is well documented. Both tried their hands at writing screenplays and were closely associated with people in the film industry (Satō was married to a movie actress and Tanizaki had an affair with one). But perhaps the most telling evidence of the power that movies exercised upon their imaginations are the stories in which film viewing provides the central psychological experience and interest of the plot.

The mad dreams of an opium addict provide the opportunity to explore unusual visual perceptions in Satō's *Shimon* (*The fingerprint*, 1917). Rapid flowing shifts in perception, reminiscent of filmic flux, are exploited in this detective story in which the image of a fingerprint, blown up on a movie screen in an Asakusa theater, launches the character N on a quest for a watch found at the scene of a murder on which a fingerprint will prove that the murderer was none other than the American film star William Wilson, whose greatly magnified fingerprint appeared in the movie, *Gun Moll Rosario*. The disembodied fluidity of the silent flux of images, described in references to the dreams experienced by N in a Nagasaki opium den, recall an early film theorist's description of the phenomenology of film viewing:

> The massive outer world has lost its weight, it was been freed from space, time, and causality, and it has been clothed in the forms of our own consciousness. The mind has triumphed over matter and the pictures roll on with the ease of musical tones. It is a superb enjoyment which no other art can furnish us. (Munsterberg, cited in Anderson, forthcoming, p.1[12])

N's posthumous diary of his dreams is entitled *Moonbeams*, and its recurring image of bright moonlight (a "rain of silvery rays of light") evokes nothing so much as the flickering play of light upon a silent movie screen. "Lilac bushes sprout from water and quickly grow into large flowering trees and countless other trees grow and bloom and grow into a deep forest" with a speed reminiscent of high-speed imaging. And this flowery forest floating on the waves "pitches and sways ominously," with the instability of an image on a screen.[13] In another moonlit scene a troop of English dragoons advances; the earth seems filled with noise, but the spectator (as if watching a silent film) can hear nothing because he is "totally deaf." Moonlit images shine dimly in silvery gray with a radiance akin to the silver screen and are especially enchanting as, "caressing each curving line," the moonlight slides down "every wind-filled sail" of a ship gliding gently through the sea like a giant dream. "The round moon" floats "on still water that is like a sheet of glass"; far away houses cast "shadows perfect in every detail." At times the moonlit night is "green, like movie film. "The cluster of sails slips behind antique houses lit by the moon and past a towering black gothic steeple. A fountain gleams in the moonlight, "its bright

---

[12]   The quote appears in a chapter of the book that was in manuscript form at the time. The quote is from Munsterberg's 1916 essay, *The photoplay; A psychological study*.

[13]   *Shimon* has been translated into English as "The Fingerprint" by Frances Tenny (Satō, H.,1996); quoted material in this paragraph is from Satō.

silver threads entwined in dirty white velvet." A pale white figure dressed in a big black robe appears from the small black doorway of a large stone house.[14]

Shimon's phantom figures, moonlit castle ramparts and turrets, and the gleaming white sails of a ship that slips silently through streets between the roofs of western houses with roofs piled upward and outward may be visual "echoes" of images of the old quarter of Prague that dominates the screen in Paul Wegener's early Expressionist film, *Der Student von Prag*, (*The student of Prague*, 1913). Cited by some film critics as "probably the first legitimate example of the flowering of the horror genre" and as furnishing the basis for most of the major horror films to come (Hanson, 1982, pp. 1071, 1074), *The student of Prague* plays on the doppelgänger theme of the supernatural double, as does Satō's *Shimon*, and exploits the film media's potential for depicting dream states and strange realms of the imagination.[15] Phantasmagorical manipulation of chiaroscuro effects meant to reflect a morbid psychology, characteristic of early experimental German films such as *The student of Prague*, *Der golem*, and *The cabinet of Doktor Caligari*, are found in many of Satō's images. They are exploited in a more consistent novelistic fashion by Tanizaki.

"Desire" in many of Tanizaki's novels "is structured through" acts of voyeurism, that is, "the imposition of distance" between the viewer and the object of his (or on occasion, her) seeing, a distance which creates a cleavage between observation and participation.[16] The object may be bathed in a golden light, which enhances its distance and desirability. The Tanizaki protagonist often experiences himself as simultaneously inside and outside the experience of viewing: inside as he self-consciously records his reactions to the act of viewing; outside as he is, through the act of voyeurism, distanced and excluded from the magic circle from which desire emanates.

Perhaps no Tanizaki story exploits the idea of viewing as theatrically and bizarrely, or displays the lucid inventiveness with which he set about constructing and preserving the ocular illusion as a central inspiration for his work, as does *Jinmensō* (*The carbuncle with a human face*, 1918), a story about the mysterious, haunted film. *The boil with a human face* [*Ningen no kao o motta dekimono*], the film described at length in the story, is a movie about an ugly beggar who implants himself as a boil on the knee of a beautiful woman he loves.

---

[14]   High comments on the mesmerizing effect of early films, shown on projectors that were "geared down to an almost glacial speed, hypnotizing audiences with flickering light." (High, 1984, p. 50).

[15]   The theme of the supernatural double was a popular one in film and literature at the time. Paul Wegener's film, "Der Student von Prag" (1913, The Student of Prague), of which Satō is said to have been very fond, is about a student, Baldwin, who gives his mirror reflection to a sorcerer in exchange for worldly happiness. The sorcerer turns the student's mirror reflection into Baldwin's double, which takes on a life of its own and eventually destroys the student.

[16]   See Christian Metz (1982), especially chapter 4, "The Passion of Perceiving," for a theoretical discussion of the relationship between cinematic viewing, distance, and desire.

As Satō's *Shimon*, the title is named after an image magnified in a close up shot in a movie. And like the fingerprint in *Shimon*, an image projected onto a movie screen — that of a boil with human features — is pursued by a character bent upon unraveling an unsolvable mystery. Whereas the protagonist of *Shimon* pursues the image of a movie actor's fingerprint to solve the mystery of a murder, the protagonist of *Jinmensō*, a movie actress, pursues the image of an actor's face in an attempt to solve the mystery of a film in which she starred but of which she has no recollection.

The five reel film, *The boil with a human face*, is said to have been produced by the Grove Film Company of Los Angeles five or six years ago during a time when the Japanese actress Utagawa Yurie made a number of pictures for them. After its completion, the film disappeared from circulation, then reappeared in Southeast Asia. It surfaced next in Japan, where it had been allegedly purchased by a Japanese distribution company from a French businessman, and shown in small theaters in Shibuya and Shinjuku under the title, *Shūnen* (*Tenacity*). Beyond the fact that Yurie who appears in it has no memory of ever making it, the film is rendered even more mysterious by viewers' inability to identity the Japanese actor whose face appears in the film, first as a beggar, and then as a human-faced boil.

Like the golem in Wegerner's *Der Golem* (one of Tanizaki's favorite movies),[17] the boil is a revolting creature that becomes willfully more destructive when its desire for the courtesan Ayume (played by Yurie) is thwarted.[18] Although *The carbuncle with a human face* has been termed an early horror story, it is also farcical in the perversely playful manner that readers have come to associate with Tanizaki. The hideous boil, located on the Ayume's knee, assumes the facial features of the beggar who threw himself off a cliff, cursing her, after she spurned his love. The narrative describes in detail the scene in the film where the beggar's face emerges on the head of the boil as Ayume sits in her lover-seaman's chest as a stowaway en route to America.

---

[17] Italian, French, and American films (Max Sennet's *Bathing Beauties* and movies of Mary Pickford and Charlie Chaplin in particular) were popular in Japan during Taishō, but the movies that Tanizaki is said to have loved most were Paul Wegener's *The student of Prague*, starring Paul Wegener as the student; and *Der Golem* (*The golem*, 1915), followed by *Der Golem und die Tanzerin* (*The golem and the dancing girl*, 1917), with Wegener playing the role of the Golem. (Kawamoto, 1990, p. 88) Between the two versions of "The Golem" another German director, Otto Rippert, made a similar six-part serial film about monstrous human-like beings entitled, *Homunculus* (1916). Kawamoto also suggests that it was through the medium of the silent film that Tanizaki learned to appreciate the aesthetic/psychological quality of shadows and darkness (*yami*) that he later celebrated in his famous statement on Japanese aesthetics (Kawamoto, 1990, p. 86).

[18] In *The golem* the Rabbi of the Jewish quarter of Prague uses secret lore to construct from clay a powerful giant-sized man that comes to life when fragments of an ancient Hebrew word emerge from its large "demoniac" head. Through demonstration of feats of strength the golem prevents the expulsion of the Jewish community from the city, but the Rabbi's plans go awry when the golem falls in love with the Rabbi's daughter. Refused the affection it desires, the golem embarks on a rampage to avenge itself on the Rabbi and his people.

The first thing to appear on the screen was the leather trunk in which she was hiding. It had been thrown into a corner of the ship's hold together with various miscellaneous pieces of cargo. Then came a cross section of the constricted space of the trunk's interior, in which she was hunched over, clasping both legs, her neck resting on top of her knee caps, as she hung to life subsisting on nothing more than the bread and water that had been laid in store ahead of time. In two or three days time, a strange boil formed on her right kneecap and began to swell in an alarming fashion. Then four additional small boil heads began to protrude from the boil's soft swollen surface. Strangely, the boil seemed not to pain her at all. She tried pressing down on the swollen part and beating it with her hand. Was it because she was too cruelly insistent in her attempt to crush and destroy it that the surface of the boil, which had been soft, grew harder and tougher with each passing day, and the four small boil heads gradually assumed clear distinct outlines? Of the four heads, the two on top became round as jewels; the one in the center expanded vertically and took on a long thin shape; and the one on the bottom spread sideways and assumed a strange shape like a caterpillar crawling. It would have been pitch black inside the trunk, but for a shaft of sunlight filtering through a small crack that had been made to let in air. Floating in the air around her, the beam of light spread over her right knee, forming a bright circle, like the halo of a moon, and gradually blurring like a drop of spreading water. One time as she gazed at the disordered spot on her knee she couldn't help but feel somehow that the two upper protuberances looked like living eyeballs. The next time she discovered that the boil in the center was like a long thin nose and that the one shaped like a caterpillar was like a pair of lips. There was no mistake about it. The entire swollen surface had turned into a human face. "Am I going mad?" she asked herself. Yes, it was a human face. What disgusted her even more was the fact that although the face was formed of simple lines, much as a child's cartoon, it bore a close resemblance to the beggar's face. The moment she realized this she was overcome with a nameless fear and swooned. (Tanizaki, 1968a, pp. 288–289)

The beggar's curse takes effect soon after the couple set up housekeeping in San Francisco. When the sailor (who is referred to throughout the story as *hakujin* 'white man) catches sight of the boil which she has kept hidden and tries to run away from her, she clings to him, and endowed with superhuman power by the spirit of the boil, accidentally strangles him. Already far more beautiful than most Japanese women (Yurie the actress who plays her is described as combining Western style coquetry with Oriental "neatness of form"), once Ayume is possessed by the beggar's demonic spirit, she becomes even more beautiful, seductive, and degenerate. She leads a wild, dissolute life as a prostitute, vaudeville performer, and stage actress in San Francisco and New York, attracting to her side European aristocrats, wealthy industrialists, and diplomats (all of them *hakujin*), whom she fleeces before destroying them. In the last reel of the film as Ayume whirls and twirls wildly at an evening soirée before her guests, the boil on her knee gnaws its way through the concealing bandages and then through her silk stocking. When her current husband, a European viscount, bends over to look at it, the boil, blood streaming down its face, sticks out its tongue and laughs raucously (*geragera*). Driven mad, Ayume locks herself in her room and plunges a dagger into her breast as the face on the boil guffaws the movie to its end.

Acts of voyeurism, central to the cinematic process itself (Ellis, 1982, p. 88), initiate and sustain both the plot of the story, *Jinmensō*, and the movie *The boil with a human face*. The film begins as the ugly beggar (called simply *kojiki*) plays a flute in the shadows of a wharf in order to lure Ayume onto the moonlit balcony of a port brothel where he can fasten his eyes upon her as she, in turn, gazes out to sea, searching for the ship that will bring her American sailor lover back to her. The beggar tries in vain to get a close look at Ayume as he guards the trunk in which she is hidden. But *hakujin*, who has induced him to transport the trunk to a deserted temple, where he will pick her up prior to sneaking her aboard his ship, has taken the key. And when *hakujin* arrives to collect Ayume and the beggar demands his reward, that is, to "see" the courtesan, she spurns his request, leading him to throw himself into the sea.

While looking upon the boil's face leads to death for *hakujin* in the film, viewing the haunted film brings on physical illness and madness for men who watch it alone late at night in a closed room. Try as they might, the Japanese film distributors are unable to identify or locate the Japanese actor who played the role of the beggar. Unlike other images in the film, that of the face on the boil corresponds to nothing in the outside world. Existing only on celluloid, it underlines cinema's illusion of referentiality. The description of the face of the boil — round, fat, goggle-eyed, and so swarthy that it is impossible to tell whether he is a Japanese or a South Sea islander — does, however, bear a resemblance to Tanizaki's own face, thereby pointing not to the existential world of the story, but to the realm of the author's caprice.

Like Satō and Tanizaki, Akutagawa Ryūnosuke and Uno Kōji also created film-like phantasmagoria in their narratives and presented experiences in the world as a series of disembodied simulacra. Akutagawa Ryūnosuke's characteristic use of montage within carefully framed scenes bears evidence to the applicability of the principle formulated by film maker and theorist Sergei Eisenstein that "the juxtaposition of two fragments resembles their product more than it does their sum." (Eisenstein, cited in Aumont, 1987, p. 35). Already in his early story, *Rashōmon* (1914), scenes are built up of carefully articulated images juxtaposed against each other to create subtle, and at times not so subtle, ironic commentary upon those scenes. A flock of crows flying in the evening sky in the distance, for example, is set against the close up view of "crumbling stone steps, with rank grass growing in their crevices, and dotted with white droppings" — to undercut the awesomeness of the scene of the blood red sky framed by the Rashō gate (Akutagawa, 1952, p. 36). His framed perspectives, together with the rapid alternations in distance perspective — from long shot to close up, from images that draw the gaze upward followed by images that pull the eye downward — are reminiscent of the moving eye of the camera. These filmic perspectives become yet more pronounced in Akutagawa's late writings, in particular, works such as *Asakusa kōen* (*Asakusa Park*, 1927), which is subtitled *Aru shinario* (A scenario).

Asakusa kōen shares the radical resistance to plot and narrativity that characterizes Akutagawa's last works. In place of naturalistic verisimilitude, embedded in a story, the work emphasizes the autonomy of the visual image. The scenario is constructed of a series of shots consisting of fragmented and by and large disconnected frames, linked together only by the setting of the Asakusa entertainment district in Tokyo, and by the camera-eye perspective that follows a young boy through the area. Within these frames the focus is not on the boy, but on what the boy sees as he wanders through the arcades. The scenario is framed by long distance shots of the Nio Gate leading into the neighborhood followed by a close up of the giant lantern hanging in the gate that gradually rises at the beginning of the scenario like a show curtain going up. Within the frames of the scenario, scenes lit by artificial illumination giving way to scenes in which images float up from a black background enhance the filmic quality, as do the many perspectival changes that occur as distance shots give way to close ups, angle views zoom into frontal views, pans give way to wipes, and objects magically transmogrify into completely unrelated shapes.

The narrative, like cinema before sound track, is virtually "silent"; no human voice breaks this spell. The ordinary is thus made strange by this silence that envelops the piece, in which voices in the disconnected vignettes exist only as hallucinatory sounds: lines that the boy imagines to be uttered by items in showcase windows.

The viewing gaze, of both the boy and his father, holds and is held by desire: the boy leaves the father's side and gazes at the show case of a toy shop; the father forgets to scold the boy and gazes at the showcase of a hat shop. The theme of specularity is highlighted by the recurrence of images having to do with "viewing" in the form of movie houses, a photography shop, and shop windows displays of microscopes, binoculars, telescopes, and eye-glasses.

The unreal disembodied ambiance of the frames is further underlined by the artificiality of the items showcased behind the plate glass windows (i.e., handmade flowers, artificial tresses [kamoji], toy animals, and dolls); by the *air gun* the boy shoots at a shooting gallery; by the hallucinatory way in which people suddenly appear wearing masks; by the way objects become transparent; and by the transformation before the boy's eyes of passersby into animals and then back into human beings. The world is transparent. Images alone exist and they are unstable and insubstantial. Reality is an appearance that is an illusion, a series of disembodied simulacra that change with the angle of vision and the condition of the illumination.

Noteworthy is the filmic phantasmagoria at the end Uno Kōji's novel *Renaigassen* (*Love contest*, 1923), where the protagonist's visual memory of his recent experiences collapses into a kaleidoscopic whirl, in which images of the actors and actresses of a *shingeki* troupe with which he has been associating merge with images of soldiers drilling in a field before his eyes. The play with the eye, accompanied by a dematerialization of the body, is also to be found in Uno's novel *Shusse gonin otoko* (*Five men go out in the world*, 1926), whose characters appear in portraits, as actors on the stage, and as cinematic images on the screen of an Asakusa movie house. In the following scene the film star Hirayama Matsuyuemon (a thinly disguised allusion to Japan's most famous and popular film actor of the early twentieth century, Onoue Matsunosuke) stands in front of another actor, who looks like Charlie Chaplin, but in fact is a Japanese impersonating Chaplin.[19]

> Matsuyuemon saluted the audience once and just as he was about to withdraw, the curtain behind him suddenly opened and Chaplin's head with the derby hat appeared. He turned his head several times to the left and right, and after looking in all directions, he leaped onto the rostrum with a single bound and took off his hat and bowed.
>
> Indeed he looked almost exactly but not quite like Chaplin. At that time the spectators, who until then had thought they were seeing Chaplin, began to have doubts. But before they could ascertain their suspicions, Chaplin, his head still bowed, holding his hat in his right hand and his cane in his left, slowly backed away into the curtain behind him; as he did so, the picture changed, and one saw Chaplin waving his hat from a swinging balloon as it rose from the earth. There was an instant's close up when Chaplin's face appeared clearly. It was without question another man. The balloon climbed. He continued waving his hat, but as his moustache grew smaller he looked more and more like a fake Charlie Chaplin. (Uno, 1968b, p. 385)

Meiji and particularly Taishō marked the moment when new vision technologies (film in particular) began to transform the relationship between the eye and the world and open new possibilities of consciousness and literary art. Detached from the moorings of realistic representation, the writings of the authors discussed here represent a movement, which has been ongoing, toward a condition in which "the optical is no longer necessarily the real, and seeing is no longer necessarily believing." (Horton, 1995, p. 16) They were writers who actively sought the disjunctures between thought, visual experience, and reality for the stimulations they afforded, both psychologically and aesthetically. These men turned the technology created through the application of instrumental reason — the same pragmatic rationalism that was transforming the country — into a tool for keeping fantasy and illusion alive.

REFERENCES

Akutagawa, R. (1952). Rashōmon. In T. Kojima (Trans.), *Rashōmon and other stories* (pp. 34–44). New York: Liveright. (Original work published in 1914)

Anderson, J. D. (forthcoming). *The reality of illusion: An ecological approach to cognitive film theory.* Carbondale: Southern Illinois University Press.

Aumont, J. (1987). *Montage Eisenstein* (L. Hildreth, C. Penley, and A. Ross, Trans.). Bloomington: Indiana University Press.

Castle, T. (1988). Phantasmagoria: Spectral technology and the metaphysics of modern reverie. *Critical Inquiry, (15)*l, 26–61.

Crary, J. (1990). *Techniques of the observer: On vision and modernity in the nineteenth century.* Cambridge: MIT Press.

---

[19] During Taishō, while the Japanese film industry was still mastering the techniques of film making, it was a common practice for Japanese film studios to make imitative versions of western films (Satō T., 1995, p. 68–69).

Dodd, S. (1994). Fantasies, fairies, and electric dreams: Satō Haruo's critique of Taishō. *Monumenta Nipponica, (49)*3, 287–314.

Fowler, E. (1988). *The rhetoric of confession: Shishōsetsu in early twentieth century Japanese fiction.* Berkeley: University of California Press.

Fujii, J. (1993). *Complicit fiction: The subject in the modern Japanese prose narrative.* Berkeley: University of California Press.

Hanson, S. L. (1982). The student of Prague. In F. N. McGills (Ed.), *MaGills' Survey of Cinema* (Vol. 3, pp. 1070–1074). Englewood, NY: Salem Press.

Hattori, B. (1956). The Western peep show. Donald Keene (Trans.). In D. Keene (Ed.), *Modern Japanese literature* (pp. 34–36). New York: Grove Press, Inc. (Original work published in 1874)

High, P. (1984). The dawn of cinema in Japan. *Journal of Contemporary History, (19),* 23–57.

Horton, S. R. (1995). Were they having fun yet? Victorian optical gadgetry, modernist selves. In C. T. Christ & J. O. Jordan (Eds.). *Victorian literature and the Victorian visual imagination* (pp. 1–26). Berkeley: University of California Press.

Kawamoto, S. (1990). *Taishō gen'ei* [Taishō phantasms]. Tokyo: Shinchōsha.

Keene, D. (Ed.). (1956). *Modern Japanese literature.* New York: Grove Press, Inc.

Metz, C. (1982). *The imaginary signifier: Psychoanalysis and the cinema.* (C. Britton, A. Williams, B. Brewster, & A. Buzzette, Trans.). Bloomington: Indiana University Press.

Sarra, E. B. (1994). A poetics of the gaze in *Makura no sōshi.* In E. Sekine (Ed.), *The desire for* Monogatari: *Proceedings of the Second Midwest Research/Pedagogy Seminar on Japanese Literature.* Purdue University.

Satō, H. (1962). House of a Spanish dog. (George Saito, Trans.). In I. Morris (Ed.), *Modern Japanese stories, an anthology* (pp. 162–172). Rutland, VT: Charles E. Tuttle. (Original work published in 1916)

Satō, H. (1993). Gloom in the country. In F. B. Tenny (Trans.) *The sick rose, a pastoral elegy, or gloom in the country.* Honolulu: University of Hawai'i Press. (Original work published in 1918)

Satō, H. (1996). *Beautiful town: Stories and essays by Satō Haruo* (F. Tenny, Trans.). Honolulu: University of Hawai'i Press.

Satō, T. (1995). *Nihon eiga shi* [The history of Japaneses movies] (Vol. l). Tokyo: Iwanami Shoten.

Silverberg, M. (1993). Constructing a new cultural history of prewar Japan. In M. Miyoshi & H. D. Harootunian (Eds.), *Japan in the world.* (pp. 115–143). Durham: Duke University Press.

Tanaka, S. (1993). *Japan's orient: Rendering pasts into history.* Berkeley: University of California Press.

Tanizaki J. (1968a). Jinmensō [The carbuncle with a human face]. In *Tanizaki Jun'ichirō zenshū* [The collected works of Tanizaki Jun'ichirō] (Vol. 5, pp. 283–305). Tokyo: Chūō Kōronsha. (Original work published in 1918)

Tanizaki J. (1968b). Katsudō shashin no genzai to shorai [The present and future of motion pictures]. In *Tanizaki Jun'ichirō zenshū* [The collected works of Tanizaki Jun'ichirō] (Vol. 20, pp. 21–28). Tokyo: Chūō Kōronsha. (Original work published in 1917)

Tanizaki J. (1968c). Tokyo o omou [Thinking of Tokyo]. In *Tanizaki Jun'ichirō zenshū* [The collected works of Tanizaki Jun'ichirō] (Vol. 21). Tokyo: Chūō Kōronsha. (Original work published in 1920)

Uno K. (1968a). Yamagoi [Love of Mountains]. In *Uno Kōji zenshū* [The collected works of Uno Kōji] (Vol. 3, pp. 330–411). Tokyo: Chūō Kōronsha. (Original work published in 1922)

Uno K. (1968b). Shusse gonin otoko [Five men rise in the world]. In *Uno Kōji zenshū* [The collected works of Uno Kōji] (Vol. 5). Tokyo: Chūō Kōronsha. (Original work published in 1926)

Uno, K. (1997) *Love of mountains:Two stories* (E. Gerbert, Trans.). Honolulu: University of Hawai'i Press.

Yukie Aida
University of Texas at Austin

ELECTRONIC NETWORKING ACTIVITIES IN JAPANESE LANGUAGE CLASSROOMS

INTRODUCTION

Through use of the Internet, computers have become tools that transcend geographical and cultural boundaries to allow students to experience direct contact with people using the same technology in different cultures. The March issue (1996) of *Syllabus*, a magazine dedicated to technology for education, reported that the percentage of college courses using e-mail and multimedia resources more than doubled from 1994 to 1995. It is also reported that university faculty and student ownership of computers in 1994 was 41% and 27%, respectively (Cotton, 1995). These statistics show that technology integration seems to surely be on the rise. Recent advances in computer technology provide a valuable supplement to conventional classroom instruction while making students computer literate and better prepared for the job market of the future, which will be information technology oriented.

In this paper, I will discuss how computers and technology can be integrated into Japanese classrooms as an adjunct to the conventional language classroom. I will describe four activities that I used for my second-year Japanese and advanced conversation classes. The four activities are:

1. the use of personal computers (Macs and PCs) for students' composing and editing Japanese essays;

2. electronic discussion and conferencing in Japanese among students of Japanese on the *Nihongo-Hiroba* mailing list;

3. the use of e-mail as a tool for quality control of classroom routines and assignments; and

4. reading authentic materials found in fj* (from Japan) newsgroups and Japanese WWW (World Wide Web) pages.

The software necessary for each activity is listed in Appendix A.

WRITING JAPANESE COMPOSITIONS USING A COMPUTER

In my classes, students are required to write two essays (about 1200 characters) using a Japanese word processor at our language lab on campus or using their own

Aida, Y. (1997). Electronic networking activities in Japanese language classrooms. In H. M. Cook, K. Hijirida, & M. Tahara (Eds.), *New trends and issues in teaching Japanese language and culture* (Technical Report #15, pp. 31–43). Honolulu: University of Hawai'i, Second Language Teaching and Curriculum Center.

computers at home. At the beginning of the fall semester, students participated in two 1-hour computer sessions to learn how to use Power Macs, NisusWriter (1996) (commercial word processing software) and MacJDic (1995) (on-line freeware dictionary). For those who own PCs, I provided handouts describing where to get software to display Japanese characters on their PCs (see Appendix B).

The second essay is a rewrite of the first essay. Instructors do not correct errors found in students' essays, but rather provide them with feedback using a set of editing codes. Please see the examples of the codes (Appendix C). Students self-correct their essays according to the feedback codes given by the instructors. In Fall 1995, students wrote on one of the following topics:

1. 最近、よく考えること
   What I have been most recently thinking about
2. 私の人生に一番えいきょうをあたえた出来事　/人
   What things (or people) have impressed (or influenced) me most in life

For following semester, the title options were:

1. 世界を変えるとしたら、どう変えますか？
   How would you change the world?
2. 一番うねしかったこと
   The happiest moment of my life
3. 一番かなしかったと
   The saddest moment of my life

Please see Appendix D for examples of students' compositions. Those two essays are original and were not corrected for publication.

At the beginning, some students were reluctant to use computers. In fall 1995, I allowed students to use *genkooyooshi* (writing paper with an imprinted grid) for the first essay but asked them to use a computer for the second essay. One third of the students used *genkooyooshi* for their first essay. This semester, only one student used *genkooyooshi* for the first essay.

It appears that students are less apprehensive about using computers now. Some of the students use a computer even for assignments which do not require the use of one, such as homework assignments and writing drafts for the group presentation skit. Some of the reasons they like to use a computer, according to students, are (a) the assignments look neat when typewritten, (b) the students can reduce spelling errors, and (c) it's fun to use more *kanji* in their writing. Therefore, computers can motivate students to improve their writing skills. In addition, computer printouts are much easier for teachers to read and grade.

In the future, I would like to try peer editing. In peer editing, students at Japanese universities read University of Texas at Austin (UT) students' Japanese writing and provide feedback using the editing codes. In return, UT students do the same for Japanese students' English writing using a variation of the Japanese editing marks. The exchange between the two groups can be done by e-mail. In peer editing, both Japanese and American students can help each other with their writing and learn different cultural perspectives from each other's writing. Another possibility for the future exemplified by the University of Tsukuba's exchange program (Ishida, 1996). The University of Tsukuba receives students' compositions via e-mail from several universities overseas, including the University of Stirling (Scotland), the University of Durham (England), and the University of Melbourne (Australia). Students in the teacher training program in Tsukuba correct the compositions and return them with explanations via e-mail. Students of Japanese will benefit from this program by having their compositions corrected by native speakers of Japanese other than their instructors. As well, the students in training programs to become teachers of Japanese can gain valuable experience in evaluating work of students of Japanese in other countries.

THE *NIHONGO-HIROBA* MAILING LIST

In summer 1995, 15 students in my summer intensive class participated in the e-mail exchange project set up by Professor Komori at Chubu University in Nagoya, Japan. In the project, foreign students studying Japanese at Chubu University and UT students communicated in Japanese via e-mail several times during the period of five weeks. It was a fun experience for me and for my students. This experience inspired me to create a new mailing list called *Nihongo-Hiroba* at the University of Texas at Austin. I thought that the mailing list would be a great way for students to communicate in Japanese with fellow learners of Japanese all over the world and to exchange cultural and linguistic information over the Internet. Currently, about 170 people from 18 countries (e.g., Japan, Australia, Canada, France, Brazil, England, and Hong Kong) are on the *Nihongo-Hiroba* mailing list. This semester, I required Advanced Conversation students to join the *Hiroba*, but for second-year Japanese classes, it was voluntary. The subscribers include students, teachers, other professionals such as computer programmers, physicists, chemist, biologists, financial brokers, accountants, and so forth. They talk about all kinds of things.

We use Eudora-J for e-mailing. Students bring a floppy disk and we install Eudora-J's 電子メール設定、受信簿、送信簿、ゴミ箱、電子メールニックネーム on the floppy disks. The language lab computers have the Eudora-J application installed. Students drag and drop 電子メール設定 from their floppy disk onto the Eudora-J application in the lab computer. Information on Nihongo-Hiroba is available on the UT Department of Asian Studies' WWW Home page:

http://asnic.utexas.edu/asnic/countries/japan/hirobaad.html

Not all student subscribers post messages regularly to the *Hiroba*. This is not necessarily a problem; they enjoy reading other people's Japanese messages, and in that way increase their exposure to written texts.

Information about *Nihongo-Hiroba* is available from our department's homepage: (http://asnic.utexas.edu/asnic/countries/japan/hirobaad.html).

E-MAIL AS A TOOL FOR QUALITY CONTROL OF CLASSROOM ROUTINES

Another way of using e-mail in the classroom is to use it as a tool for quality control in classroom routines. E-mail can be used as an alternative way to reach out to students and keep open communication with them. I encourage my students to use e-mail to reach me

- when they have questions about unclear points in the day's lecture;
- when they want to discuss personal matters with me;
- when they just want to check with me for assignments or due dates; or
- when they have to miss a class.

The instructors certainly can make great use of e-mail

- when they want to remind the students of an important due date or a schedule change;
- when they wish to check the academic progress of students individually; and
- when they wish to provide information on special lectures or seminars given by the department, on scholarships and grants, or club meetings (Anime Club, Culture Club, Conversation Club, etc.). Using e-mail, you save paper and time spent writing on the blackboard.

READING WORLD WIDE WEB PAGES AND FJ* NEWSGROUPS

The fj* newsgroup articles and World Wide Web (WWW) pages are excellent sources for Japanese language instruction because they contain a variety of authentic materials (original and unedited) written by actual people in Japan (vs. textbook writers or editors). A teacher can surf through those pages to select and compile reading materials appropriate for his or her class' level. The following is an example that I used for my classes:

第18回オリンピック冬季競技大会　長野冬季オリンピックマスコット

長野オリンピックの基本理念をシンボル化し、子どもから大人まで、
また国際的にも親しまれる大会マスコットとして、フクロウをモチーフとし
た「スノーレッツ」が生まれました。
フクロウは日本をはじめ、広く世界に分布し、古くから「森の知恵者」とい
われてきました。　古代ギリシャでは英知の女神アテナの従者であり、ギリ
シャ神話にも登場します。
「スノーレッツ(SNOWLETS)」という名称には、いくつかの意味がこめら
れています。まず、冬季オリンピックをイメージさせる「雪」(SNOW)、
「さあ、一緒に！」と元気よく呼びかけることば(LET'S)、そして「フクロ
ウのこどもたち」(OWLETS)です。「4」という数は、4年に一度の開催であ
るオリンピックの記号でもあります。
メンバーそれぞれが、ちがった個性を持つ「スノーレッツ」。これまでの
オリンピックマスコットにはなかった愉快で新しい雰囲気を、きっと作り
出すことでしょう。

The text was taken from "Official Mascot of the XVIII Olympic Winter Games in Nagano, Japan" located at http://www.nagano.olympic.org/welcome/welcome-j.html (Nagano Olympic Organizing Committee, 1997). It is a fairly short text and fun to read. You can create a list of new vocabulary (see Appendix D) using AutoGloss/J (Hatasa, 1994). AutoGloss/J is designed to automatically produce a glossary (pronunciation and meaning(s) of each word) in Japanese from a list of words taken from authentic reading materials. Sometimes AutoGloss/J can not find a word in its dictionary. In that case, you can use MacJdic, an on-line dictionary.

After reading the text, students are asked several questions concerning the content. For example,

1. What are "Snowlets"? (Answer: Owls.)

2. What did the writer say about the owls? (It is often said that owls are wise men of the forest. In Greek mythology, owls served Athena, the Goddess of Intelligence.)

3. List four meanings of the name "Snowlets", according to the text.

    (Answers:
    1. Snow: an important component of the winter Olympics;
    2. let's: everyone is involved;
    3. owlets: young owls;
    4. the four members of the Snowlets: symbolizes the quadrennial cycle of the Olympics)

Other interesting WWW pages include:

Yomiden 　(読伝)
(http://www.tomio.com/YOMIDEN/yomiden.html)

今月の星占い
(http://www.ascii.co.jp/misc/zodiac/index.html)

ふるさとネットワーク
(http://www.iijnet.or.jp/sankei/kurasi/week4/furusato/furhome.html).

Other excellent sources of authentic reading materials are fj* newsgroups, especially, fj.rec.animation and fj.rec.travel.japan. Again, you can use AutoGloss/J and/or MacJDic to generate a glossary for each reading. For those schools that do not carry fj* newsgroups, there are two public access servers, ume.cc.tsukuba.ac.jp and pubnews.demon.co.uk.

BENEFITS OBSERVED AND PROBLEMS ENCOUNTERED

In the process of integrating computer activities into regular classrooms, we have observed some benefits and encountered several problems. First, I would like to share the problems with you.

- There was a small group of students who had never used a computer before and were not really willing to try. The instructors had to be very patient with those who are reluctant to use computers.

- There are many students who prefer PCs over Macs. I did not, and still do not, know much about PCs, so I had to research and learn more about PCs and the software for PCs. We have 17 PowerMacs on campus with Japanese software installed, however, there are no PCs on campus for public use that have Japanese software. So, I have to convince students to use Macs, or provide information on how to Japanize their own PCs at home.

- Since more and more instructors from other foreign language areas are integrating computer use into their curricula, access to computers on campus and to the main line off campus is a huge problem, as there is always a long waiting line. Right now, our department is trying to set up a separate computer room in our building for students who are enrolled in classes offered by our department. This will alleviate the crowding a little.

Despite such drawbacks, we can still see some benefits.

- As I mentioned earlier, most of the students say that they like typed compositions. They feel that the use of computers helps them improve their writing (*kanji* recognition skill and spelling). Plus, they say that it is easy to redraft, since the compositions they write are saved on floppy disks. In *genkooyooshi*, they have to rewrite them all over again.

- All students who never used electronic communication before say they will continue to use it and are glad to have learned it. One of the students got a job at the Consulate-General of Houston last fall. She said that she was happy that she knew how to use Japanese software and e-mail, because the Consulate uses the same software.

- Students like the materials taken from WWW and fj* newsgroups. They say that those readings are challenging but not too intimidating ("comprehensive input + 1", Krashen, 1982), they deal with the current issues, and that the accompanying visual effects are attractive. The pictures and illustrations often make the students want to check the web sites themselves.

FUTURE PLANS

For future activities, I plan to integrate other media tools for communications tasks such as using CU-SeeMe (1995) for video-conferencing, and creating a WWW home page for Japanese classes. It provides video and audio transmission from Mac or Windows platforms. Through CU-SeeMe, American students can engage in direct oral communication with native speakers of Japanese. They can hear correct pronunciation, see facial expressions and gestures, and can learn from each other about life, culture, music, and customs.

Recently, two of my students had a 45-minute conversation in Japanese via CU-SeeMe with two students of Professor Nakajima at the University of Toronto as a part of a demonstration for participants at the conference, "Global Learning Networks in the Language Curriculum" held at the Language Learning Research Centre at New College, Canada. It was originally scheduled for only 15 minutes, but the students enjoyed talking to each other so much that they continued the conversation for an extra 30 minutes. At the beginning, both sides were a little nervous and awkward talking through the microphone. However, the ice was quickly broken and they became more relaxed. One of the students even sang a Japanese song. I hope that this kind of interaction among students of Japanese in different countries and cultures will take place on a regular basis in the future.

Although time differences between the US and Japan may be an obstacle, the interactive possibilities provided by CU-SeeMe are very appealing. It would be great for composition editing partners in Japan and Texas to talk to each other and discuss their writing via CU-SeeMe. The world is surely getting smaller.

REFERENCES

Cogger, D. (1995). CU-SeeMe0.83b2 [Computer software]. Cornell University: Author. Available FTP: CU-SeeMe.cornell.edu/pub/CU-SeeMe or http://cu-seeme.cornell.edu/get_cuseeme.html).

Cotton, C. (1995, June). Technology-mediated learning: Are we there yet? *Syllabus*, 26–27.

Crevier, D. (1995). MacJDic1.3.4 [Computer software]. Harvard University: Author.

Hatasa, K. (1994) AutoGloss/J [Computer Software]. Purdue University: Author.

Noon, J. (Ed.). (1996, March). Instructional use of technology dramatically increases in colleges and universities. *Syllabus, 10*.

Ishida, T. (1996). E-mail for distance Japanese language learning and teacher training. In M. Warschauer (Ed.) *Virtual connections: On-line activities and projects for networking language learners*. (Technical Report #8). Honolulu: University of Hawai'i, Second Language Teaching and Curriculum Center.

Krashen, S. D. (1982). *Principles and practice in second language learning*. New York: Pergamon.

Nagano Olympic Organizing Committee (1995). *Official mascot of the XVIII Olympic Winter Games in Nagano, Japan* [HTML document]. Retrieved 1997 from the World Wide Web: http://www.nagano.olympic.org/welcome/welcome-j.html

Nakata, S. (1995). Eudora-J 1.3.8.5 [Computer software]. Asics Corporation: Author.

NisusWriter 5.0. (1996) [Computer software]. Paragon Concepts, Inc.

APPENDIX A: SOFTWARE AND OTHER RESOURCES
FOR COMPUTER ACTIVITIES

Software for composing and editing Japanese students' essays:

Macintosh platform

NisusWriter5.0 (commercial product)

MacJDic1.3.4 (on-line dictionary)
    available at ftp.sedl.org/pub/mirrors/nihongo (a U.S. mirror site of Monash U.)
    ftp.monash.edu.au/pub/nihongo

PC platform

JWP1.31 (freeware word processor for PCs) available at
    ftp.sedl.org/pub/mirrors/nihongo (a U.S. mirror site of Monash U.)
    or ftp.monash.edu.au/pub/nihongo

Software for electronic discussion and conferencing in Japanese among students of Japanese on the *Nihongo-Hiroba* mailing list:

Macintosh platform

Eudora-J1.3.8.5 (e-mailing), available at
    ftp.uwtc.washington.edu/pub/Japanese/Macintosh/Communications

PC platform

JWP1.31 (word processor for PCs), MView1.20 (Japanese viewer) both available at
    ftp.sedl.org/pub/mirrors/nihongo
    ftp.monash.edu.au/pub/nihongo

Authentic reading materials found in fj* (from Japan) newsgroups and Japanese WWW (World Wide Web) pages:

Macintosh platform

Netscape Navigator (WWW browser) available at
    ftp2.netscape.com/pub/navigator
    http://www.netscape.com/comprod/mirror/index.html

Newswatcher-J16 (newsgroup reader) available at
    ftp.uwtc.washington.edu/pub/Japanese/Macintosh/Communications

AutoGloss/J1.0 (glossary generator) available at
    http://www.sla.purdue.edu/academic/fll/JapanProj/AutoGloss.html

E-mail for quality control of classroom routines and assignments

Miscellaneous:

fj* (From Japan) hierarchy public access at
ume.cc.tsukuba.ac.jp or pubnews.demon.co.uk

Austin Japan Association information is available at
http://www.utexas.edu/students/aja/jlinkjpn.html

Information on Nihongo-Hiroba is available at
http://asnic.utexas.edu/asnic/countries/japan/hirobaad.html

APPENDIX B: HOW TO DISPLAY JAPANESE CHARACTERS ON NON-JAPANESE WINDOWS PCS

1. Get JWP1.31 (a Japanese word processor) — freeware

2. Get all the JWP13*.zip files (approx. 6 Mb in all) from
    ftp.sedl.org/pub/mirrors/nihongo
    ftp.cdrom.com/japanese/monash

3. You also need MView1.20 (Japanese viewer) — shareware, $5

    You can get mview12.zip (1.7Mb) from the above sites.

4. To read e-mail, just start MView before you start Eudora (or other e-mail utility.)

    To send e-mail, type your message in JWP and cut/paste onto Eudora. You should use the new JIS codes for your message.

To write Japanese e-mail, make sure your JWP option for "clipboard format" is set to newJIS. Then compose the message in JWP, use menu items "edit/select all" and "edit/copy" to copy the message to the clipboard. Then go to your mail reader and use "edit/paste" to place the message in the text area.

To find out about other methods for using Japanese on PCs visit the following WWW page: http://www.panix.com/~tn/j-pc.html

APPENDIX C: ESSAY FEEDBACK CODES

5	K	*kanji* errors or *kanji* needed to be used.	卌
3	SP	spelling errors	ⅠⅠⅠ
7	VOC	error in the selection of vocabulary	卌 ⅠⅠ

4	G	grammar errors	ⅠⅠⅠⅠ
3	CJ	conjugation error	ⅠⅠⅠ
1	T	tense error (present, past, future)	Ⅰ
7	R	relational error	卌 ⅠⅠ
1	L	logic error	Ⅰ
5	FM	form error (-*masu* form, plain form,- *te* form, -*nai* form, -*ba* form, etc.)	卌
2	?	awkward or incomprehensible sentence or expression	ⅠⅠ
4	==	delete	ⅠⅠⅠⅠ
2	^	insert	ⅠⅠ

TOTAL grammar errors (the sum of G through ^) __29__

	very poor									excellent
kanji	1	2	3	4	5	6	7	8	9	10
spelling	1	2	3	4	5	6	7	8	9	10
voc	1	2	3	4	5	6	7	8	9	10
grammar	1	2	3	4	5	6	7	8	9	10
content quality/	1	2	3	4	5	6	7	8	9	10
creativity/originality mechanics	1	2	3	4	5	6	7	8	9	10

(title, name, date, spacing, margins, length of essay)

TOTAL: _____/60 = _____%

COMMENTS: _____

第	だい	ordinal (prefix)
回	かい	counter for occurrences
冬季	とうき	(season of) winter
競技	きょうぎ	game/match/contest
大会	たいかい	convention/tournament/mass meeting/rally
基本	きほん	foundation/basis/standard
理念	りねん	idea
シンボル		symbol
化する	かする	to change into, to convert into, to transform, to be reduced, to influence, to, improve(someone)
国際的	こくさいてき	international
親しむ	したしむ	to be intimate with/to befriend
マスコット		mascot
フクロウ	ふくろう	owl
分布	ぶんぷ	distribution
森	もり	forest/Mori (pronoun)
知恵者	ちえしゃ	wise person
古代	こだい	ancient
英知	えいち	intelligence
女神	めがみ	goddess
従者	じゅうしゃ	follower/attendant/valet/servant
神話	しんわ	myth/legend
登場	とうじょう	entry (on stage)
名称	めいしょう	name
意味	いみ	meaning/significance
開催	かいさい	holding a meeting/open an exhibition
記号	きごう	symbol/code
個性	こせい	individuality/personality/idiosyncrasy
愉快	ゆかい	pleasant
雰囲気	ふんいき	atmosphere (e.g. musical)/mood/ambience

Hideko Shimizu
Vanderbilt University, Tennessee

PSYCHOLINGUISTIC RESEARCH ON WORD IDENTIFICATION IN JAPANESE *KANJI:* IMPLICATIONS FOR JFL PEDAGOGY

INTRODUCTION

Learning *kanji* is a significant challenge for many students of Japanese who are not native speakers. At the same time, building knowledge of *kanji* is crucial because *kanji* are used to read and write most Japanese vocabulary items. In order to develop an effective instructional design for teaching *kanji*, it could be beneficial for instructors of Japanese to understand the cognitive processes that are involved in learning *kanji*. The goal of this paper is to review current empirical research on Japanese *kanji* in psycholinguistics and to draw important pedagogical implications for teaching *kanji*. First, psycholinguistic research on word identification in general will be discussed, along with the central theories of word identification based on the connection between orthographies and phonology. These theories of word identification have been developed based on empirical research and thus may provide accurate insight into the mental processes involved in the learning and use of *kanji*. Second, the specific characteristics of Japanese and Chinese orthographies relevant to word identification will be reviewed. Third, the findings of some of the most recent studies specifically involving Japanese and Chinese word identification will be reviewed and summarized. Finally, some potential implications of these research results for developing more effective Japanese as a Foreign Language (JFL) educational pedagogy will be discussed.

SIGNIFICANCE OF *KANJI* RESEARCH

What is the significance of *kanji* research? There are a number of reasons why people who are interested in word identification might look at *kanji*. For those who are involved in curriculum development and JFL teaching, the results of research on *kanji* identification may help to develop more effective curricula. Most research on word identification makes use of alphabetic orthographies. From a researcher's perspective, the Japanese and Chinese orthographies provide very important research alternatives to alphabetic orthographies. In order to determine what is universal in terms of language processing, it is important to have something with which to compare alphabetic orthographies. The logographic orthographies of the Japanese and Chinese language could be used for such a comparison. The results of this sort of research will provide us with important insights into understanding the cognitive processes that are involved in learning language in general and may also

Shimizu, H. (1997). Psycholinguistic research on word identification in Japanese *kanji*. In H. M. Cook, K. Hijirida, & M. Tahara (Eds.), *New trends and issues in teaching Japanese language and culture* (Technical Report #15, pp. 45–59). Honolulu: University of Hawai'i, Second Language Teaching and Curriculum Center.

help us to develop more effective and efficient curricula and instructional methods for teaching in the classroom.

CURRENT THEORIES

There are several theories of word identification that have been developed based on research on alphabetic writing systems. In the case of alphabetic writing systems, the dominant view of word processing is that of the dual-route model in which there are two separate processes. The meaning of a word may be identified by these two processes (Patterson & Coltheart, 1987; Seidenberg, 1985). One is the lexical route via direct visual access of whole-word meaning and the other is the mediated-access route, in which a string of graphemes is first converted into phonemes using grapheme to phoneme correspondence (GPC) rules. Rooted in this dual-route model is also a developmental model called the bypass hypothesis, which assumes that beginning readers use phonologic mediation, and that over time reading proficiency eventually results in a bypass where direct associations are established between orthographic codes and lexical codes (Baron, 1973; McCusker, Hillinger, & Bias, 1981). Other researchers suggest that the phonologically mediated and direct-access routes to word meaning are not mutually exclusive, and that it is quite possible that the two processes operate together (Coltheart, 1985; Seidenberg & McClelland, 1989). Another view is the independent-process hypothesis in which the phonological word codes are automatically (rather than optionally) activated during word identification. Evidence for such a system is based on various observed phenomena (Pollatsek, Lesch, Morris, & Rayner, 1992; Van Orden, 1987). Van Orden has also proposed a verification model, in which written words are first translated into phonological codes and are then compared to the spellings of words in memory. Response time with homophones is longer because errors are not recognized until the mental "spell-check" is done. Figure 1 presents a diagram of the dual route model.

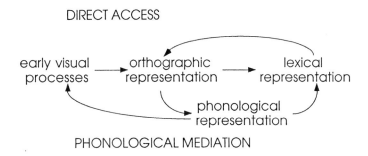

DIRECT ACCESS

early visual processes → orthographic representation → lexical representation

phonological representation

PHONOLOGICAL MEDIATION

Figure 1. Word identification processes

VAN ORDEN'S EXPERIMENTS: HOMOPHONY EFFECTS

Van Orden (1987 and 1991) investigated the effects of homophony and orthographic similarity between category exemplars and incorrect target words on judgment tasks in English. In these experiments, subjects were asked to judge whether the target homophone word *meet* and the spelling control target *melt* belonged to the category "a type of food." The correct answer would be "no." Van Orden's assumption is that if an orthographic representation is used directly in the word identification processes, there should be no difference in either the error rate or the response time for the homophone *meet.* or spelling control target *melt* relative to the correct exemplar *meat.* The results of these experiments, however, suggest a homophony effect. Significantly more errors were reported for homophone than control foils. The data, therefore, support the phonological mediation model. Further supporting the involvement of phonological mediation, studies conducted by Van Orden, Johnston, and Hale (1988) found significant homophony effects in experiments that used non-words as targets. False-positive-type errors with pseudohomophone targets (e.g., **brane* for the category "a part of the human body") were found to occur far more frequently than false positive errors to word spelling controls. It is hypothesized that such categorization errors arise because an automatic phonological code is activated pre-lexically. Phonological coding, therefore, appears to have a central role in the identification of printed words in English.

Does this hold true for languages other than English? The symbol-sound-meaning relationships of non-alphabetic languages such as Japanese and Chinese are different from those of English, so investigation of the processing mechanisms in these languages may contribute additional insight into language processing in general.

CHINESE AND JAPANESE WRITING SYSTEMS

CHINESE LOGOGRAPHIC ORTHOGRAPHY

Modern Chinese characters may be divided into four categories: (a) pictographs, (b) self-explanatory characters (simple ideographs), (c) associative compounds (compound ideographs), and (d) phonetic compounds (phonetic ideographs) (Shi & Yang, 1984, in Tan, Hoosain, & Peng, 1995). Except for phonetic compounds, all other characters convey meaning directly by graphic symbols. For example, 山 (meaning "mountain") is a character which is a pictographic depiction of mountain. Phonetic compounds consist of a phonemic radical (the phonetic), which normally provides some hint about the pronunciation of the compound, and a semantic radical, which normally provides some indication of the meaning of the total character. About 90% of Chinese characters are phonetic compounds (Zhu, 1988). Fan (1986) investigated the semantic cueing value of the semantic radical 糸 The basic meaning of 糸 is "silk" or "things relating to fabric." According to studies by Fan, of the more than 160 characters containing the 糸 radical, approximately 65% have meanings associated with that of the semantic radical.

JAPANESE *KANJI* ORTHOGRAPHY

Japanese orthography consists of syllabic *kana* and logographic *kanji*. There are two key characteristics of words written in *kanji* that are important to an understanding of how the orthography might be translated to phonology and meaning. First, nearly all *kanji* characters have at least two pronunciations, one which is distinctly Japanese and the other which reflects the original Chinese pronunciation devoid of accents and tones. Without accents and tones the pronunciation of many of these characters now form homophones. *Kanji* compounds consisting of two or more characters usually utilize the Chinese pronunciation of the character. By themselves, individual characters are usually assigned the Japanese pronunciation. Second, *kanji* characters do not have separate phonemic components, so *kanji* characters cannot be decomposed phonemically in the manner of an alphabetic word. Because phonological representations are word-specific, it has generally been thought that meaning is directly accessed from *kanji*.

PHONOLOGICAL AND SEMANTIC ACTIVATION BY JAPANESE *KANJI*

Why do people generally believe that reading of *kanji* involves access to word meanings without the use of a phonological route (Barron, 1978; Coltheart, 1978, in Tan, et al., 1995)? There are three reasons: (a) the pictorial characters of *kanji* are based on the association of word meanings, (b) the appropriate pronunciation of *kanji* is very word-specific, and (c) *kanji* cannot be decomposed or broken down into phonemes in the same way that an alphabetic word can be broken down.

Wydell, Patterson, and Humphreys (1993) used Van Orden's homophone verification task to investigate phonology and meaning acquisition with Japanese *kanji*. They conducted two experiments with ten Japanese native speakers to determine (a) whether homophony had any impact beyond visual similarity, and (b) whether the homophony and word frequency relationship matched that of Van Orden's 1987 study of English. If the same word identification processes are involved in non-alphabetic word identification, it would be expected that homophones would be associated with longer reaction times (RT) and higher error rates than control words.

Table 1 shows examples of the categories and foils used by Wydell's group in the study. First is an example of a visually similar homophone foil. The category for this foil is "a type of debt." The correct exemplar is the *kanji* compound *akaj* meaning 'an overdraft.' The target homophone is *akaji* meaning 'red cloth.' These words are visually similar since they both share the character *aka*. Subjects were asked to decide whether the target word *akaji* (*i.e.* 'red cloth') belonged to the category "*fusai no issu*" meaning "a kind of debt." A subject is expected to correctly reject a target word by saying "no."

Table 1: Phonological access to *kanji*

category	target	correct exemplar
visually similar homophone 負債の一種 "type of debt"	赤地	赤字
visually similar control 国政の役割 "government official"	大根	大臣
visually dissimilar homophone 土の一種 "kind of dirt"	年度	粘土

from Wydell, Patterson & Humphreys (1993)

The second example in Table 1 is of a visually similar control foil. The non-homophone compounds *daikon* and *daijin* are visually similar because they share the character for *big*. Finally, *nendo* which means 'year' and the correct exemplar of *nendo* meaning 'clay' is an example in Table 1 of a visually dissimilar homophone foil; the two words have no character in common. Wydell, et al. reported that both the mean reaction time for correct rejections and the error rates showed reliable homophony effects. Response times were significantly longer for homophone foils (862 ms) than for control foils (795 ms), and more errors were made with homophone foils (14.5%) than with control foils (8.1%). These findings are contrary to the common assumption that access of meaning from *kanji* is mediated only by orthographic access to semantic meaning. Still, the data also showed a significant effect of visual similarity in all experiments. This serves to remind us that the orthographic processing of *kanji* is different from alphabetic processing in some ways. For example, incorrect target characters that were visually similar to a correct character were associated with longer RTs and higher error rates. The effects of both visual similarity and homophony were observed even under conditions of pattern masking through errors. The authors suggest that the results mean that (a) access from orthography to meaning is partially via phonological coding, and (b) categorization decisions require subsequent verification. It was argued that normal reading does not involve immediate backward visual masking so outcomes are applicable only to masking conditions, and that the major impacts of visual similarity survive masking in *kanji*. The lack of a target word frequency effect on homophone errors may be due to the common use of fairly narrow categories in these types of experiments. They concluded that the data suggest that the reading of *kanji* is characterized by parallel access to semantics from orthographic and phonological representation.

Another study by Flores d'Arcais, Saito, and Kawakami (1995) investigated recognition of single complex *kanji* characters. In these types of characters, the left radical gives some information about the meaning of the whole character, and the right radical gives information on pronunciation. An important and fundamental assumption was that each of the radicals alone is capable of activating either semantic or phonological information. If activation of this information by the separate radicals occurs at different rates, this could indicate that one particular type of information, either semantic or phonetic, is accepted before the other. In their experiments, subjects were exposed to the phonetic or semantic radical before being presented with a target character containing the radical. Subjects then had to name the character as rapidly as possible. An example of an experimental set is given in Table 2.

The main purpose of this experiment was to explore the effects of pre-exposure of each of the semantic or phonetic radicals on character naming. The results showed that phonetic radical pre-exposure facilitated correct responses, while semantic radical pre-exposure had only a weak degree of facilitation. What this means is that while both phonological and semantic pathways are apparently activated, phonological information seems to be far more readily available. A valid criticism of this work is that the task required naming and that to perform this task, the subjects had to retrieve phonological information.

Table 2: Phonological and semantic activation

character	meaning	pronunciation
校	"school"	kou
松	"pine"	shou
木	"tree"	moku
公	"public"	kou
交	"cross"	kou

from Flores d'Arcais, Saito, & Kawakami (1995)

PHONOLOGICAL ACTIVATION IN CHINESE READING

It seems that even for the logographic orthography of the Japanese word, meaning is accessed first through a phonological route. This is, however, based on the results of research on a single logographic orthography. The question now is whether Japanese *kanji* represents a unique situation among non-alphabetic orthographies. To address this question, experiments were conducted by Perfetti and Zhang (1995). Their results provide evidence that phonological information is also activated in Chinese character identification. Perfetti, Zhang, and Berent (1992) had argued earlier that a phonological principle applies to reading on a universal level. To support their position, they conducted experiments designed to determine whether Chinese readers use phonology in a semantic judgment task in which phonological information is interfering. In their studies, subjects were required to make two kinds of decisions: (a) a semantic decision — subjects were asked whether or not two characters had similar meanings (homophones create phonological interference), and (b) a phonological decision-subjects were asked whether two characters have the same pronunciation (characters with the same meaning create semantic interference).

The objective was to look for evidence of both phonological and semantic interference. Table 3 contains examples of the pairs of characters used in their synonym and homophone judgment tasks. The first two characters, which are both pronounced "shi," should generate a "yes" response in the homophone judgment task and a "no" response in the synonym judgment task. The opposite set of responses would be expressed for the two characters shown at the bottom when one judges synonyms but not homophones. For the control foil, shown here, the pair of characters are neither synonymous nor homophones.

Table 3: Phonological activation in Chinese

character	pronunciation	meaning	synonym judgement	homophone judgement
homophone				
事	shi	"master"	no	yes
視	shi	"see"		
control				
清	qing	"clear"	no	no
視	shi	"see"		
synonym				
看	kan	"look"	yes	no
視	shi	"see"		

from Perfetti & Zhang (1995)

Subjects took longer to reject homophone foils than controls in the synonym judgment tasks and longer to reject synonym foils than control foils in the homophone judgment tasks. In the synonym tasks, subjects had a higher error rate with homophone foils (2.6%) than with controls (0.5%). In the homophone judgment tasks, there was a higher error rate with synonym foils (2.3%) than with control foils (0.5%). These results suggest the existence of both semantic interference in homophone judgment tasks and homophone interference in semantic judgment tasks. It was posited that homophone interference was unavoidable because phonological information cannot be suppressed. While the lack of a common similarity scale makes it impossible to compare synonym judgment tasks with homophone judgments tasks, the responses with the synonym tasks were slower than with the homophone tasks. Perfetti and Zhang concluded, "it is reasonable to infer from the results that homophone judgments are more easily made than meaning judgments" (Perfetti & Zhang, 1995).

In another set of experiments, Perfetti and Zhang (1995) looked at the time course of phonological/semantic activation. No indication was found to suggest that phonological activation occurs at the expense of semantic activation. Chinese readers, therefore, do not appear to bypass phonology. The results of these experiments provide support for the existence of a universal principle of phonological processing in reading.

Finally, Tan, et al. (1995) examined phonological processing in Chinese character identification using a backward-masking procedure. There are three types of masking: (a) graphic mask (visually similar to the target), (b) homophonic/phonological mask (homophonic, but neither orthographically nor semantically related to the target), and (c) semantic mask (masks that were synonymous with the target). The experiments looked for the activation of phonology before access to meaning in Chinese character identification. The results of these studies showed that with short exposure times, graphic but not homophonic or semantic masks affected target recognition. Longer target and mask exposure times resulted in a significant phonological mask facilitation effect. Furthermore, with high-frequency targets having well-defined meanings, semantic masks facilitated target identification. By contrast, high-frequency targets with fuzzy meanings were not associated with a semantic mask effect. These results strongly suggest that character frequency is an important factor in the time course of phonetic and semantic activation.

DISCUSSION

Overall, studies of word identification in Chinese and Japanese orthographies have produced evidence that the reading of Chinese and Japanese *kanji* characters involves phonological recording similar to that employed with alphabetic orthography. The results of some of these studies, however, appear to be contradictory or at least ambiguous depending on the selection of characters and tasks. With respect to the study by Wydell, et al. (1993) it should be noted that several category names had characters in common with the target and/or exemplar.

An example of this can be seen between the category name *yoi kekka* 'a good result' and the visually similar homophone foils *seika* 'fruits and vegetables' and *seika* 'an achievement'. Both foils share the same *kanji* for *ka*, making them visually similar. The same character, however, is also found in the category name. When a subject sees this character in the category name *kekka* before being exposed to target or the exemplar, there may be a significant priming effect. The effect of this commonalty on response time and error rate is unknown but is of potential concern. In the study by Flores d'Arcais, et al. (1995), the use of single Japanese characters presents the potential for problems, because a *kanji* character, by itself, has at least two and often more pronunciations: an *on*-reading (derived from Chinese) and a *kun*-reading (derived from Japanese). The choice of pronunciation that should be used depends on the context and types of compounds that the character is usually associated with. This may affect the retrieval of phonological information in a naming task. Another concern was that the study by Perfetti and Zhang (1995) controlled the mean number of strokes in each character while the study of Tan, et al. (1995) did not control for the number of strokes. Furthermore, neither study provided any definitive evidence of whether the number of strokes had any impact on the amount of time required to identify a character.

IMPLICATIONS FOR JFL PEDAGOGY

On the basis of a review of the latest research, some major and pedagogically important implications for teaching Japanese *kanji* can be suggested. First, all types of information, including orthographic, phonologic, and semantic, appear to be involved in processing Japanese *kanji*, and thus instruction should take advantage of these different routes of information processing. Second, a recurring theme seems to be that phonological factors play an important and universal role in word identification regardless of differences in languages' writing systems.

The results of empirical research also have important pedagogical implications for the development of curriculum for the teaching of *kanji* to L2 and JFL learners. When considering these pedagogical implications for curriculum development, however, it is important to discuss whether these findings involving L1 learners are equally applicable to L2 and JFL learners. Koda (1994) examined L1 reading theories from the perspective of L2 learners. She identified three distinctions between L1 and L2 learners: (a) the consequences of prior reading experience, (b) the effects of cross-linguistic processing, and (c) the compensatory devices stemming from the efforts of learners with limited linguistic knowledge to solve comprehension problems. However, instructional research on *kanji* word identification in L2 learners is virtually absent in the literature. What is known is that a phonological coding system seems to be a dominant feature of the short-term memory (STM) encoding process regardless of a student's linguistic background. The direct teaching of L2 cognitive strategies to L2 learners would be expected to constitute effective pedagogy since L1 cognitive strategies are retained in L2 reading (Koda, 1989, 1990).

Hayes (1988) conducted experiments to compare the differences in phonological, visual, and semantic processing strategies used in STM between native and non-native readers of Chinese. The results of these studies revealed that native readers phonologically encode material at the character level, while the non-native speakers failed to show a clear-cut preference for phonological, visual, or semantic strategies, apparently using a mixed strategy of phonological and graphic encoding because they still feel uncertain dealing with characters. This led Hayes to suggest that students might increase fluency by paying less attention to the visual characteristics of characters. He also suggests providing students with background information on textual materials before the students actually begin to read the texts, so that they do not have to rely exclusively on the printed characters. Providing cultural information is also expected to help students to read and better understand their textual materials. Another strategy might involve an emphasis on the spoken language before students begin working with characters. This approach should enable students to develop the requisite phonological inferencing skills for learning *kanji*.

Matsunaga (1995) investigated the role of phonological coding in reading *kanji*. Her results suggested that for Japanese native speakers, pronunciation plays a significant role in reading *kanji*. The most direct interpretation of this is that *kanji* do not appear to act as ideographs at the psycholinguistic level. One of the pedagogical implications of this is that it might be more beneficial to introduce and emphasize speaking skills before efforts are made to develop reading and writing skills. This can be viewed as a more natural learning process, since native speakers acquire spoken oral language skills long before they learn to write their L1 orthography.

An excellent illustration of this can be found in a study of *kanji* learning in a Chinese L2 classroom at a US university (Packard, 1990). Students with a three-week time lag between the introduction of oral-aural Chinese and their introduction to logographic characters in their elementary Chinese program performed better in terms of phonetic discrimination and spoken Chinese than the students who had not been allowed a lag period. Very early emphasis on the orthographic elements of a character may reduce the learners' awareness of the phonological components of the target language. Thus, in terms of pedagogical implications, delaying introduction of orthographic materials and emphasis on the phonology may facilitate improved phonological discrimination and spoken fluency.

The results of the studies reviewed here indicate that greater effectiveness in the development of *kanji* identification skills may be achieved if learners are exposed to *kanji* in a more visually and phonologically meaningful way. The bulk of instructional materials that have been published, however, emphasize semantic and orthographic approaches to the study of *kanji*. For example

Basic Kanji Book (Kano, Shimizu, Takenaka, & Ishii, 1993) This book provides explanations about the origins and meanings of many individual *kanji*. The *on-kun* readings, strokes and radicals are all covered. The book is designed to help students to develop the skills to infer the meaning of a *kanji* from its construction. The book also teaches effective ways to memorize 500 *kanji* that were selected based on their frequency of use and utility in forming new words.

A Guide to Remembering Japanese Characters (Henshall, 1988) This book covers 1,945 *joyo kanji* and presents them in an order that is in accordance with the guidelines of the Japanese Ministry of Education. It provides extensive explanations of the origins and meanings of individual characters. The book also offers a number of valuable suggestions and mnemonic devices that students can use to learn individual characters.

Kanji Pict-O-Graphix: Over 1,000 Japanese Kanji and Kana Mnemonics (Rowley, 1992) This book also makes full use of pictographs and visual mnemonic devices many of which reflect the creativity of the book's authors.

The books mentioned above are essentially dedicated to the study of *kanji*. Perhaps a more important question for Japanese language teachers is how these books are integrated into an overall instructional program and how (and when) the various college Japanese language textbooks introduce *kanji*.

Situational Functional Japanese (Tsukuba Language Group, 1992) This popular textbook introduces the Japanese writing system, including all *hiragana* and *katakana*, early in volume one. Each lesson starts with a situational "model conversation" which introduces several *kanji* characters without any *furigana* pronunciation aids. On the pages that follow, several additional *kanji* are introduced, including pictographs, simple ideographs, compound ideographs, and phonetic ideographs. This book emphasizes overall communicative proficiency more than just the learning of *kanji*.

Shimizu & Kano (1992) developed a curriculum using *Situational Functional Japanese* in combination with the *Basic Kanji Book* as a supplemental text. They also developed a computer *kanji* instruction program as part of their intensive Japanese course consisting of 500 hours of instruction over a period of six months. The students start learning *kanji* three weeks into the course. The students are first provided with the computer program detailing the shapes of the individual *kanji* characters so they can prepare for the classroom lessons. The students are then encouraged to use the program outside of class to practice their pronunciation and semantic usage. Using the computer program motivates students to learn *kanji* on their own. The program also helps instructors to select specific characters for each lesson, monitor student progress in the course, develop effective *kanji* lessons, and fine-tune them to student needs and progress.

Yokoso: An Invitation to Contemporary Japanese (Tohsaku, 1994) This is another popular book that starts with a section which is designed to develop skill in spoken Japanese, including daily greetings and common expressions. The instructor's manual recommends that teachers spend two or three weeks on simple spoken Japanese (about 10 to 15 classroom hours). After this section, each chapter introduces about 25 *kanji* for a total of 169 characters in the textbook. The workbook/laboratory manual contains information about character strokes, and exercises in which students copy over *kanji* templates in order to gain writing proficiency. The instructor's manual suggests that instructors provide meaning and information about the intra- and extra-context of the *kanji* characters, connect the *on-kun* readings of *kanji* to spoken vocabulary, and initially emphasize recognition skills.

This review of several textbooks reveals that phonological material is not often emphasized. It is perhaps to be expected that this emphasis would be absent since by their very nature textbooks provide visually-oriented information. An area where immediate improvement could be made, however, would be to have *furigana* at least over all new *kanji* characters when they are first introduced. Some texts already provide this, but using those that do not, beginning students are unable to read a character unless they look the character up in a dictionary. Most texts rely heavily on the instructors to develop their own curricula for teaching *kanji*. Integration of *kanji* into the existing textual materials might benefit many instructors. The results of research into the mental processing of *kanji* can provide some insight into the development of effective curricula for teaching *kanji*.

We might seriously reconsider the value of introducing beginning students immediately to *kanji*. If it is true, as suggested by the research, that phonology plays a central role in the identification of *kanji*, then it may be better to delay introduction of *kanji* until students have a more substantial phonological base of language proficiency. At this point, further research using beginning learners of Japanese (rather than Packard's Chinese learners) would be most welcome.

Using a delay method in the classroom, new vocabulary would be introduced orally first. Then the orthographic form of those new words can be introduced in a manner that links the written characters to the earlier learned pronunciation and meaning. Students can be encouraged to practice *kanji* usage in contextually relevant short sentences so that they become familiar with the natural usage of the new vocabulary. After the learners are familiar with use of the new vocabulary in speech, the character's pronunciation can be written on the board in *furigana* in order to enable the student to match sound, meaning, and orthography.

In the classroom, additional activities and instructional materials should be used (in addition to textbooks) to develop *kanji* recognition skills and to facilitate mapping between the *kun* and *on* readings for specific *kanji* and *kanji* compounds. Such activities might include the use of flash cards and/or illustrated books (*manga*) which introduce *kanji* and the corresponding *furigana* in a contextually meaningful format (Yanagimachi, 1996, June).

Even more promising may be the use of innovative computer programs that allow for virtually unlimited latitude in the development of interactive software for *kanji* instruction. There are several computer programs for teaching *kanji* now available but most of them focus on orthography and the meaning of single *kanji*. As an illustration of what could be developed as the next generation of instructional software, dialogues and other situations in which *kanji* are being introduced in the textbook can be adapted to the computer, utilizing audio as well as animation and other video samples. *Kanji* presented to students in an attractive, meaningful, and multimedia format may help the many foreign language students who do not have adequate opportunities to hear authentic language outside of the classroom. Through the use of computers, students will be able to hear the pronunciation of *kanji* characters alone and in contextually-appropriate compounds. This will help students to map among *kanji* orthography, phonology, and semantics. The interactive nature of computer programs also allows each student to progress at his or her own pace and to better develop linguistic proficiency.

Finally, it is important that we recognize the value of psycholinguistic research that has been reviewed here. Certainly further research remains to be conducted and such research deserves our enthusiastic support. For example, there are exciting studies currently underway to determine whether adult learners of Japanese as a foreign language process *kanji* in the same way as native speakers. Japanese language educators are optimistic that ultimately these studies will make it possible to design and develop the most efficient and motivating language education programs, by using approaches that take advantage of underlying language-processing mechanisms that are part of the natural foundation of human cognition.

REFERENCES

Baron, J. (1973). *Words in the mind*. Oxford. England: Basil Blackwell.

Barron, R. W. (1978). Access to the meanings of printed words: Some implications for reading and learning to read. In F. B. Murray (Ed.), *The recognition of words: IRA series on the development of the reading process* (pp. 34–56). Newark, DE: International Reading Association.

Coltheart, M. (1978). Lexical access in simple reading tasks. In G. Underwood (Ed.), *Strategies of information processing* (pp. 151–216). London: Academic Press.

Coltheart, M. (1985). In defense of dual-route models of reading. *The Behavioral and Brain Sciences, 8*, 709–710.

Fan, K. Y. (1986). *Graphic symbol of the Chinese character*. A paper presented at the Symposium of Chinese Character Modernization, Beijing, China.

Flores d'Arcais, G. B., Saito, H., & Kawakami, M. (1995). Phonological and semantic activation in reading *kanji* characters. *Journal of Experimental Psychology: Learning, Memory, and Cognition, 21*, 34–42.

Hayes, E. B. (1988). Encoding strategies used by native and non-native readers of Chinese Mandarin. *The Modern Language Journal, 72*, 188–195.

Henshall, K. G., (1988). *A guide to remembering Japanese characters*. Tokyo: Tuttle Language Library.

Kano, C., Shimizu, Y., Takenaka, H., & Ishii, E. (1993). *Basic kanji book*. Tokyo: Bonjinsha.

Koda, K. (1989). Effects of L1 orthographic representation on L2 phonological coding strategies. *Journal of Psycholinguistic Research, 18* (2), 201–222.

Koda, K. (1990).The use of L1 reading strategies in L2 reading: Effects of L1 orthographic structures on L2 phonological recording strategies. *Studies in Second Language Acquisition, 12* (4), 393–410.

Koda, K. (1994). Second language reading research: Problems and possibilities. *Applied Psycholinguistics, 15,* 1–28.

Matsunaga, S. (1995). *The role of phonological coding in reading kanji: A research report and some pedagogical implications* (Technical Report #6). Honolulu: University of Hawai'i, Second Language Teaching & Curriculum Center.

McCusker, L. X., Hillinger, M. L., & Bias, R. G. (1981) . Phonological recording and reading. *Psychological Bulletin, 89,* 217–245.

Packard, J. L. (1990). Effects of time lag in the introduction of characters into Chinese language curriculum. *The Modern Language Journal, 74,* 167–175.

Patterson, K. E., & Coltheart, V. (1987). Phonological processes in reading: A tutorial review. In M. Coltheart (Ed.), *Attention and performance XII: The psychology of reading* (pp. 421–447). Hillsdale, NJ: Erlbaum.

Perfetti, C. A., & Zhang, S. (1995). Very early phonological activation in Chinese reading. *Journal of Experimental Psychology: Learning, Memory, and Cognition, 21,* 24–33.

Perfetti, C. A., Zhang, S., & Berent, I. (1992). Reading in English and Chinese: evidence for a "universal" phonological principle. In R. Frost & L. Kats (Eds.), *Orthography, phonology, morphology, and meaning* (pp. 227–248). Amsterdam: North-Holland.

Pollatsek, A., Lesch, M., Morris, R. K., & Rayner, K. (1992). Phonological codes are used in integrating information across saccades in word identification and reading. *Journal of Experimental Psychology: Human Perception and Performance, 18,* 148–162.

Rowley, M. (1992). *Kanji pict-o-graphix: Over 1,000 Japanese kanji and kana mnemonics.* Berkeley: Stone Bridge Press.

Seidenberg, M. S. (1985). The time course of phonological code activation in two writing systems. *Cognition, 19,* 1–30.

Seidenberg, M. S., & McClelland, J. L. (1989). A distributed, developmental model of word recognition and naming. *Psychological Review, 96,* 523–568.

Shi, X. Y., & Yang, Q. H. (1984). *Xian dai han yu* [Modern Chinese language]. Beijing, China: Beijing Normal University Press.

Shimizu, Y., & Kano, C. (1992). Using computers in *kanji* lessons. *Nihongo Kyoiku, 78,* 92–105.

Tan, L. H., Hoosain, R., & Peng, D. (1995). Role of early presemantic phonological code. *Journal of Experimental Psychology: Learning, Memory and Cognition, 21,* 43–54.

Tohsaku, Y. (1994). *Yokoso: An invitation to contemporary Japanese.* New York: MacGraw-Hill.

Van Orden, G. C. (1987). A rose is a rose: Spelling, sound and reading. *Memory & Cognition, 15,* 181–198.

Van Orden, G. C. (1991). Phonologic mediation is fundamental to reading. In D. Besner & G. W. Humphreys (Eds.), *Basic processes in reading.* (pp. 77–103). Hillsdale, NJ: Erlbaum.

Van Orden, G. C., Johnston, J. C., & Hale, B. L. (1988) Word identification in reading proceeds from spelling to sound to meaning. *Journal of Experimental Psychology: Learning, Memory, and Cognition, 14*, 371–386.

Wydell, T. N., Patterson, K. E. & Humphreys, G. W. (1993). Phonologically mediated access to meaning for *kanji*: Is a rows still a rose in Japanese *kanji*? *Journal of Experimental Psychology: Learning, Memory, and Cognition, 19*, 491–514.

Yanagimachi, T. (1996, June). *The phonology based decoding of meaning in kanji and its implications for teaching Japanese*. Paper presented at the Tenth New England Japanese Pedagogy Workshop, Cambridge, MA.

Zhu, X. (1988, August). Xiandai hanzi xingshengzi shengpang biaoyin gongneng de fenxi [Analyses of the cueing function of the phonetic in modern Chinese]. In X. Yuan (Ed.), *Proceedings of the Symposium on the Chinese Language and Character* (pp. 260–288). Beijing: Guang Ming Daily Press.

Yoko Okita
University of Hawai'i at Mānoa and University of Texas at Austin

STUDENTS' BELIEFS ABOUT LEARNING JAPANESE ORTHOGRAPHY: BEYOND THE TEXTBOOKS

INTRODUCTION

The present study addresses two questions: (a) whether students' beliefs about learning *kanji* change when the textbooks are changed, and (b) whether Japanese language learning experience affects students' beliefs about learning *kanji*. Belief has been acknowledged as an important construct of individual differences (IDs) that influence learning outcomes in second language acquisition (SLA) (Ellis, 1994). Students, especially adults, come to the classroom with strong beliefs, "mini theories," on language learning (Horwitz, 1987). Students' beliefs on language learning affect their approach to learning (e.g., choice of learning strategies) and consequently may affect their learning outcomes (Ellis, 1994). Figure 1 shows the schematic interrelationship between IDs, strategy use, and learning outcomes proposed by Ellis (1994, p. 473).

The three factors are interrelated. One of the purposes of second language acquisition research research is to understand the nature of interrelationships between these factors (Ellis, 1994).

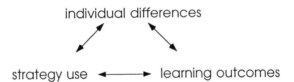

Figure 1. **The relationship between individual differences, strategy use, and learning outcomes**

Further, IDs (e.g., age, sex, experience, cognitive styles, motivation, and beliefs) themselves are interrelated. Several studies report that learning environments and experience affect students' beliefs on learning foreign languages. For example, Elbaum, Berg, and Dodd (1993) investigated the relationships between language learning strategy use, beliefs of the efficacy of strategies, and previous learning experience among American college students who were taking foreign language classes. They found that students with formal instruction strongly believed the

Okita, Y. (1997). Students' beliefs about learning Japanese orthography: Beyond the textbooks. In H. M. Cook, K. Hijirida, & M. Tahara (Eds.), *New trends and issues in teaching Japanese language and culture* (Technical Report #15, pp. 61–75). Honolulu: University of Hawai'i, Second Language Teaching and Curriculum Center.

efficacy of using rule-following strategies, whereas students in immersion programs or with no formal instruction strongly believed the efficacy of using functional strategies. However, interrelationships between IDs still have not been well explored in second language acquisition (Ellis, 1994).

In Japanese as a foreign language (JFL), not much interest has been placed on students' beliefs on learning Japanese. Learning *kanji* (Chinese characters in Japanese) has been regarded as one of the most difficult tasks in learning Japanese especially for students whose native languages do not use Chinese characters. When *kanji* should be introduced or how to teach *kanji* has been a hot topic in teaching JFL in the US. However, students' beliefs and their influence on *kanji* learning processes have been absent from educators' arguments.

Educators who believe in speech primacy argue that students must learn the spoken language first as children learn spoken language first in their first language. For example, Unger, Lorish, Noda, and Wada (1993) argue that literacy is not a prerequisite of learning linguistic competence and a solid foundation of the spoken language best ensures steady reading progress (p. 12). Further, they argue that using romanized texts reduces the burden of learning Japanese at the initial stage. Those educators who prefer romanized texts strongly recommend introducing Japanese orthography (*kana* and *kanji*) after students have developed substantial oral and aural skills (e.g., Unger, et al., 1993). Under the speech primacy premise, romanized Japanese texts are used at the beginning; Japanese orthography is introduced later.

On the other hand, some educators question the use of non-authentic texts. For example, Koda (1992) claims that if students are exposed to non-authentic script at the beginning, they develop the sound-visual decoding system which is linked to non-authentic script. And students have to reconstruct the sound-visual decoding system when the authentic writing system is introduced later. Therefore, early exposure to non-authentic print might make learning authentic writing systems complex, difficult, and might hinder the development of a student's reading proficiency, even though non-authentic print may facilitate initial learning. Recent psycholinguistic studies show that the most basic and essential skill in reading is word recognition, extracting visual information from print (e.g., Adams, 1990). Increasing the degree of exposure to print is thought to be one of the best ways to improve word recognition skills (Stanovich & West, 1989). Early introduction of authentic print definitely increases the amount of exposure to print (Koda, 1992).

The University of Hawai'i at Mānoa (UHM) shifted the beginning level textbooks from *Japanese: The Spoken Language* (JSL) (Vols. 1–2) (Jorden & Noda, 1987–1988) to *Situational Functional Japanese* (SFJ) (Vols. I–III) (Tsukuba Language Group, 1992) in 1994. The former textbook, JSL, is based on the speech primacy premise and uses only romanized Japanese texts. Conversations, new vocabulary, and example sentences for grammar explanations are all romanized. The Japanese writing systems and reading were taught using separate handouts. That is, spoken and written Japanese were taught separately by using different materials that employ different writing systems. At UHM, conversations in JSL were transcribed in *kanji* and *kana* and were provided as an additional material. Students had an opportunity to be exposed to Japanese orthography. However, the degree of exposure to Japanese orthography using *JSL* was very limited. Most of the classroom activities that were used for grammar and conversation exercises did not involve Japanese orthography much. Further, given this author's teaching experience using *JSL* and observing students from other Japanese classes, what students usually used was the textbook, not handouts. For example, students read the textbook before oral examinations. Thin separate handouts were easily ignored.

On the other hand, the latter textbook, *SFJ*, uses Japanese orthography (*hiragana*, *katakana*, and *kanji*) from Lesson 1. Students are exposed to Japanese orthography not only when they learn reading and writing but also when they learn grammar and conversations. Students using *SFJ* are more exposed to the Japanese writing system than those students using *JSL*. Since the two textbooks are drastically different in the degree of exposure to Japanese orthography, they provide a good and rare opportunity to investigate solo effect of the degree of exposure to Japanese texts of the textbook on students' beliefs on learning the Japanese writing system.

The present study examines whether students' beliefs about learning *kanji* changed when the new textbook was adopted and whether their Japanese learning experiences in the past affected their beliefs about learning *kanji* in regard to the following five beliefs which have been widely recommended by educators in Japan and the US. The following are the five beliefs.

Belief 1: Instructors should provide information on how to learn *kanji*.

Belief 2: I know how to learn *kanji*.

Belief 3: The Japanese orthography should be introduced from the beginning of the instruction of Japanese.

Belief 4: The Japanese orthography should be introduced after substantial spoken Japanese has been acquired.

Belief 5: Knowledge of radicals will enhance *kanji* learning.

METHOD

PARTICIPANTS

The participants were 337 students enrolled in one of the basic Japanese language courses, 102, 201, or 202 at the University of Hawai'i at Mānoa from 1994 to 1996. 208 participants used *JSL* and 129 used *SFJ*. None of the participants had learned Chinese characters in their native languages. None of the classes were taught by this author. The textbook used in all the courses in 1994 was *Japanese: The Spoken Language Part 1, or 2* (JSL) (Jorden & Noda, 1987). The textbook used in all the courses in 1995 and 1996 was *Situational Functional Japanese Vol. I, II, or III* (SFJ) (Tsukuba Language Group, 1992).

Table 1 shows the number of participants with or without previous learning experience of *kanji* before entering UHM. Most of the students (85% in 1994 and 94.5% in 1995 and 1996) had learned Japanese before entering UHM. However, most of them (96.6% in 1994 and 97% in 1995 and 1996) did not learn *kanji* before UHM. Table 2 shows the ethnic backgrounds of the participants. About 70% of the students (69.7% in 1994 and 71.3% in 1995 and 1996) were Japanese-American or related to Japanese. Table 3 shows the native languages of the participants. About ninety percent of the students (88.5% in 1994 and 90.5% in 1995 and 1996) reported their native language as English.

Table 1: Number of participants with/without Japanese language experience

learning experience	94	95/96
yes	176	122
no	31	7

Table 2: Ethnic background of participants

ethnicity	94	95/96
Japanese	107 (51.4%)	77 (59.7%)
Japanese mixed	38 (18.3%)	15 (11.6%)
Caucasian	18	10
Chinese	16	13
Korean	8	5
Pacific	15	9
other	6	0

Table 3: Native languages of participants

native language	94	95/96
English	184 (88.5%)	117 (90.7%)
English + Japanese	18 (8.7%)	4 (3.1%)
English + other	3	3
Chinese	2	4
Korean	1	1

Table 4 shows the number of *kanji* which are introduced in each textbook. The total number of *kanji* introduced during the two years of instruction in *SFJ* is 500, whereas that in *JSL* is 325. The number of *kanji* introduced in *SFJ* is almost twice as many as that in *JSL*.

Table 4: Number of *kanji* introduced in each course

class	number of *kanji* introduced in JSL	number of *kanji* introduced in SFJ
JPN 102	73	140
JPN 201	110	160
JPN 202	142	200
TOTAL	325	500

METHODOLOGY

The instrument used in this study was a questionnaire developed by this author. The questionnaire consists of the five questions about beliefs about learning *kanji*. Each question was followed by a five-point Likert response scale, labeled: 1 "strongly disagree", 2 "disagree", 3 "neither", 4 "agree", and 5 "strongly agree." The validity of students' reports might be questioned, for students may not report what they really do or believe. However, researchers can gather data based on a large number of participants in a short time of period using written reports. A large number of participants reduces the risk of threatening the internal validity due to the truthfulness of students' self-reports. Further scaled measurement allows the researcher to obtain data constantly regardless of time differences.

Instructors were asked to hand out and collect the questionnaire in the classroom. The questionnaire was assigned as homework. Participation was strictly voluntary.

DATA ANALYSIS

Chi-square tests were used to examine all five items in the questionnaire for significance by year (textbook difference) and Japanese language learning experience. For the chi-square tests, responses 1 and 2 ("strongly disagree" and "agree") were consolidated into one "disagree" category, and responses 4 and 5 ("agree" and "strongly agree") were consolidated into one "agree" category.

Results of the chi-square tests were considered statistically significant with an alpha level of .05.

RESULTS

In this section we will test Question 1, "Did students' beliefs about learning *kanji* change when the textbooks changed?," on the five beliefs mentioned above.

Belief 1: Instructors should provide information on how to learn *kanji*.

Figure 2 shows the percentage change by year. The chi-square test was not significant, $\chi^2(2, N=336)=4.49$, $p<.2$. Students' beliefs did not change when the textbook was changed. Students wanted instructors to provide information how to learn *kanji* regardless of the textbook.

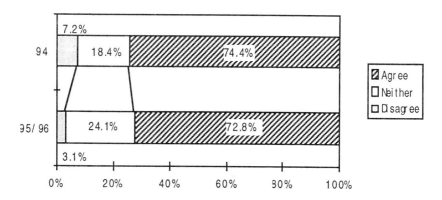

Figure 2. Percentage change by year for Belief 1

Belief 2: I know how to learn *kanji*.

Figure 3 shows the percentage change by year. The chi-square test was not significant, $\chi^2(2, N=333)=1.64$, $p<.8$. Students' beliefs did not change when the textbook was changed. About 40% of the students thought they knew how to learn *kanji* and about 45% of the students were not sure whether they knew how to learn *kanji* regardless of the textbook.

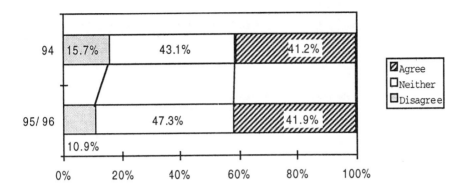

Figure 3. Percentage change by year for Belief 2

Belief 3: Japanese orthography should be introduced from the beginning of the instruction of Japanese.

Figure 4 shows the percentage change by year. The chi-square test was not significant, $\chi^2(2, N=335)=1.58$, $p<.7$. Students' beliefs did not change when the textbook was changed. About 70% of the students wanted Japanese orthography to be introduced from the beginning of instruction regardless of the textbook.

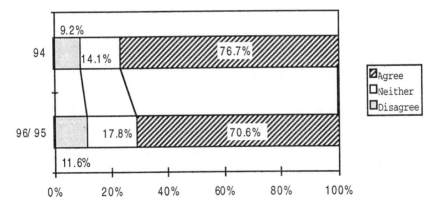

Figure 4. Percentage change by year for Belief 3

Belief 4: Japanese orthography should be introduced after substantial spoken Japanese has been acquired.

Figure 5 shows the percentage change by year. The chi-square test was not significant, $\chi^2(2, N=335)=2.80$, $p<.5$. Students' beliefs did not change when the textbook was changed. About half of the students disagreed with learning Japanese orthography after acquiring substantial spoken Japanese regardless of the textbook.

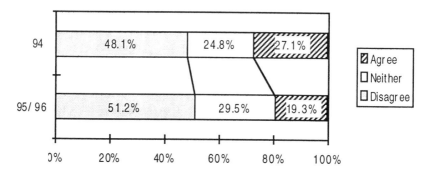

Figure 5. Percentage change by year for Belief 4

Belief 5: Knowledge of radicals will enhance *kanji* learning.

Figure 6 shows the percentage change by year. The chi-square test was not significant, $\chi^2(2, N=334)=2.80$, $p<.5$. Students' beliefs did not change when the textbook was changed. About 60% of the students wanted to learn about radicals regardless of the textbook.

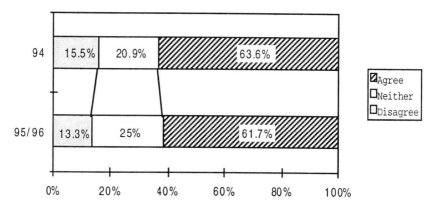

Figure 6. Percentage change by year for Belief 5

In this section we will test Question 2, "Do students' beliefs about learning *kanji* differ between participants with and without Japanese learning experience?," on the five beliefs.

Belief 1: Instructors should provide information on how to learn *kanji*.

Figure 7 shows the percentage comparison between participants with and without Japanese learning experience. The chi-square test was significant, $\chi^2(2, N=335)=6.19$, $p<.05$. Post hoc comparisons using residual analysis revealed that students who did not have Japanese learning experience chose "neither" significantly less and chose "agree" significantly more. Table 5 shows the results of residual analysis. Significantly more students without Japanese learning experience wanted instruction on how to learn *kanji*.

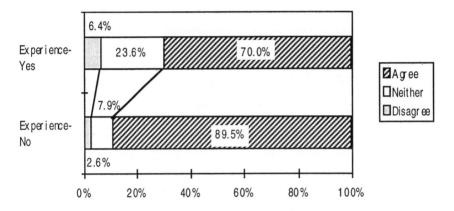

Figure 7. Percentage comparison between participants with and without Japanese learning experience for Belief 1

Table 5: Results of residual analysis by Japanese learning experience for Belief 1

experience	disagree	neither	agree
yes	n.s.	n.s.	n.s.
no	n.s.	–s	+s

note: n.s. = no significance
–s = significantly less frequent
+s = significantly more frequent

Belief 2: I know how to learn *kanji*.

Figure 8 shows the percentage comparison between participants with and without Japanese learning experience. The chi-square test was not significant, $\chi^2(2, N=332)=4.25$, $p<.2$. Students' beliefs did not differ between students with and students without Japanese learning experience. About 45% of the students were not sure whether they knew how to learn *kanji* and about 40% of the students were sure that they knew how to learn *kanji*.

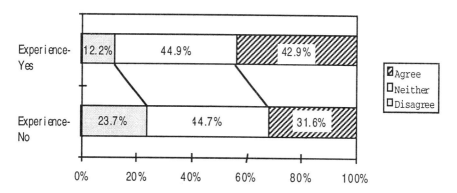

Figure 8. Percentage comparison between participants with and without Japanese learning experience for Belief 2

Belief 3: Japanese orthography should be introduced from the beginning of the instruction of Japanese.

Figure 9 shows the percentage comparison between participants with and without Japanese learning experience. The chi-square test was not significant, $\chi^2(2, N=335)=1.07$, $p<.7$. Students' beliefs did not differ between students with and students without Japanese learning experience. About 70% of the students wanted Japanese orthography to be introduced from the beginning of instruction regardless of their learning experience.

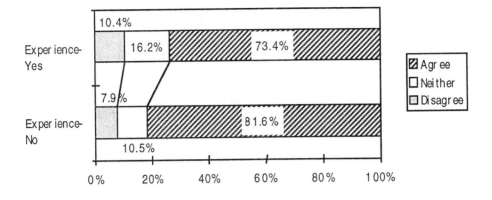

Figure 9. Percentage comparison between participants with and without Japanese learning experience for Belief 3

Belief 4: Japanese orthography should be introduced after substantial spoken Japanese has been acquired.

Figure 10 shows the percentage comparison between participants with and without Japanese learning experience. The chi-square test was not significant, $\chi^2(2, N=335)=1.07$, $p<.7$. Students' beliefs did not differ between students with and students without Japanese learning experience. About half of the students disagreed with the speech primacy promise.

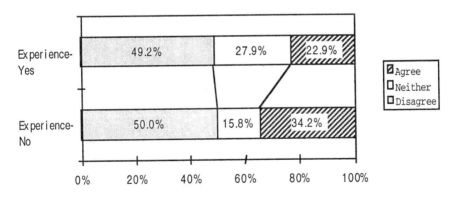

Figure 10. Percentage comparison between participants with and without Japanese learning experience for Belief 4

Belief 5: Knowledge of radicals will enhance *kanji* learning.

Figure 11 shows the percentage comparison between participants with and without Japanese learning experience. The chi-square test was significant, $\chi^2(2, N=334)=13.17$, $p<.01$. Post hoc comparisons using residual analysis revealed that students who did not have Japanese learning experience chose "disagree" significantly less and chose "neither" significantly more. Table 6 shows the results of residual analysis. Significantly more students without Japanese learning experience seem to be confused by learning *kanji*.

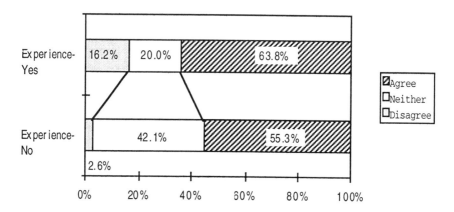

Figure 11. Percentage comparison between participants with and without Japanese learning experience for Belief 5

Table 6: Results of residual analysis by Japanese learning experience for Belief 5

experience	disagree	neither	agree
yes	n.s.	n.s.	n.s.
no	−s.	+s	n.s.

note: n.s. = no significance
−s = significantly less frequent
+s = significantly more frequent

DISCUSSION

The five beliefs which were investigated in this study did not change when the students' textbooks changed. This finding suggests that students' beliefs about learning *kanji* are independent of the type of textbook or teachers' beliefs about learning *kanji* that underlie the textbooks. It can be said that textbooks in and of themselves do not affect students' beliefs about learning *kanji*. However, all the participants of the present study were students at the University of Hawai'i at Mānoa. Therefore, the finding of the present study might reflect teaching methodology at UHM. That is, teaching at UHM did not change with the textbook change. Further studies at other institutions are necessary to determine more conclusively whether different textbooks affect students' beliefs or not.

This author's preliminary research data (Okita, 1996a) show that students' preference for early introduction of Japanese orthography positively correlates with *kanji* achievement test scores, $r=0.596$, $N=33$, $p<0.001$, whereas students' preferences for speech primacy negatively correlates with *kanji* achievement test scores, $r=-0.524$, $N=33$, $p<0.002$. Further, Okita (1996b) reports that there were no relationships between students' beliefs on speech primacy and the verbal and visual learning styles. These results suggest that the students' beliefs on speech primacy might influence *kanji* learning achievement, whereas the students' beliefs on speech primacy do not relate to the verbal and visual learning styles and the degree of exposure to Japanese orthography by the textbooks. What determines the students' beliefs on speech primacy? Further research is needed to understand the mechanism of forming the beliefs on speech primacy and the relationship between speech primacy preference and *kanji* learning success.

Belief in speech primacy in JFL is strong in the US (e.g., Unger, et al., p. 46). However, most students surveyed in this study did not support the concept of speech primacy whether or not the textbook used was speech primacy based. The students' beliefs on speech primacy also did not differ whether or not they had past Japanese learning experience. The majority of the participants (approximately 70%) agreed with introducing Japanese orthography from the very beginning of instruction. Approximately half of the students disagreed with introducing Japanese orthography after acquisition of spoken Japanese (i.e., speech primacy). Further, speech primacy might negatively affect *kanji* learning (Okita, 1996a). These findings suggest that the speech primacy premise might hinder *kanji* learning and teachers should reconsider applying the speech primacy premise to teaching Japanese.

Interestingly the frequency distributions of Belief 3, "Japanese orthography should be introduced from the beginning of the instruction of Japanese," and Belief 4, "Japanese orthography should be introduced after substantial spoken Japanese has been acquired," were not complementary. About 70% of the students agreed to introduce Japanese orthography from the beginning, whereas about 50% of the students disagreed with the speech primacy premise. Given that about 30% of the students could not make a decision on the speech primacy premise, many students seem not to be able to determine whether the speech primacy is beneficial or not, even though most of them support early introduction of Japanese orthography as a principle.

Past learning experience did affect the students' beliefs about learning *kanji*. Significantly more students without Japanese learning experience wanted instructors to provide information on how to learn *kanji*. Significantly more students without Japanese learning experience were not certain whether knowledge of radicals would enhance *kanji* learning. This finding suggests that students without Japanese learning experience wanted considerable guidance from instructors. According to Hatasa's (1989) survey, half of the institutions in the US did not teach *kanji* systematically (e.g., teaching radicals or explaining etymology). The finding of the present study suggests the necessity of systematic *kanji* instruction.

The present study showed that the type of textbook does not affect the students' beliefs about learning *kanji*, rather students' beliefs were affected by their past Japanese learning experience. The present study supports the finding of Elbaum, et al. (1993) that foreign language learning experience does affect students' beliefs on language learning.

The social and geographical environments of the present study are unique. The majority of the participants were Japanese-Americans and had previous Japanese learning experience. The number of participants who did not have previous Japanese language learning experience was quite small. Therefore, further studies in other social and geographical environments are necessary for a more conclusive generalization.

CONCLUSION

Students' beliefs about learning *kanji* did not differ regardless of the textbook. Rather students' beliefs were affected by their past Japanese learning experience. The finding of this study supports the idea that language learning experience affects students' beliefs on language learning. Students without Japanese learning experience wanted guidance to learn *kanji*. This finding suggests that instruction on how to learn *kanji* is necessary, especially for beginning students. Speech primacy was not supported by the majority of the participants regardless of the textbook. Speech primacy preference does not relate to the degree of exposure to Japanese orthography of the textbook and the verbal and visual learning styles, even though speech primacy preference might negatively affect *kanji* learning outcomes. Further research is necessary to investigate how students' beliefs on speech primacy are formed and relate to *kanji* learning success. Most participants of the present study were Japanese-Americans in Hawai'i with past Japanese learning experience. They do not represent students of Japanese in general. Therefore, further studies in other situations are necessary to generalize the findings of the present study more conclusively.

REFERENCES

Adams, M. J. (1990). *Beginning to read: Thinking and learning about print*. Cambridge, MA: MIT Press.

Elbaum, B., Berg, C., & Dodd, D. (1993). Previous learning experience, strategy beliefs, and task definition in self-regulated foreign language learning. *Contemporary Educational Psychology, 18*, 318–336.

Ellis, R. (1994). *The study of second language acquisition*. Oxford, UK: Oxford University Press.

Jorden, E., & Noda, M. (1987–1988). *Japanese: The spoken language* (Parts 1 and 2). New Haven, CT: Yale University Press.

Hatasa, K. (1989). A study of learning and teaching of *kanji* for nonnative learners of Japanese. *Dissertation Abstracts International, 50*, 1238A.

Horwitz, E. (1987). Surveying student beliefs about language learning. In A. Wenden, & J. Rubin (Eds.), *Learner Strategies in Language Learning* (pp. 119–129). Englewood Cliffs, NJ: Prentice Hall.

Koda, K. (1992). The effects of lower-level processing skills on FL reading performance: Implications for instruction. *Modern Language Journal, 76*(4), 502–512.

Okita, Y. (1996a). *Kanji gakushuu sutoratejii to kanji gakushuu shinnen to kanji seiseki tono kankei* [Correlations between *kanji* learning achievement test scores and students' beliefs on *kanji* learning]. Unpublished raw data.

Okita, Y. (1996b). *Students' beliefs on kanji and verbal and visual learning styles*. Manuscript submitted for publication.

Stanovich, K. E. & West, R. F. (1989). Exposure to print and orthographic processing. *Reading Research Quarterly, 24*(4), 402–433.

Unger, J. M., Lorish, F. C., Noda, M., & Wada, Y. (1993). *A framework for introductory Japanese language curricula in American high schools and colleges*. Washington, DC: National Foreign Language Center.

Tsukuba Language Group. (1992). *Situational functional Japanese* (Vols. 1–3, Note and Drill). Tokyo: Bonjinsha.

Yukiko Abe Hatasa
University of Iowa
Yasu-Hiko Tohsaku
University of California, San Diego

SPOT AS A PLACEMENT TEST

INTRODUCTION

SPOT (Simple Performance Oriented Test) is a type of indirect test designed to measure an ongoing processing ability of grammar (Ford, Kobayashi, & Yamamoto, 1994; Kobayashi, Ford, & Yamamoto, 1996). It consists of a set of sentences in which one *hiragana* letter is deleted. The sentences are read at a natural speed consecutively, and the test taker is to supply missing *hiragana* as he/she listens to them. Reliability and discriminability of SPOT has been studied in Japan (Ford, Kobayashi, & Yamamoto, 1995; Kobayashi, Ford, & Yamamoto, 1995), but very little research has been conducted elsewhere. Since 1995, a group of researchers from Australia, South Korea, and the United States have been conducting joint research to explore the applicability of SPOT in foreign language settings. This paper presents the results of two studies which investigated the test quality of SPOT, and the relationship between the scores on SPOT and learners' performance on other tests, as well as class performance. The results in both studies indicate that SPOT is a highly efficient and reliable test method which could be used as a placement test in Japanese as a foreign language in the US.

RESEARCH ON SPOT

SPOT was developed by a group of researchers at the University of Tsukuba (Kobayashi & Ford, 1991, 1992) to investigate how well learners of Japanese can process grammar while listening. They hypothesized that learners could process structures and lexical items that they had acquired but not those they had not yet acquired. For the purpose of this study, they developed such a test as follows:

1. 頭 （　） 痛いんです。

2. ごはんを食べ （　） した。

3. 東京行きのバスはど （　） ですか。

4. お金が少し （　） かないから、旅行には行きません。

5. 昨日、母にしか （　） れました。

Hatasa, Y. & Tohsaku, Y-H. (1997). SPOT as a placement test. In H. M. Cook, K. Hijirida, & M. Tahara (Eds.), *New trends and issues in teaching Japanese language and culture* (Technical Report #15, pp. 77–98). Honolulu: University of Hawai'i, Second Language Teaching and Curriculum Center.

6. 先生、にもつを（　）持ちしましょうか。

7. 明日、雨が降った（　）、うちにいます。

As shown in these examples, each question has one blank corresponding to one *hiragana* letter. Each blank selected is related to a certain grammatical item. Each test sentence is semantically independent, and there is no contextual relationship among the sentences. Test takers fill in the blanks while listening to the taped narration of sentences. On the tape, each sentence is read only once, and there is a two-second pause between sentences. Because each set of tests consists of 60 to 65 sentences, the total time required for completing the test is ten to fifteen minutes. Only the exact answers are accepted, and thus, grading is relatively simple and does not require much time.

This test format is similar to a cloze test (Oller & Conrad, 1971; Oller, 1979; Klain-Braley, 1981; Bachman, 1982, 1985; Shin, 1990) and a c-test (Klain-Braley & Raatz, 1984; Klain-Braley, 1985), but it is different from them with respect to the following features:

1. SPOT uses an audio tape, and the answer is given on the tape. Neither the cloze test nor c-test uses a tape.

2. SPOT items are independent from each other because each item appears once in a sentence and sentences in the test are all unrelated. On the other hand, in cloze and c-tests, test items are dependent on each other because more than one item is likely to be embedded in a sentence which is in the text.

3. SPOT is not affected by topic familiarity or text difficulty unlike a cloze or c-test.

4. Deleted items in SPOT are grammar items. Items on a cloze test with a rational deletion procedure may or may not be grammar items, and items on a cloze test with a random deletion procedure or those in a c-test are not necessarily grammar items.

5. A letter which represents one mora is deleted in SPOT. One word or a part of a word is deleted in a cloze or c-test.

6. SPOT is a timed test in that learners have a limited time to fill in the blanks. A cloze or c-test is not necessarily a timed test.

Kobayashi and Ford (1992) found that SPOT was highly correlated (r=.81) with the grammar section of the placement test used at the University of Tsukuba, while it was moderately correlated with the other sections of the same test (r=.75 with listening, r=.69 with reading, and r=.61 with character recognition and production). They also found that some grammatical items were not processed until the learners reached a high level of proficiency. In a subsequent study, Kobayashi, Ford, and Yamamoto, (1994) investigated whether the orthography used in the test makes any difference. They compared the performance of two versions of SPOT. The two versions were identical except that one was written in Japanese syllabaries (the *hiragana* version), whereas the other version was written in syllabaries and Chinese characters (the *kanji* and *kana* version). The results showed that the orthography did not affect the test performance. Since over eighty percent of the subjects were Asian students who use Chinese characters in their native language, the lack of significance may be attributed to the fact that they were used to reading Chinese characters. The results may have been different if the subjects had come from languages with alphabets (e.g., English).

Ford, et al. (1995) compared the performance on SPOT with or without the audio tape stimuli. They gave the same test to two different groups (a total of 240 subjects) whose proficiency ranged from beginning to intermediate levels. The results indicated that the tape did not affect the overall performance on the test for students who scored high (i.e., top 25% of students). The use of the tape seemed to positively affect the performance in this group, though the results were not statistically significant. On the other hand, the use of the audio stimuli significantly affected the performance of students who scored low (i.e. bottom 25% of students), $F(5,161)=11.65$, $p<.01$. More specifically, the latter group tended to perform better when the tape was not used. Furthermore, the items answered correctly in the taped version corresponded to those answered correctly in the untaped version only at twenty-four percent of the time. Ford, et al. (1995) concluded that SPOT may have tested different abilities between the two versions in the case of lower scores, while it did test the same ability in the case of high scorers regardless of the use of tape. They argued that lower scorers had not yet developed an ongoing language processing abilities, which resulted in a different performance. However, the high scorers had developed automaticity in an ongoing processing of language, and thus, could actually benefit from the presence of sound stimuli.

These studies indicated a differential development of grammar processing according to language proficiency, and that SPOT seems to measure ongoing processing of grammar. However, the studies were conducted at one university in Japan, and, thus, its generalizability to other testing situations is highly limited. Also, no reports on reliability or item quality have been made. Without such data, it is difficult to say how well SPOT actually measures learners' ability. Therefore, the present studies were undertaken to investigate the quality of SPOT as well as its applicability in a foreign language learning environment.

STUDY 1

Study 1 was conducted at the University of Iowa to examine the quality of SPOT. In this study, reliability, item discriminability and difficulty, and relationship with other skills have been analyzed to find out how well SPOT can distinguish different proficiency levels and how consistently such distinctions may be made. The instructional environment and student population is very different from those in Japan. Thus, these background issues will be described first.

INSTRUCTIONAL ENVIRONMENT

The University of Iowa offers four years of Japanese language courses and one review course for high school graduates. In general, four skills are emphasized in all of the courses, though there is a gradual shift in emphasis from speaking/listening to reading/writing in four years. The instructional approach is communicative, but accuracy is also emphasized. The syllabus is based on theme-function or on tasks. The first-year Japanese and the review courses put a special emphasis on communication strategies, reading and listening strategies, and learning strategies. Instructors and teaching assistants (TAs) teach most of the courses as a team, except for the review course and the fourth year, which are taught by a senior TA. There is no difference between what TAs are assigned to teach and what instructors teach. Both TAs and instructors teach grammar, activities, reading, and so on. All of the courses meet every day except for fourth-year Japanese which meets three times a week.

The majority of students are Caucasian American. Less than 10% of students come from other ethnic backgrounds. Most non-Caucasian students are Chinese and Korean. Students take these courses because of interests in Japanese culture. Approximately one third of them major in Japanese. There are virtually no opportunities to practice Japanese outside of class, so instructors and students organize conversation hours approximately three times a week outside of class.

DESIGN OF THE STUDY

Subjects

Eighty-two students who were enrolled in the Japanese language courses participated in the study. Of those, 42 students were enrolled in the second semester of first-year Japanese, 19 students were in second-year Japanese, 15 students were in third year Japanese, and five students were in fourth-year Japanese. The majority of students were native speakers of English. Two students in the first-year Japanese course were Korean, and one student was Chinese. Three students in the second-year course were Korean. Two students in the third-year course were Korean, and one student in the fourth-year course was Chinese.

Materials

Two versions of SPOT were used in this study. Version 3 was constructed for students at beginning and intermediate levels, and it was written in *kanji* with *hiragana* superscripts. Version 2 was written in *kanji* without *hiragana* superscripts and it was intended for advanced students. The placement test used at the University of Tsukuba was also administered to investigate the relationship between SPOT and other skills, as well as to compare the results of the present study with those of the University of Tsukuba. The placement test consisted of 28 listening items, 24 reading items for all levels, 30 grammar items for beginning/intermediate students, and an additional 30 items for advanced students (see Table 1). All of the items were in a multiple-choice format.

Table 1: Test materials

level	placement test (2 hours)	SPOT (15 minutes)
1st & 2nd year	Listening (28 items) Reading (24 items) Grammar: Part 1 (30 items)	Version 3 (60 items)
3rd & 4th year	Listening (28 items) Reading (24 items) Grammar: Part 1 and Part 2 (30 items + 30 items = 60 items)	Version 2 (65 items)

Procedure

During the third week of the spring semester, 1996, all of the tests were administered in class. It took approximately two hours to complete the placement test and fifteen minutes to complete SPOT.

RESULTS

The results were analyzed in terms of distributional characteristics, reliability, discriminability among levels, item difficulty, and item discriminability. Furthermore, the relationship between SPOT and the Tsukuba placement test was also analyzed.

Test difficulty and distribution

Tables 2 and 3 show the means and the standard deviations of SPOT and the Tsukuba placement test. Numbers within the parentheses indicate accuracy rates. Table 2 clearly indicates that SPOT differentiated between the first-year and second-year students with a minimum overlap between the two levels as shown in Figure 1. On the other hand, the Tsukuba placement test was too difficult to show the difference between the two groups, showing a greater overlap in distribution (cf. Figure 1). The difficulty of the placement test for the first- and second-year students is attributable to the difference in the learner population between Tsukuba and Iowa. That is, beginning and intermediate students at Tsukuba had between 100 to 500 hours of instruction, but the participants in this study had between 100 and 250 hours of instruction.

Table 2: Distribution statistics of SPOT & the placement test:
First- and second-year students

		SPOT	placement test	grammar	listening	reading
	total score	60	82	30	28	24
first year n=42						
	average (%)	14.19 (23.65%)	19.43 (23.70%)	7.95	9.38	2.97
	SD	9.27	5.98	3.36	2.95	2.39
second year n=19						
	average (%)	39.47 (65.79%)	28.84 (35.17%)	14.42	11.47	2.95
	SD	9.44	6.52	3.70	3.10	1.96
1st & 2nd year n=61						
	average (%)	23.21 (38.68%)	22.36 (22.36%)	9.97	10.07	2.97
	SD	14.49	7.51	4.58	3.13	2.24

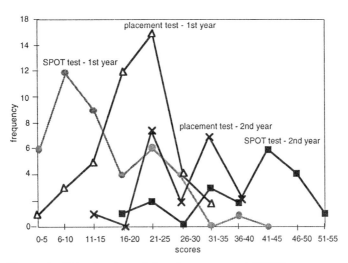

Figure 1. Distribution of the placement and SPOT tests:
First- and second-year levels

Table 3 shows the results of the third and fourth-year students. In this case, both SPOT and the Tsukuba placement test differentiated the third-year students from the fourth-year students. Furthermore, SPOT was slightly more difficult than the placement test. Figure 2 illustrates these characteristics.

Table 3: Distribution statistics of the SPOT & placement tests:
Third- and fourth-year students

	SPOT	placement test	grammar	listening	reading
total score	65	112	60	28	24
third year n=15					
average (%)	26.07 (40.11%)	45.93 (56.01%)	25.67	12.71	8.40
SD	13.31	16.45	8.19	5.48	4.67

Table 3: Distribution statistics of the SPOT & placement tests:
Third- and fourth-year students (cont.)

	SPOT	placement test	grammar	listening	reading
total score	65	112	60	28	24
fourth year n=5					
average (%)	44.00 (67.69%)	81.40 (99.27%)	42.20	21.80	17.40
SD	4.94	9.66	7.05	2.86	2.79
3rd & 4th year n=20					
average (%)	30.55 (47.00%)	54.80 (66.83%)	29.80	15.11	10.65
SD	13.76	21.07	10.40	6.19	5.66

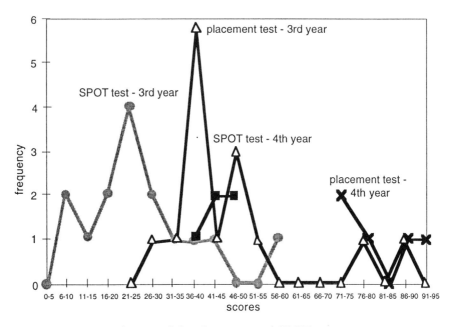

Figure 2. Distribution of the placement and SPOT tests:
Third- and fourth-year levels

Reliability

Reliability was computed using Kuder-Richardson Formula 20. Table 4 shows the reliability estimates and standard error of measurements for the placement test, its sections, and SPOT. The reliability estimates for both versions of SPOT were extremely high and exceeded .95, and they were higher than those of the placement test. The low reliability estimate of the placement test for the first and second-year students is attributable to the difficulty of this test.

Table 4: Reliability (Kuder-Richardson Formula 20) and standard error of measurement of the SPOT and placement tests

test type	version/section	reliability	standard error of measurement
placement test	1st & 2nd	0.776	3.554
	3rd & 4th	0.928	4.418
	Reading	0.882	1.660
	Listening	0.669	2.417
	Grammar: Part 1	0.816	2.410

	Grammar: Part 2	0.839	2.178
	Grammar: 3rd & 4th	0.910	3.123
	Grammar: 1st & 2nd	0.736	2.352
SPOT	Version 3 (1st & 2nd)	0.962	2.861
	Version 2 (3rd & 4th)	0.953	2.962
placement test	1st & 2nd	0.975	5.270
+ SPOT	3rd & 4th	0.947	4.782

Item difficulty and discriminability

Figures 3 and 4 illustrate the distribution of the SPOT items in terms of difficulty and discriminability. Both versions of SPOT contained items with a wide range of difficulty, most of which had a mid-range difficulty. There are a few items that seem too difficult or too easy, such as items 9, 17, and 27 in version 3, and items 19, and 47 in version 2. Item 42 in version 2 is problematic because less proficient students tended to answer more correctly than more proficient students. These ineffective items should be modified.

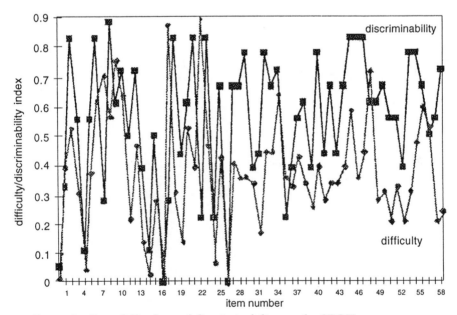

Figure 3. Item difficulty and discriminability on the SPOT test (version 3): First- and second-year levels

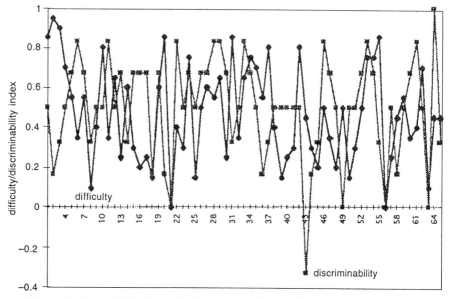

Figure 4. Item difficulty and discriminability on the SPOT test (version 2): Third- and fourth-year levels

Correlation between the Tsukuba placement test and SPOT

Tables 5 and 6 show the correlation matrix among the placement test, listening, reading, and grammar sections of the placement test, and SPOT. For the first and second-year levels, the SPOT scores were highly correlated with the total scores of the placement test though the placement itself was rather difficult. This means that SPOT seems to be able to measure students' abilities as effectively as the placement test. Table 6 also shows that SPOT was highly correlated with the grammar section. This confirms the results shown in Ford, et al. (1995), indicating that SPOT indeed measures ongoing processing of grammar. In addition, SPOT was moderately correlated with listening, but not with reading. This is not surprising because this version of SPOT had *hiragana* superscripts, and the items did not form a discourse. Thus, the knowledge of *kanji* or ability to read a text should not influence the SPOT score.

Similar tendencies were observed in the more difficult version of SPOT and the placement test. The SPOT scores were highly correlated with the total placement test scores as well as those of the grammar section, and they were moderately correlated with the scores of the listening test. The only difference is that SPOT was also moderately correlated with the reading test. Because this version of SPOT did not have any *hiragana* superscripts, each student's knowledge of *kanji* may have influenced the performance.

Table 5: Correlation between SPOT (version 3) and the placement test
(Pearson Product-Moment Correlation Coefficient):
First- and second-year levels ($n=61$)

	listening	reading	grammar	SPOT	placement test
listening	1.000				
reading	0.020	1.000			
grammar	0.403**	0.054	1.000		
SPOT	0.429**	0.054	0.783***	1.000	
placement test	0.717***	0.362**	0.857***	0.725***	1.000

*** significant at 0.001 level
** significant at 0.01 level

Table 6: Correlation between SPOT (version 2) and the placement test
(Pearson Product-Moment Correlation Coefficient):
Third- and fourth-year levels ($n=20$)

	listening	reading	grammar	SPOT	placement test
listening	1.000				
reading	0.826***	1.000			
grammar	0.765***	0.740 ***	1.000		
SPOT	0.610**	0.477*	0.767 ***	1.000	
placement test	0.853***	0.759***	0.872***	0.922***	1.000

*** significant at 0.001 level
** significant at 0.01 level
* significant at 0.05 level

STUDY 2

Study 2 was conducted at the University of California, San Diego (UCSD). The scope of this study was rather different from Study 1 in that its main objective was to investigate the practical applicability of SPOT as a placement test in foreign language settings. During the course of this study, the correlations between SPOT scores and the results of achievement tests, final course grade, and instructors' impression of students' speaking abilities were also analyzed.

INSTRUCTIONAL ENVIRONMENT

The University of California, San Diego offers four undergraduate levels of Japanese language courses and one course (Written Japanese) for those who can speak Japanese rather fluently, but cannot read or write it. In the former four courses, the development of four skills is emphasized, although the focus shifts from listening/speaking to reading/writing as the level advances. The teaching approach is communicative in that the course activities are designed and implemented with the main focus on the development of functional, communicative abilities throughout all levels. The syllabi of the first year and second year are based on topics and functions. The syllabi of the third year and fourth year are mainly based on topics, situations, and tasks. The Written Japanese course designed for bilingual, monoliteral students focuses on imparting basic reading and writing abilities, so that they will be able to enroll in the third- or fourth-year course the following year. The first three years are team-taught by lecturers and TAs. TAs teach listening/speaking, using only Japanese. Lecturers teach grammar, reading, writing in addition to listening/speaking. The fourth-year course and Written Japanese are taught by lecturers. First-year and second-year courses meet every day (the total instructional hours are six hours a week), while the third-year course meets three times a week (the total instructional hours are four hours a week). The fourth-year course and Written Japanese meet twice a week (the total instructional hours are three hours a week).

The majority of students take Japanese language courses because of general interests in Japanese language and culture, whereas a small number of students take them in order to fulfill the Japanese Studies major or minor requirement or their college's language requirement. UCSD's Japanese language program has an ethnically diverse student population. While approximately 30 to 35% of students are Caucasian Americans, the rest are mostly Asian or Asian American students including Japanese Americans, Chinese Americans, Korean Americans, Vietnamese Americans, and students from Taiwan, Korea, and Hong Kong, whose native language is not English. Many students have had previous contact with the Japanese language in one way or another, such as using or hearing Japanese at home, studying Japanese at their high school or at community colleges, teaching English in Japan, watching Japanese TV programs or animation films, and so forth. Also, students from Taiwan and Hong Kong already have a knowledge of Chinese characters. For these reasons, students' placement has been one of the crucial tasks for lecturers at the beginning of each academic year in order to manage classes smoothly throughout the year. In the past, between 35 and 50 students took a placement test each year. The placement test is in the form of an oral interview, during which lecturers ask each student about his or her background in Japanese language studies and so on in Japanese while evaluating the student's Japanese language abilities. If necessary, lecturers administer reading, writing, or *kanji* tests after the interview in order to identify the testee's reading and writing abilities accurately. The process of this placement test requires from at least 20 minutes to 1 hour and 30 minutes with each student.

DESIGN OF THE STUDY

Subjects

A total of 154 students who were enrolled in first- through fourth-year Japanese language courses took one of the two versions of SPOT at the end of the 1994/1995 academic year.[1] There were 92 students at the first-year level, 48 at the second-year level, nine at the third-year level, and five at the fourth-year level. In addition, 40 students who required a placement test at the beginning of the 1995/1996 academic year participated in this study.

Materials and procedures

In order to collect data necessary for the students' placements for the 1995/1996 academic year, SPOT was administered in first through fourth-year courses on May 31, 1995, a date near the end of the academic year. As in the study conducted at the University of Iowa, two versions of SPOT were administered at this time. Version 3 (with *hiragana* superscripts)[2] was used for first and second-year students, while version 2 (without *hiragana* superscripts) was used for third and fourth-year students (see Table 2 above). It took approximately fifteen minutes to complete SPOT.

On September 22 and 25, 1995, SPOT was administered to 40 students as a placement test. Version 3 (with *hiragana* superscripts) was used. These students were placed based on the results of SPOT administered on May 31, 1995.

RESULTS

Score distribution

The distribution statistics of SPOT administered on May 31, 1995 are shown in Table 7. Figures 5 and 6 illustrate the score distribution of the two versions of SPOT.

---

[1] SPOT was also administered in the Written Japanese class to investigate the correlation between students' reading abilities and the SPOT score, and so on. The results will be reported elsewhere.

[2] The original test developed at Tsukuba University does not include *hiragana* superscripts. Because first and second year students had been using a textbook that uses *hiragana* superscripts and were used to texts with *hiragana* superscripts, it was decided to add them.

Table 7: Distribution statistics of SPOT

	SPOT version 3		SPOT version 2	
	1st year n=92	2nd year n=48	3rd year n=9	4th year n=5
mean	19.37	39.08	26.78	43.6
maximum	50	58	52	60
minimum	0	15	7	31
standard error	1.12	1.57	4.77	6.15
standard deviation	10.71	10.85	14.30	13.76

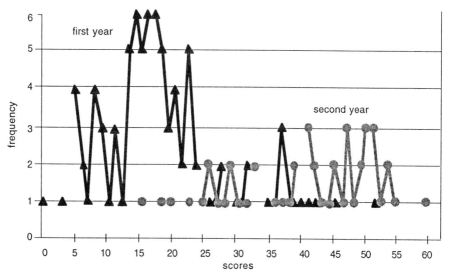

Figure 5. Distribution of the SPOT score (version 3): First- and second-year levels

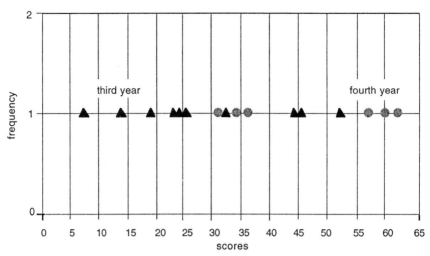

Figure 6. Distribution of the SPOT score (version 2):
Third- and fouth-year levels

Both of these figures indicate some overlap between two levels of students, although SPOT somehow successfully differentiated them. This overlap is attributable to diversified study backgrounds of UCSD's Japanese language students. Almost all first-year students who scored more than 30 points had previous study experience with Japanese or contact with Japanese before studying Japanese at UCSD. All third-year students who scored more than 30 points had lived in Japan, use Japanese at home, or had knowledge of Chinese characters through their native language.

Correlation between SPOT scores and speaking abilities

Before the administration of SPOT in May, 1995, all TAs who were teaching first through third-year courses and the lecturer who was teaching the fourth-year course were asked to rank the students in each of their sections solely based on oral communicative abilities. After SPOT was administered, these rankings were compared with the ranking of the SPOT score in each section in terms of Spearman's Rank Correlation.[3]

---

[3] The ranking lists of students based on their oral communicative abilities were collected from the TAs and lecturer before the administration of SPOT so that their ranking was not influenced by the SPOT score.

Table 8: Ranking correlation between the SPOT score and instructors' evaluation of speaking abilities

course	ranking correlation
first year	0.825*** – 1.000***
second year	0.887*** – 0.953***
third year	0.770***
forth year	1.000***

*** significant at 0.001 level

Table 8 shows that SPOT is highly correlated with the instructors' evaluation of speaking abilities. This correlation is interesting in that answering SPOT questions does not involve speaking abilities at all and SPOT is a grammar-based test. It is necessary for us in the future to study exactly what skill or ability SPOT tests and what aspect of speaking abilities (accuracy, fluency, etc.) and are correlated with SPOT[4].

Correlation between SPOT score and overall class performance

Table 9 shows the correlation between SPOT scores and students' final course grade.[5]

Table 9: Correlation between the SPOT score and final course grade

course	final course grade
first year	0.824***
second year	0.703***
third year	0.772***
forth year	0.880***

*** significant at 0.001 level

In the first- through fourth-year courses, the final course grades were determined based on students' class performance, homework assignments, daily or weekly quizzes

---

[4] Yamamoto, Ford, and Kobayashi, (1995) report a strong correlation between students' ranking in terms of the SPOT score and teachers' ranking of their Japanese abilities. Also see Kobayashi et al. (1995).

[5] In this computation, A was calculated as 7, A- as 6, B+ as 5, and so on.

(listening and *kanji*), and the results of a mid-term examination and a final examination, each of which consisted of listening, reading, grammar, and writing (*kanji*) questions, and an oral examination or an oral presentation. Thus, we can safely say that the final course grade is a good indicator of students' overall performance in the course. Again, it is interesting that SPOT is moderately or highly correlated to students' overall performance.

Correlation between SPOT and final examination

With regard to second-year students, the correlation between the SPOT score and the componential scores of their final examination were analyzed.

The lack of a significant correlation between the SPOT scores and the componential scores of the final examination, shown in Table 10, can be attributed to the different nature of SPOT and the final examination. While SPOT is a proficiency test measuring testees' ongoing language processing abilities, the final examination is an achievement test whose objective is to test students' mastery of material covered during a given quarter.

Table 10: Correlation between the SPOT score and
final exam componential scores

SPOT	1.000
final course grade	0.703***
final examination total score	0.689***
final examination *kanji*	0.325***
final examination listening	0.649***
final examination grammar	0.500
final examination reading	0.640

*** significant at 0.001 level

SPOT as a placement test

At the beginning of the 1995/1996 academic year, SPOT was administered as the only means to place 40 students[6]. who transferred from local colleges and other universities, returned from Japan, studied Japanese at high schools, or were using

---

6   The University of Tsukuba has been using SPOT questions as well as the placement test discussed above to place their students. Study 2 was the first attempt to place students solely based upon the results of SPOT.

Japanese at home. Based on the results of SPOT administered in May, the students were placed as follows:

Table 11: Placement based on SPOT

SPOT score (version 3)	placement
under 21	first year
21 – 40	second year
41 – 55	third year
over 55	fourth year or written Japanese

In the past, 35 to 50 students took a placement test each year. Among them, five to 10 students changed levels because the placement test failed to identify their appropriate level correctly, in spite of the fact that a considerable amount of time was spent for the administration of the placement test (cf. 4.1). During the 1995/1996 academic year, no students needed to change levels after two weeks from the beginning of fall quarter. Interviews with lecturers also revealed that all of those who took SPOT as a placement test had been placed into an appropriate level. The lecturers were happy not only because the placement went successfully, but also because they did not have to spend a lot of time administrating and grading placement tests.

CONCLUSION

The results of the present studies clearly demonstrate that SPOT is highly effective as a placement test of Japanese in the US. The high discriminability observed in the present studies indicates its versatility for various groups of students. Also, extremely high reliability estimates ensure the stability of its items. High correlations among SPOT, the placement test, instructors' evaluation of speaking abilities, and the final course grades provide additional support for its plausibility as a placement test. Because it only takes fifteen minutes to administer the test, SPOT is particularly useful when a large number of students need to be tested in a relatively short period of time.

However, as it is a type of indirect test, it is not easy to observe the abilities measured by SPOT from the task itself, and thus the examination of construct validity is crucial (Bachman & Palmer, 1981; Grotjahn, 1986). In order to fill in one *hiragana*, a testee must process an incoming message, read the test item, locate the position of a blank, and process or retrieve the appropriate grammatical item in a short time. Many of these processes occur in real-life situations. For instance, skimming and listening to a list at a normal speed occur quite often. Also, one may have to fill in missing letters when reading a text in which some letters are illegible or smeared. However, these processes do not necessarily take place simultaneously in real-life situations. In this sense, SPOT forces the learners to process language in an unnatural way. Thus, it is crucial to clarify exactly what SPOT measures.

In fact, previous studies suggest that abilities and knowledge measured by SPOT vary depending on items. Ming (1996) found that his subjects' errors in some items of SPOT were predominantly phonological errors. Ford (1996) reports that phonological prominence and syntactic contexts also affect the difficulty level of items. Moreover, the use of *kanji* or *kana* affects the response patterns when testees' native languages are alphabetical languages (Kobayashi, et al., 1994). Further investigation is necessary to identify the characteristics of each item in terms of the abilities and knowledge required to answer it.

Such investigations will enable test developers to create different sets of skill or knowledge-based items, which can be used for diagnostic purposes. For example, it is possible to create a SPOT test of grammar. Unlike conventional tests of grammar, SPOT allows more items to be included within a limited amount of time. Thus, an instructor can test a wide variety of grammatical items and pinpoint specific problems that examinees have.

Because the test format is unique, it is necessary to investigate psychological effects and test-taking strategies. Klain-Braley (1981) found that students who are trained to take a cloze test were more comfortable in taking the test and were able to answer more items than those who were not. In the case of SPOT, time pressure may cause testees to panic if they are not familiar with the test format. Furthermore, speech rate and pitch may affect testees' cognitive and affective states. The items in the current versions are recorded with a male voice. A female voice, however, may be more effective because a higher pitch may make it easier to listen and because students may be more comfortable with a female voice due to the large number of female teachers in our profession. Similarly, a slower speech rate may lower testees' anxiety level and affect test-taking strategies. Introspective research (Anderson, Bachman, Perkins, & Cohen, 1991; Cohen, 1984; Turner, 1989) and research involving multivariate analysis that investigate the relationship between cognitive/affective variables and test performance (Kunnan, 1995) should clarify these issues.

Despite these limitations, SPOT has been shown to be an effective instrument in measuring proficiency in Japanese, and it deserves further investigation and trial use as a placement test.

Acknowledgments

This research was supported by an International Scientific Joint Research Grant from Japan's Ministry of Education, Science and Culture to the International Student Center at the University of Tsukuba (Research Group Leader, Noriko Kobayashi, Research Project #07044003). The authors would like to express their sincere appreciation to Noriko Kobayashi, Hilofumi Yamamoto, Junko Ford, and Takako Sakai for their invaluable help throughout all stages of the present studies. The authors also wish to thank Tad Mukaihata and Carol Tohsaku for their assistance.

REFERENCES

Anderson, N. J., Bachman, L. F., Perkins, K., & Cohen, A. (1991). An exploratory study into the construct validity of a reading comprehension test: Triangulation of data source. *Language Testing, 8,1,* 41–66.

Bachman, L. F. (1982). The trait structure of cloze test scores. *TESOL Quarterly, 16, 1,* 61–70.

Bachman, L. F. (1985). Performance on cloze tests with fixed-ratio and rational deletions. *TESOL Quarterly, 19, 3,* 193–209.

Bachman, L. F., & Palmer, A. S. (1981). The construct validation of FSI Oral Interview. *Language Learning, 3, 1,* 67–86.

Cohen, A. (1984). On taking language tests: What the students report. *Language Testing, 1,1,* 70–81.

Ford, J. (1996). SPOT no mondai sakusee ni kanshite: SPOT no kuuran ichi ni kansuru ichi koosatsu yori [Position of the blank in the production of items for the SPOT]. In T. Sakai (Ed.), *Nihongo gakushuusha ni taisuru pureesumento tesuto to shite no SPOT (Simple Performance-Oriented Test): Kenkyuseeka hookokusho 1* [Development of SPOT (Simple Performance-Oriented Test) for the purpose of placing Japanese language students: Report 1]. Tsukuba: University of Tsukuba, Institute of Literature and Linguistics.

Ford, J., & Kobayashi, N. (1993). Nihongo gakushuusha ni yoru bunpoo koomoku no shuutoku ni kansuru ichikoosatsu [Differences in degree of acquisition of grammatical items by learners of Japanese according to levels of grammatical ability]. *Tsukuba Daigaku Ryuugakusee Sentaa Nihongo Kyooiku Ronshuu* [Journal of Japanese Language Teaching], 8, 185–200.

Ford, J. Kobayashi, N., & Yamamoto, H. (1994). Nihongo nooryoku kan'i shiken (SPOT) ni okeru onsee teepu no yakuwari ni kansuru kenkyuu. [Study of the tape listening factor on Simple Performance-Oriented Test of Japanese (SPOT)]. *Nihongo Kyooiku Hoohoo Kenkyuukai* [Meeting of Japanese Language Education], *1,* 3.

Ford, J., Kobayashi, N., & Yamamoto, H. (1995). Nihongo nooryoku kan'i shiken (SPOT) wa nai o sokutee shite iru ka: Onsee teepu yooin no kaiseki [What does Simple Performance-Oriented Test (SPOT) measure?: A study of the tape listening factor]. *Nihongo Kyooiku* [Journal of Japanese Language Teaching], 86, 93–102.

Grotjahn, R. (1986). Test validation and cognitive psychology: Some methodological considerations. *Language Testing, 5, 1,* 1–18.

Klain-Braley, C. (1981). *Empirical investigation of cloze tests: An examination of the validity of cloze tests as tests of general language proficiency in English for German university students.* Unpublished doctoral dissertation. University of Duisburg.

Klain-Braley, C. (1985). A cloze-up on the c-test: A study in the construct validation of authentic tests. *Language Testing, 2, 1*, 76–104.

Klain-Braley, C. and U. Raatz,. (1984). A survey of research on the C-test. Language Testing, 1, 134–146.

Kobayashi, N., & Ford, J. (1992). Bunpoo koomoku no onsee chooshuu ni kansuru jisshooteki kenkyuu [An empirical study of aural recognition of grammatical items]. *Nihongo Kyooiku* [Journal of Japanese Language Teaching], 78, 167–177.

Kobayashi, N., Ford, J., & Yamamoto, H. (1994). Nihongo nooryoku kan'i shiken to shite no kikitesuto: Kaitoo keeshiki no kanji yooin ni kansuru bunseki [Aural recognition test as a simple test of Japanese language abilities: Analysis of effects of *kanji* on answer sheets]. *Tsukuba Daigaku Ryuugakusee Sentaa Nihongo Kyooiku Ronshuu* [Journal of Japanese Language Teaching], 9, 149–158.

Kobayashi, N., Ford, J., & Yamamoto, H. (1995). Nihongo nooryoku kan'i shiken (SPOT) no tokuten bunpoo keekoo: Chuukyuu-muke tesuto to shokyuu-muke tesuto [Distribution of scores in the Simple Performance-Oriented Test (SPOT): Comparison of scores between easy and difficult versions of SPOT]. *Tsukuba Daigaku Ryuugakusee Sentaa Nihongo Kyooiku Ronshuu* [Journal of Japanese Language Teaching], 10, 107–120.

Kobayashi, N., Ford, J., & Yamamoto, H. (1996). *Nihongo nooryoku no atarashii sokuteehoo: SPOT* [SPOT: Anew testing method of Japanese language proficiency]. *Nihongo gakushuusha ni taisuru pureesumento tesuto to shite no SPOT (Simple Performance-Oriented Test: Kenkyuseeka hookokusho 1* [Development of SPOT (Simple Performance-Oriented Test) for the purpose of placing Japanese language students: Report 1]. Tsukuba: University of Tsukuba, Institute of Literature and Linguistics.

Kunnan, A. J. (1995). *Test taker characteristics and test performance: A structural modeling approach*. Cambridge, UK: Cambridge University Press.

Ming, Kwang-Joon. (1996). Kankoku Chonbok Daigakkoo ni okeru SPOT [SPOT at Chonbok University in Korea]. *Nihongo gakushuusha ni taisuru pureesumento tesuto to shite no SPOT (Simple Performance-Oriented Test: Kenkyuseeka hookokusho 1* [Development of SPOT (Simple Performance-Oriented Test) for the purpose of placing Japanese language students: Report 1]. Tsukuba: University of Tsukuba, Institute of Literature and Linguistics.

Oller, J. W., Jr. (1979). *Language tests at school: A pragmatic approach*. London: Longman.

Oller, J. W., Jr., & Conrad, C.A. (1971). The cloze technique and ESL proficiency. *Language Learning, 21, 2*, 183–194.

Shin, K. (1990). Nihongo cloze test kara nihongo henkee c-test e: Saitenhoo no mondai o chuushin ni [From Japanese cloze test to Japanese modified c-test: Focus on scoring method]. *Naogoya Daigaku Soogoo Gengo Sentaa Gengo Bunka Ronshuu* [Journal of Language and Culture], 11, 2, 213–225.

Turner, C. E. (1989). The underlying factor structure of L2 cloze test performance in francophone, university-level students: Casual modeling as an approach to construct validation. *Language Testing, 6, 2*, 172–197.

Yamamoto, H., Ford, J., & Kobayashi, N. (1995). *Nihongo nooryoku kan'i shiken (SPOT) to kyooshi no hyooka ni kansuru kenkyuu* [Study of Simple Performance-Oriented Test (SPOT) and teacher evaluation]. Unpublished manuscript.

Sayoko Yamashita
International Christian University, Japan

CLOZE TEST PERFORMANCE OF JSL LEARNERS AND NATIVE FIRST GRADERS

INTRODUCTION

The cloze procedure was first used by Taylor (1953) to assess the readability of texts for native English speakers. In a typical cloze test, the participants fill in words that have been deleted from a reading selection. A number of studies have been conducted using native speakers of English to investigate the effectiveness of cloze as a test of reading proficiency (Bormuth, 1965; Miller & Coleman, 1967; Shiba, 1957; Taylor, 1957). Later, the cloze procedure was applied to testing ESL students' reading proficiency (for an overview, see Oller, 1979; Hinofotis, 1987). Chihara, Oller, Weaver, & Chavez-Oller (1977) compared native speakers and ESL students, using a cloze procedure, and found that the percent of correct answers was higher for groups with higher language proficiency (i.e., native speakers and higher level ESL students) than for ESL groups with lower proficiency. Alderson (1980) also reported similar findings in a study comparing the performances of native speakers of English with performances of non-native speakers.

A group of researchers (Bachman, 1982; Brown, 1983; Chavez-Oller, Chihara, Weaver, & Oller, 1985; Jonz, 1987, 1990) argued that cloze is a stable, reliable, and sensitive measure of the inter-sentential components of the language. Brown (1992) summarizes that cloze items assess a wide range of language points from morphemic and clausal level grammar rules to discourse and pragmatic rules of cohesion and coherence (p. 2). Also, researchers have studied reliability, validity, mean item facility and discrimination, and usability of various types of scoring methods (Bachman, 1985; Brown, 1980, 1983, 1984, 1988, 1992; Chapelle & Abraham, 1990; Darnell, 1970; Feldmann & Stemmer, 1987; Klein-Braley, 1985; Markham, 1985; Shin, 1983, 1990).

In a Japanese language cloze, Yamashita (1994) used the fixed-ratio deletion method (with blanks substituted for every ninth character) and the acceptable-word scoring method after Brown (1980) in her comparison study of native children and Japanese as a second language (JSL) learners. This study (Yamashita, 1994) compared native Japanese children's reading comprehension performance to university JSL students, and investigated whether there was a difference in reading comprehension performance between native children and JSL learners. Disturbingly, the performance scores of the advanced and intermediate JSL students overlapped considerably. The minimum score for the intermediate level was 28, whereas the minimum score for the advanced level was 32; and the maximum score

Yamashita, S. (1997). Cloze test performance of JSL learners and native first graders. In H. M. Cook, K. Hijirida, & M. Tahara (Eds.), *New trends and issues in teaching Japanese language and culture* (Technical Report #15, pp. 99–117). Honolulu: University of Hawai'i, Second Language Teaching and Curriculum Center.

for the intermediate level was 64, whereas that for the advanced level was 71. As a result, scores between 32 and 64 overlapped completely for the two groups (i.e., scores of some of the advanced level JSL participants were lower than intermediate students' scores and/or some of the intermediate JSL participants' scores were higher than the scores of average advanced participants). Overall, Yamashita (1994) found that there was a significant difference between the native first graders and the intermediate JSL learners, but no significant difference was found between the native first graders and the advanced JSL learners. As explained above, however, it was difficult to generalize the findings on the basis of two course levels where there was a big variance (i.e., the scores were overlapped between intermediate levels and advanced levels).

The purpose of the present study is to find differences in performance between upper and lower level students strictly based on their cloze test scores, not the course levels to which they belonged. In order to do that, new participants from a wider range of ability levels were added to the JSL group ($n=167$), and all of the participants were categorized into three groups — bottom, middle, and high — based strictly on their cloze scores. Differences between the upper and lower groups of both native first graders (GR1) and JSL students are examined item by item (leaving the middle third out). In that way, the item performances of the upper and lower students within each group could be compared while at the same time contrasting the performances of the GR1 and JSL students. To help organize this new study, the following research questions were posited:

1. Which types of items are difficult on the cloze test for the upper JSL learners, lower JSL learners, upper native first graders, and lower first graders?

2. Which types of items show differences (larger than 40%) between the upper and lower groups for the JSL students and first graders?

3. Which types of items are difficult for both the JSL group and native first graders?

4. To what extent are there differences in item performance between JSL learners and native first graders?

5. Is the cloze test an appropriate measure for assessing JSL learners' overall Japanese proficiency?

METHOD

SUBJECTS

The subjects in this study were: (a) a group of native Japanese first graders (GR1, aged six to seven, $n=43$) in a public elementary school in Tokyo, and (b) a group of non-native learners of Japanese as a second language (JSL, or learners who live in a target country, $n=167$). The test for the GR1 group was administered at the end of the school year, which means that they had completed all of their work for the first grade. They are supposed to have mastered all *hiragana, katakana,* and the 76 basic *kanji* learned by all first graders. The JSL participants were predominantly Americans who had lived in Japan at least three months. The average was three years, Most of them were university students, but some were non-students from various professional backgrounds, and their levels of proficiency varied from rank beginners to very advanced.

MATERIALS

A cloze test with every ninth character deleted was used for this study. It was the same cloze procedure used in Yamashita (1994). The test was designed from a well-known traditional folk tale called *Momotaroo* (known as "Peach Boy" in English). This version of the story was taken from Yamashita and Ogawa (1994). There were two reasons that *Momotaroo* was selected as the material: (a) the passage and topic were suitable for all learners because the vocabulary which appears is relatively easier than that of newspapers or magazines, and (b) even though *Momotaroo* is a traditional folktale, cultural background knowledge is part of proficiency in the target language. If the test was to be strictly used for the purpose of estimating reading ability, perhaps the choice of this topic would not be the best, but since this cloze test also measures overall proficiency including grammatical correctness, word choice, and so on, any negative effects from the type of passage should be minimal.

The current cloze test had 72 blanks, distributed to create an every-ninth-character deletion pattern (see Appendix A). A typical English language cloze test would have every six or seventh word deleted with several sentences intact at the beginning and end of the passage to provide context (Hinofotis, 1987). The passage was written predominantly in *hiragana* (with a few simple *kanji*) so it was deemed necessary to use a ninth-character deletion pattern in the current test because Japanese sentences do not have spaces between words and more characters are needed to carry meaning as compared to English words (see also Ogawa, 1992). The grammatical categories involved in the characters appearing in the blanks included adjectives, adverbs, conjunctions, demonstrative words, nouns, onomatopoeia, particles, prefixes, and verbs.

The acceptable-answer scoring method (see Brown, 1980) was used. The glossary of acceptable answers was based on the responses of native-speaker university students in a pilot study. As a result, any character that was used by more than 40% of the native students was counted as correct. Such words were *waroo* 'to divide' (52%), *kiroo* 'to cut' (48%), *pakutto* (an onomatopoetic expression) (52%), and *pakurito* (an onomatopoetic expression) (42%).

PROCEDURE

The GR1 group's data were gathered from two intact classes of a public elementary school in the western part of Tokyo in March (for a total *n* of 49). The time limit was 30 minutes. Six out of 49 answer sheets were incomplete (probably due to the

---

time limit), and these six with incomplete data were eliminated from the study. Most of the GR1 group finished the test in less than 30 minutes, whereas the advanced JSL learners took from 10 to 20 minutes, and the lower level learners took up to 30 minutes. There were no invalid answer sheets for the advanced level learners, whereas eight lower level learners did not finish the test in 30 minutes. These eight with incomplete data were eliminated from the study.

ANALYSIS

The descriptive statistics in this study included the mean, standard deviation (SD), minimum and maximum scores, range, variance, number of subjects (n), and number of items (k). The K-R20 reliability coefficient was also calculated. Item facility (IF, the percentage of students who correctly answer a given item, Brown, 1996, p. 64) and item discrimination (ID, the degree to which an item separates the students who performed well from those who performed poorly, Brown, 1996, p. 66) for each of the 72 items were calculated separately for each group (GR1 and JSL learners). Based on their cloze tests scores, each group was divided into three levels (approximately one-third each) to establish upper, middle, and lower levels for estimating item discrimination. To determine if specific differences among the group means were significant, a one-way ANOVA was performed, and post-hoc comparisons were made with the Scheffé test.

RESULTS

The descriptive statistics for the test results of each group are reported in Table 1.

The difference between the means of the GR1 and JSL was 11.24 (the first graders' mean was higher). However, the first graders' minimum score was 18, whereas minimum score of the JSL group was 28 (10 points higher), which made the range of the GR1 group much larger than that of the JSL group. The K-R20 statistic indicated that the reliability of the test was remarkably high for both the GR1 and JSL groups (.94 and .91, respectively), which means that the test is very reliable for both groups.

Table 1: Descriptive statistics

	Japanese first graders(GR1)	JSL learners (JSL)
k	72	72
n	43	167
mean	62.77	51.53
SD	9.82	9.34

minimum	18	28
maximum	72	72
range	54.00	44.00
K–R20	0.94	0.91

Item facility (*IF*) and item discrimination (*ID*) statistics were also calculated for each group. The item statistics are listed in Appendix C. Research Question 1 asks what the difficult items on the cloze test for the upper JSL group and upper GR1 group, as well as for the lower JSL and GR1 groups are. A difficult item was defined as any item whose *IF* score was .60 or less. Research Question 2 asks in which items the responses of the upper and lower learners of each of the two groups (JSL and GR1) differed greatly (i.e., *ID* was more than .40). Research Question 3 asks what the items which were difficult (i.e., *IF* score was .60 or less) for both groups are. Table 2 shows the results related to Research Questions 1, 2, and 3. The items of the cloze test which were originally written in Japanese are written in Roman characters in the "Results" and "Discussion" sections of this paper using the Hepburn system and grammatical rules suggested by the CHILDES Japanese system (Oshima-Takane & MacWhinney, 1995).

Research Question 4 asked to what extent there are differences in performance between JSL learners and GR1. Here, three groups, JSL TOP, GR1 TOP, and GR1 BOT, groups were compared. The rationale for omitting the JSL BOT group is that the correct response rate was too low compared with the other two groups (see Table 2). Also, in the previous study (Yamashita, 1994), the bottom JSL group was significantly different from both upper groups (i.e., JSL and GR1). The overall ANOVA procedure indicated that there was a significant difference among the individual item comparisons, $F(2)=21.49$; $p<.05$, between the group means. The Scheffé procedure further indicated that, overall, all three groups (JSL TOP, GR1 TOP, and GR1 BOT) were significantly different. Further discussion about the above findings and Research Question 5 ("Is the cloze test an appropriate measure for assessing the JSL learners' Japanese proficiency?") will follow in the discussion section.

Table 2: Difficult items for each group

		GR1			JSL			RQ3
		TOP	BOT	TOP-BOT (I D)	TOP	BOT	TOP-BOT (I D)	
I 01	*[a]rutokoro*					x	x	
I 03	*obaasan[ga]*					x	x	
I 08	*sentaku[o]*		x	x				
I 09	*soko[e]*		x	x	x	x		x

Table 2: Difficult items for each group (cont.)

		GR1			JSL			RQ3
		TOP	BOT	TOP-BOT (I D)	TOP	BOT	TOP-BOT (I D)	
I 10	don[bu]rako		x	x		x	x	
I 12	kore[wa]		x					
I 16	[mo]tte				x			
I 20	bikkurishi[te]					x	x	
I 24	[wa]rooto					x	x	
I 25	[su]ruto				x	x	x	
I 27	paku[t]to		x	x	x	x	x	
I 28	[ka]waii					x	x	
I 30	[u]maremashita					x	x	
I 32	obaasan[wa]		x					
I 35	[so]noko				x	x		x
I 36	so[da]teru					x	x	
I 43	so[no]koro				x			
I 44	warui[o]ni					x	x	
I 45	tabemono[ya]	x	x		x	x		x
I 46	totte[i]ki					x	x	
I 47	[ko]maraseru		x	x		x	x	
I 49	taijishi[ni]				x	x		
I 50	I [ku]kotoni		x	x		x	x	
I 53	a[bu]naikoto		x	x		x	x	x
I 54	yamete[o]kure		x	x	x	x		x
I 55	tabe[ra]rete		x	x				
I 56	to[i]tte					x	x	
I 60	kittobo[ku]ga			x		x	x	
I 61	[te]kimasu					x	x	
I 66	ha[ta]		x	x	x	x	x	x
I 67	kibi[da]ngo				x	x	x	
I 68	[mo]taseteyaru		x	x	x	x		
I 69	ha[ta]		x	x	x	x	x	x
I 70	kibi[da]ngo				x	x	x	
I 72	genkiyo[ku]				x	x	x	

TOP = top or higher group; BOT = bottom or lower group
Note: The translation or function of each item is given in Appendix B.

DISCUSSION

THE JSL TOP GROUP

The JSL TOP group had difficulty with I09, I25, I27, I35, I45, I49, I54, I66, I67, I68, I69, I70, and I72. It seems that the reason the IF (item facility) of I09 (particle use of *e*) was low compared to the performance of the GR1 group was not that there was the mixture of the writing system. The most frequent particle mistakenly used here by the JSL group was *de* as in *soko[de] momo ga nagarete kimashita*. In the JSL group (including the lower group), particles such as *no, mo, wa, kara, o,* and *ni* were placed here. Only *e* was considered an acceptable answer for I09, which carries the subtle meaning defined by Makino and Tsutsui (1986) ("*e*: a particle that indicates the direction toward which some directional movement or action proceeds," p. 116) (see Appendix B).

Item I25 (*[su]ruto*) is "a coordinate conjunction which connects two sentences used in such a condition that the second sentence describes an event which takes place right after the event described in the first sentence" (Makino & Tsutsui, 1986, p. 437). The word *suruto* used as described above is often found in storytelling rhetoric, and is introduced in JSL teaching in a later stage.

There were two onomatopoeias in the text, *don[bu]rako* (I10) and *paku[tt]to* (I27). The JSL TOP group did poorly only on I27. Onomatopoeias such as *donburako* and *pakutto* are rarely introduced to the JSL learners either in daily life or in Japanese texts. The reason that the JSL TOP group did well in I10 (95%) seems to be that they guessed well that the word that appeared right after I10 was recursive *donburako donburako*. Even the JSL BOT group performed correctly at a similar rate as the GR1 BOT (51% and 53% respectively).

Item I35 (*[so]noko*) is a part of a demonstrative word (as underlined). Mistaken answers for blank I35 were *ko* and *a*. Item I45 was *ya*, on which all the participants in this study (i.e., GR1 TOP, BOT, JSL TOP, and BOT) did poorly. Discussion of this item will be given below in GR1 TOP group.

Item I49 (the particle use of *ni* as in *taijishi[ni]*) was a rather unique item which was difficult only for the JSL group. The most frequent error which was made by the JSL learners was *te* (*taijishi[te]*). The usages *taijishini* and *taijishite* describe opposite situations. The former is to do something "in order to (conquer devils)" whereas the latter implies "conquer (devils) and then afterward do something else." The IF for the total JSL group was only .18 (18% correct) with the ID (differences between TOP and BOT groups) only .07, which means that there was a small difference between the JSL TOP and BOT groups. On the other hand, the total IF for the GR1 group was .86. More interestingly, the ID of the GR1 group was −.15, which means that the BOT group did slightly better than the TOP group (which means that it is a poor item). The acquisition of the particle in such a case seems to have been taken place at a fairly early age in the first language group (see also Clancy,

1986). To use such particles as *ni* for expressing a purpose seems to be difficult for the JSL learners.

Item 154 (use of honorific *o* before a verb, or *[o]kure*) is a unique usage. It is not used very often in modern Japanese. A mother may tell her child *otabe* 'eat!' to get the child to eat, but such usage is very limited, and JSL learners probably do not have a chance to learn such an expression. It is also salient that the GR1 BOT did poorly (.27) in this item whereas the GR1 TOP did fairly well (.86) in the usage of 154.

The JSL TOP group did poorly on four noun items — two items where *[ha]ta* 'flag' in English appeared (166 and 169), and two where *kibi[da]ngo*, 'millet ball' in English appeared (167 and 170). One alternative answer that appeared in 167 and 170 was *[ri]ngo*, 'apple'. No such answer was found in the GR1 group. Those words were tightly related to the *Momotaroo* story. It is quite understandable that the JSL learners had difficulty with such special folk tale terms.

Two other words where the JSL TOP group did poorly were 168 (*[mo]tasete*, IF=.38) and 172 (*genkiyo[ku]*, IF=.58), both of which were grammar related items. Item 168 was a causative construction. A causative form is introduced at a relatively late stage in textbooks for beginners. Some texts do not introduce the causative form until the students are advanced into the intermediate level. Although the blank did not directly hit the causative part (i.e., *se*), it might have affected the choice of the character which should fit in the blank. Item 172 gave striking results. The most frequent errors that appeared in item 172 were *genkiyo[o]*, *genkiyo[ni]*, *genkiyo[de]*, and *genkiyo[i]*. While it is natural for native Japanese to select *yo[ku]* in this context (e.g., IF of the total GR1 was .91), both JSL TOP (IF=.58) and BOT (IF=.05) produced the incorrect responses listed above. It indicates to the JSL teachers the need for more research about how and when to teach JSL learners the use of adjectives and their proper conjugation system. Most of the current Japanese textbooks introduce the adverbial usage of adjective (*-ku*) at the same time as adjectives are first introduced, in an earlier stage of beginning Japanese.

THE JSL BOTTOM GROUP

The JSL BOT group performed poorly (i.e., IF was less than .60) in 31 items out of 72 total items. It means that the percentage of correct answers was 43%. Although most of the characteristics of the responses of the JSL BOT group had much in common with those of the JSL TOP group discussed above, a couple of special comments should be made: (a) the JSL BOT group did better than GR1 BOT in handling the writing system — examples are 108 (particle *o*), 109 (*soko e*), 112 (*kore wa*), 114 (*issho*), 115 (*shiyoo*), 123 (*issho*), 132 (*obaasan wa*), 155 (*taberarete*), and 156 (*itte*); and (b) recursive words (proper nouns) such as *Ojiisan*, *Obaasan*, *Momotaroo* were also reproduced better in many occasions (i.e., 15, 122, 139, 151, 158, and 163). The JSL BOT group probably used better strategies in reading passages than the GR1 BOT group used.

THE GR1 TOP GROUP

The GR1 TOP group performed very well on the test. Most of the items had more than 85% correct responses (most of which reached 100%), except items I09, I35, I45, I49, and I53. The only item which was below .60 accuracy was I45 (IF=.57). I45 was also the only item on which all the groups (JSL TOP, BOT, GR1 TOP, and BOT) achieved less than .60 accuracy. The item was the conjunctive particle *ya* which indicates "two or more items," in a non-exhaustive list. It is distinct from *to* which is used in exhaustive lists. In this particular context where "devils came to take valuables from the village," it may well be more than the two valuables specifically mentioned (i.e., *tabemono* 'food' and *kirumono* 'clothing'). Ninety-three percent (93%) of adult native Japanese university students used *ya* and 15% of the native university students used *to* in this context (Yamashita, 1994).

THE GR1 BOTTOM GROUP

There were several problems which were idiosyncratic to the GR1 BOT group. They seemed to have difficulty following the writing system where spelling and sounds did not match. Such examples were found in the rules for particles and some words. The particles *wa* written as *ha* by convention, *e* written as *he*, and *o* written as *wo* were mixed by GR1 BOT group (see I08, I09, I12, and I32), whereas very few such errors were found in the GR1 TOP and both groups of JSL (i.e., TOP and BOT JSL groups). Errors found in I09 in the JSL TOP and BOT did not seem to be caused by the difficulty in writing sounds which was found in the GR1 BOT group (discussed in the above section). The GR1 BOT group did not show as wide a variety of vocabulary as the GR1 TOP group did. For example, the group performed poorly on items I10 (*donburako*, IF=.53), I53 (*abunai*, IF=.20), I54 (*okure*, IF=.27), and I66 and I69 (*hata* or *flag*, IF=.07). None of the above items were problematic for the GR1 TOP group. The GR1 BOT group did not do the items well in passive and causative construction (e.g., [*ko*]*maraseru* in I47, *tabe*[*ra*]*rete* in I55, and [*mo*]*taseteyaru* in I68)—the above constructions are underlined — all of which had ID (differences from the GR1 TOP group) larger than .40, which means that there was a large differences between the GR1 TOP group and GR1 BOT group in the particular construction). Some of the errors appearing in I55 were due to the writing system, again. Several cases were found in the GR1 TOP group where they used da instead of ra as in tabe[da]rete, which was not found in either of the JSL groups.

ITEMS WHOSE *ID* WAS LARGER THAN .40 IN THE JSL GROUP

Those items with large ID (more than .40) indicate that mastering or acquiring the items is developmental, or that the JSL learners understand the usage better when they advance to higher levels. Such items are presented in Table 2, and categorized as follows: adjectives (I28, I53 and I72), adverbs/ onomatopoetic expressions (I10 and I27), conjunctions (I25), demonstrative words (I1 and I35), nouns (I44, I60, I66/I69, and I67/I70), particles (I03), verbs (I24, I30, I36, I46, I47, I50, and I56), and special functions, te (I20 and I61 as in *bikkurishi*[*te*] and *yattsuke*[*te*]*kimasu* consecutively). Most of the items have been discussed in the above section to answer Research Question 1 concerning the difficult items. For adjectives, the JSL

TOP group did 96% correctly in I28 and 95% correctly in I53, but only 58% correctly in I72. It seems to take time for the JSL learners to master I72. The nouns that the JSL TOP did better than the JSL BOT were *oni* (devil), *boku* 'I' (used by a male), *hata* 'flag', and *kibidango* 'millet balls'. All of these words except boku are related to the Momotaroo story. Advanced JSL students probably had more chances to hear or read old folk tales, and experiences and naturally acquired knowledge may have helped to improve their language proficiency. This text (i.e., Momotaroo) clearly differentiates between upper and lower level JSL learners. Some of the verbs had not yet been introduced to the lower level learners in Japanese textbooks or elsewhere (e.g., *[wa]roo* 'let us divide', *[u]mareru* 'to be born', *so[da]teru* 'to raise', and *[ko]maraseru* 'to cause trouble'). One is a compound verb (i.e., *totte-[i]ki* 'to get and go'), and another is a verb used in phrase *i[ku]-koto ni shimashita* 'decided to go'. The verb usage listed above are all difficult items for the JSL BOT group, and thus distinguish them from the JSL TOP group. There are variety of usages of *te* form, and it is naturally difficult for the lower learners to master each usage.

ITEMS WHOSE *ID* WAS LARGER THAN .40 IN THE GR1 GROUP

As shown under the column of GR1 TOP-BOT (*ID*) in Table 2, there were 12 items whose *ID* were larger than .40. Items I10, I27, I47, I50, I53, I60, and I66/I69 were the same items listed in the JSL group. I10 and I27 were onomatopoetic words (*donburako* and *pakutto*), I47 (*komaraseru*) was the verb with a causative form, I50 (*ikukoto ni*) was a phrase, I53 (*abunai*) was an adjective, I60 (*boku*) and I66/I69 (*hata*) were nouns. The items (*ID*>.40) which only occurred in the GR1 group were I08 (*sentaku[o]*), I09 (*soko[e]*), I54 (*[o]kure*), I55 (*tabe[ra]rete*), and I68 (*[mo] taseteyaru*). The discussion on these items was already given in the above section, but it is notable that for the native Japanese children in learning their first language, there seems to be a distinctive developmental pattern linking the TOP and the BOT groups. Some items were difficult for the GR1 BOT group but not for the JSL groups.

DIFFICULT ITEMS FOR BOTH GROUPS

As listed in the far right column in Table 2, there were 7 items whose IFs were less than .60 for both groups (I09, I35, I45, I53, I54, and I66/I69). Among the 7 items, I09(*soko[e]*), I35(*[so]noko*), and I45 (*[ya]*) were difficult for both groups because they carried the delicate shades of meaning discussed above (i.e., differences between *e* and *de*, *so-* and *ko-*, *ya* and *to*). Item I53 (*a[bu]nai* 'dangerous') was an item which differentiated the TOP and BOT groups widely. Both I54 (*okure* 'give') and I66/I69 (*hata* 'flag') were the words which are not heard very often. In addition to that, it is interesting that I66 had the total IF=.47, IFTOP=.93, and IFBOT=.07, whereas I69 (the same word repeated again in the next sentence), the total IF score changed and increased to .56, the score of the IFTOP also increased to 1.00 (100% correct), and the score of IFBOT increased to .20. It seems that more GR1 children knew the word than actually responded in the first blank, but became able to write the correct answer as they read the text further. The JSL groups had the same IF scores for both I66 and I69.

DIFFERENCES BETWEEN THE JSL AND THE GR1

From Table 2 and the above discussion, there are a few differences in performance of the cloze test between the JSL and GR1 groups. The JSL learners performed better in using the writing system appropriately through learning in the classroom (e.g., the writing of particles). Also, the JSL learners can use the better strategies to fill in the blanks based on the context (e.g., recursive words such as *donburako*, onomatopoetic expression, and words such as *Momotaroo* and *Obaasan* 'old lady' which were used repeatedly in the text). The JSL learners performed well in some typical usages (or grammatical items) that they had learned in the classroom (e.g., *sentaku[o]suru* 'to wash clothes', and *tabe[ra]rete*, a passive form of verb for "to eat," which are grammatical constructions often introduced in Japanese textbooks for beginners). Finally, there are certain items which need to be learned by the JSL learners but not by the GR1 group (i.e., both GR1 TOP and BOT groups did well, probably because that they had acquired the items as an earlier stage as native speakers, but there was a big ID between the JSL TOP and BOT, which means that the JSL BOT group are still on the stage of learning these items). Examples of (d) are 101 (*[a]rutokoro ni* 'somewhere'), 103 (*obaasan[ga] sunde imashita* 'an old lady was living') — note that there were many JSL participants who used *wa* instead of *ga* in this context), 172 (*genkiyo[ku]* 'energetically'), and so forth. It seems that the processes of learning or acquiring a first language and a second language are not totally identical.

CLOZE AS A MEASURE OF JAPANESE PROFICIENCY

Research question 5 asked whether or not the cloze test is an appropriate measure for assessing the JSL learners' Japanese proficiency. As we saw in the results, there were clear differences between the performances of the higher JSL group (JSL TOP) and the lower JSL group (JSL-BOT). Some items which are often introduced in early beginning Japanese textbook were performed well by both higher and lower groups, whereas some difficult items were clearly performed differently by the two groups. The cloze test, even though the blanks were set mechanically (i.e., every ninth character without consideration of the choice of items), hit a wide variety of grammatical items as well as phrases and word-stems. The cloze test requires not only grammatical knowledge, but also syntactic or reading comprehension skills to fill in the small blanks with the best choices. In addition, it takes only a short period of time (most of the JSL learners finished the test within 30 minutes) in order to complete the test. It is a practical and handy tool for measuring Japanese proficiency.

CONCLUSION

This study investigated whether there were differences in performance of the cloze test between learners of Japanese as a second language (JSL) and native Japanese first graders (GR1). Statistical analysis indicated that there were significant differences among three groups (the higher JSL, higher GR1, and lower GR1 groups). Each item performed by each group was carefully examined. The JSL

---

learners and the native Japanese children performed some of the items similarly, and others differently. Here the summary findings from this study:

1. The JSL learners were more correct in following writing rules than lower level native children for some items such as the geminative consonant (small *tsu*); particle usage of *wa* and *o*; and the distinction between *ra* and *da*, which is due to the mixture of the alveolar and dental phonemes.

2. The JSL learners used reasonable guesses or higher level strategies for solving problems in such cases as filling-in recursive words.

3. Classroom learning for JSL may improve JSL performance (e.g., passive form).

4. The native children performed better with idiomatic or cultural expressions or words (e.g., *mukashi mukashi [a]rutokoroni* 'once upon a time').

5. Some multi-functional particles were hard to master for JSL learners (e.g., usage of *ni* which indicates 'purpose' as well as 'location,' 'point of time,' 'indirect object marker,' etc.).

6. Some grammatical items were difficult for the JSL learners to master even though the concepts had been introduced in the beginning to intermediate stages (e.g., the adverbial usage of adjectives as in *genki yo[ku]*, and the causative usage).

7. Both JSL learners and native children have difficulty with words which carry subtle shades of meaning, a result which contrasts with native university students' performance (e.g., usage of the particle *ya*).

The above findings imply that first and second language development is different. It should also be mentioned that this study has limitations. First, although the cloze test used in this study had 72 blanks which covered a wide variety of grammatical categories as well as vocabulary, the examples which appeared in this study were still limited, and it is difficult to generalize the findings. Second, even though there were clear differences between the upper and lower groups in both JSL and GR1, we should be prudent about drawing the conclusion that the difference in performance was due to acquisition. This paper did not discuss the relationship between performance and acquisition closely enough. Further study is necessary.

Even with the limitations described above, the study has implications for the evaluation of JSL teaching. The study has shown that learning has taken place. The test results revealed that there were difficult items as well as easy ones. JSL teachers can examine the items which were difficult only for lower students as well as those for both upper and lower students. The grammatical categories could be examined more carefully by conducting another cloze test made from a different text. The items studied in the cloze tests could reflect syllabus design (e.g., a case of JSL high level students' poor performance of adverbial adjective, *yoku*).

In addition, the statistical analyses of this study indicated that the reliability of the cloze test for the JSL participants was remarkably high (.91), which means that the test as a whole discriminates between the upper and lower groups well. That means that the test can be used for such purposes as testing or diagnosing the students' Japanese language proficiency.

Acknowledgments

I would like to thank Dr. J. D. Brown of the University of Hawai'i at Mānoa for patiently assisting me with my statistical analysis and for his insightful comments and suggestions.

REFERENCES

Alderson, J. C. (1980). Native and nonnative speaker performance on cloze tests. *Language Learning, 30,* 59–76.

Bachman, L. F. (1982). The trait structure of cloze test scores. *TESOL Quarterly, 16,* 61–70.

Bachman, L. F. (1985). Performance on cloze tests with fixed-ratio and rational deletions. *TESOL Quarterly, 19,* 535–556.

Bormuth, J. R. (1965). Optimum sample size and cloze test length in readability measurement. *Journal of Educational Measurement, 2,* 111–116.

Brown, J. D. (1980). Relative merits of four methods for scoring cloze tests. *Modern Language Journal, 64,* 311–317.

Brown, J. D. (1983). A closer look at cloze: Validity and reliability. In J. W. Oller, Jr. (Ed.). *Issues in Language testing research* (pp. 237–250). Rowley, MA: Newbury House.

Brown, J. D. (1984). A cloze is a cloze is a cloze? In J. Handscombe, R. A. Orem, & B. P. Taylor (Eds.). *On TESOL '83* (pp. 109–119). Washington, DC: TESOL.

Brown, J. D. (1988). Tailored cloze: Improved with classical item analysis techniques. *Language Testing, 5,* 19–31.

Brown, J. D. (1992). What text characteristics predict human performance on cloze test items. In the *Proceedings of the Third Conference on Language Research in Japan* (pp. 1-26). Urasa, Japan: International University Japan.

Brown, J. D. (1996). *Testing in language programs.* Upper Saddle River, NJ: Prentice Hall Regents.

Chapelle, C. A., & Abraham, R. (1990). Cloze method: What difference does it make? *Language Testing, 7*(2), 121–146.

Chavez-Oller, M. A., Chihara, T., Weaver, K., & Oller, J. W., Jr. (1985). When are cloze items sensitive to constraints across sentences? *Language Learning, 35,* 181–206.

Chihara, T., Oller, J., Weaver, K., & Chavez-Oller, M. (1977). Are cloze items sensitive to constraints across sentences? *Language Learning, 27* (1), 63–73.

Clancy, P. M. (1986). The acquisition of Japanese. In D. I. Slobin (Ed.). *The crosslinguistic study of language acquisition. Vol. 1: The data* (pp. 373–524). Hillsdale, NJ: Erlbaum.

Darnell, D. K. (1970). Clozentropy: A procedure for testing English language proficiency of foreign students. *Speech Monographs, 37,* 36–46.

Hinofotis, F. B. (1987). Cloze testing: An overview. In M. Long & J. Richards, (Eds.) *Methodology in TESOL: A book of readings* (pp. 412–417). Rowley, Mass: Newbury House.

Jonz, J. (1987). Textual cohesion and second-language comprehension. *Language Learning, 37,* 409–438.

Jonz, J. (1990). Another turn in the conversation: What does cloze measure? *TESOL Quarterly, 24*(1), 61–83.

Klein-Braley, C. (1985). A cloze-up on the C-Test: a study in the construct validation of authentic tests. *Language Testing, 2,* 76–104.

Makino, S., & Tsutsui, M. (1986). *A dictionary of basic Japanese grammar.* Tokyo: Japan Times.

Markham, P. L. (1985). The rational deletion cloze and global comprehension in German. *Language Learning, 35*(3), 423–430.

Miller, G. R., & Coleman, E. B. (1967). A set of thirty-six prose passages calibrated for complexity. *Journal of Verbal Learning and Verbal Behavior, 6,* 851–854.

Ogawa, T. (1992). Placement toshite no cloze test [A cloze test as a placement test]. *Tsukuba University Ryugakusei Center Nihongo Kyoiku Ronshu, 8,* 201–214.

Oller, J. W., Jr. (1979). *Language tests at school: A pragmatic approach.* London: Longman.

Oshima-Takane, Y., & MacWhinney, B. (Eds.). (1995). *CHILDES Manual for Japanese.* Montreal: McGill University.

Shiba, S. (1957). Yomiyasusa no hakarikata: Cloze-hou no nihongo e no tekiyoo [How to assess readability: Application of cloze to Japanese language]. *Shinrigaku Kenkyu* [Japanese Journal of Psychology], *28,* 67–73.

Shin, K. (1983). Cloze-hou ni yoru nihongo nooryoku no sokutee [Assessing Japanese proficiency by cloze]. *Kyoiku Kenkyu: ICU Gakuho, 25,* 141–177.

Shin, K. (1990). Nihongo cloze test kara Nihongo henkee C-Test e: Saitenhoo no mondai o chuushin ni [From Japanese cloze to Japanese C-Test: Some problems on rating]. *Nagoya University Soogoo Gengo Center Gengo Bunka Ronshuu, 11–2,* 213–225.

Taylor, W. L. (1953). "Cloze procedure": A new tool for measuring readability. *Journalism Quarterly, 30,* 414–438.

Taylor, W. L. (1957). "Cloze" readability scores as indices of individual differences in comprehension and aptitude. *Journal of Applied Psychology, 41*(1), 19–26.

Yamashita, S. (1994). Is the reading comprehension performance of learners of Japanese as a second language the same as that of Japanese children? An analysis using a cloze test. *Japanese-Language Education around the Globe*, 4, 133–146.

Yamashita, S., & Ogawa, S. (1994). *Interview projects for intermediate to advanced JSL students*. Tokyo: Kuroshio Publishers.

APPENDIX A: CLOZE TEST

　　　　　　　1　　　　　　　　　　　2　　　　　　　　　　　3
むかしむかし、（あ）るところに、おじ（い）さんとおばあさん（が）すんでいました。
　　　　　　　　4　　　　　　　　5　　　　　　　　　　6
おじいさんはまい（日）山へしばかりに、（お）ばあさんは川へせ（ん）たくにいきました。
　　　　　　　7　　　　　　　　8　　　　　　　9　　　　　　　　　　10
　ある日、おばあ（さ）んが川でせんたく（を）していると、そこ（へ）大きなももがどん（ぶ）
　　　　　　　　　　　　　　11　　　　　　　　　　　　　　　　　　12
らこ、どんぶらこ　、　とながれてきまし（た）。おばあさんは、「　　おや、まあ、これ（は）
　　　　　　　　　　　　　　13　　　　　　　14　　　　　　　　15
大きなももだこと　。　いえへもってかえ（っ）ておじいさんとい（っ）しょにたべましょ（う）」
　　　　16
といって、いえへ（も）ってかえりました。
　　　　　　　　17　　　　　　　　　　18　　　　　　　　　　19
　夕がた、おじい（さ）んは山からかえっ（て）きました。おじい（さ）んはももを見ると　、
　　　　　　　20　　　　　　　　21　　　　　　　22　　　　　　　　23
大そうびっくりし（て）、「おやおや、こ（れ）は大きなももだ。（お）ばあさん、いっし（ょ）
　　　　　　　　　　　　24　　　　　　　　　25　　　　　　　　26
にたべるとしよう　」　といって、ももを（わ）ろうとしました。（す）るとそのとき、も（も）
　　　　27　　　　　　　　　28　　　　　　　29　　　　　　　　30
がまん中からばく（っ）とわれて、中から（か）わいい男の赤ちゃ（ん）が「おぎゃー」と（う）
　　　　　　　　31　　　　　　　　32　　　　　　　33　　　　　　34
まれました。おじ（い）さんとおばあさん（は）とてもおどろきま（し）た。けれども、子（ど）
　　　　　　35　　　　　　　　36　　　　　　　37　　　　　　　38
もがいないので、（そ）の子を大せつにそ（だ）てることにしまし（た）。名まえは、もも（か）
　　　　　　39　　　　　　　40
ら生まれたので「（も）もたろう」にしま（し）た。
　　　　　　　41　　　　　　　　42　　　　　　　43　　　　　　　　44
　ももたろうはま（い）日、まい日大きく（な）っていきます。そ（の）ころ、村にわるい（お）
　　　　　　　　　　　45　　　　　　　　46　　　　　　　47
にがやってきては　　村人からたべもの（や）きるものをとって（い）き、村人を大へん（こ）
　　　　　　　　　　48　　　　　　　　49　　　　　　　50
まらせていました　。　そこで、ももたろ（う）はおにをたいじし（に）、おにがしまへい（く）
　　　　51　　　　　　　　52　　　　　　　53　　　　　　　　54
ことにしました。（お）じいさんと、おば（あ）さんは「そんなあ（ぶ）ないことはやめて（お）
　　　　　55　　　　　　　　56　　　　　　　57　　　　　　　58
くれ。おににたべ（ら）れてしまうよ」と（い）ってしんぱいしま（し）た。けれども、も（も）
　　　　　59　　　　　　　60　　　　　　　61　　　　　　62
たろうは、「だい（じ）ょうぶ、きっとぼ（く）がおにをやっつけ（て）きます」といいま（し）
　　　　63　　　　　　　64　　　　　　　65　　　　　　　66
た。おじいさんと（お）ばあさんは、もも（た）ろうのために、「（日）本一　とかいたは（た）
　　　　　67　　　　　　　68
と、日本一のきび（だ）んごをつくって、（も）たせてやりました。
　　　　　69　　　　　　　　70　　　　　　　71　　　　　　　72
　「日本一」のは（た）と、日本一のきび（だ）んごをもったもも（た）ろうは、げん気よ（く）

あるいていきました。

APPENDIX B: CLOZE TEST EXACT ANSWER KEY

I 01 [a]rutokoro   somewhere
I 02 oji[i]san   old man
I 03 obaasan[ga]   <case particle: subject marker>
I 04 mai[NICHI](kanji)   every day
I 05 [o]baasan   old lady
I 06 se[n]taku   washing (clothes)
I 07 obaa[sa]n   see I 05
I 08 sentaku[o]   <case particle: object marker>
I 09 soko[e]   <directional particle>
I 10 don[bu]rako   onomatopoeia (something floats)
I 11 kimashi[ta]   came <past tense>
I 12 kore[wa]   <adverbial particle>
I 13 kae[tt]e   return (home)
I 14 I[ss]ho   together
I 15 tabemasho[o]   let us eat
I 16 [mo]ttekaeri...   return with something
I 17 ojii[sa]n   see I 02
I 18 kaet[te]   return
I 19 ojii[sa]n   see I 02
I 20 bikkurishi[te]   surprised
I 21 ko[re]wa   this
I 22 [o]baasan   see I 05
I 23 is[sho]   together
I 24 [wa]roo   let us divide
I 25 [su]ruto   then
I 26 mo[mo]   peach
I 27 paku[tt]o   onomatopoeia (sound to open)
I 28 [ka]waii   cute
I 29 akacha[n]   baby
I 30 [u]maremashita   was born
I 31 oji[i]san   see I 02
I 32 obaasan[wa]   <adverbial particle>
I 33 -ma[shi]ta   <past>
I 34 ko[do]mo   child
I 35 [so]noko   the child
I 36 so[da]teru   raise
I 37 -mashi[ta]   see I 33

I 38	momo[kara]umareta	from a peach <directional particle>
I 39	[mo]motaroo	name of a boy in the folk tale
I 40	-mashi[ta]	see I 33
I 41	ma[i]nichi	every day
I 42	ookiku[na]tte	become big
I 43	so[no]koro	at that time
I 44	[o]ni	devil
I 45	tabemono[ya]kirumono	food, clothes, and so forth <conjunctive particle>
I 46	totte[i]ki	take and go
I 47	[ko]marasete	cause trouble
I 48	momotaro[o]	see I 39
I 49	taijishi[ni]	conquer <case particle: purpose>
I 50	i[ku]	go
I 51	[o]jiisan	see I 02
I 52	oba[a]san	see I 05
I 53	a[bu]nai	dangerous
I 54	yamete[o]kure	please quit or stop (request)
I 55	tabe[ra]rete	eaten (passive form)
I 56	...to[i]tte	say
I 57	shinpai[shi]mashita	worried
I 58	mo[mo]taroo	see I 39
I 59	dai[jo]obu	all right
I 60	bo[ku]ga	I (a boy calls himself)
I 61	yattsuke[te]kimasu	beat (conquer)
I 62	iima[shi]ta	said
I 63	[o]baasan	see I 05
I 64	momo[ta]roo	see I 39
I 65	[ni]honichi	Japan number one
I 66	ha[ta]	flag
I 67	kibi[da]ngo	millet ball
I 68	[mo]tasete	let (someone) have (causative form)
I 69	ha[ta]	see I 66
I 70	kibi[da]ngo	see I 67
I 71	momo[ta]roo	see I 39
I 72	genkiyo[ku]	energetically, well

THE *MOMOTAROO* STORY (VERBATIM TRANSLATION)

Once upon a time, there lived an Old Man and an Old Lady. The Old Man went to a mountain everyday to collect branches, and the Old Lady went to a river to wash clothes. Old day, while the Old Lady was washing at the river, a big peach came floating toward her, *donburako donburako*. The Old Lady said, "My, this is a big peach! I will take it home and eat with the Old Man," and took it home.

The Old Man came home in the evening. He was very surprised and said, "This is such a big peach! Let's eat it, my Old Lady," and tried to cut it. Right at the moment, the peach divided by itself and a pretty baby boy was born with a cry, "*ogyaa!*". The Old Man and the Old Lady were very surprised, but since they did not have child of their own, they decided to raise the child with great care. They named the child Momotaroo (Peach Boy) because he was born from the peach.

Momotaroo became bigger and bigger every day. At that time, bad devils came to the village, took food, clothes, etc. from the village people, so the people were in big trouble. Momotaroo decided to go to the Devils' Island to conquer the devils. The Old Man and the Old Lady were worried about him very much and begged him, "Please do not do such a dangerous thing. You might be eaten by the devils." However, Momotaroo said, "I will be all right. I will conquer the devils." So, the Old Man and the Old Lady made a flag saying "Japan Number One" and the best Japanese millet balls and let him take them with him.

Momotaroo took the flag and millet balls and walked along very energetically...

Naoya Fujita
Pacific University, Oregon

SITUATION-DRIVEN OR STRUCTURE-DRIVEN?: TEACHING JAPANESE AT THE COLLEGE LEVEL IN THE UNITED STATES

INTRODUCTION

In language pedagogy, there are two prominent methodologies: (a) a target language is taught on the basis of situations or themes, and (b) a target language is taught on the basis of structural patterns. For the sake of convenience, I will henceforth refer to the former as "Situation-Driven Approach" and the latter as "Structure-Driven Approach" (Shrum and Glisan 1994, pp. 24–25). To summarize, under the Situation-Driven Approach students manipulate a target language to communicate thoughts by using situational skills before attending to particular language structures with the use of grammatical skills, whereas under the Structure-Driven Approach students first learn grammatical rules and vocabulary and later practice using them in communication.

Whether one approach is superior to the other is not a universal matter; rather, it is a language-specific issue. The way children acquire their first language seems uncontroversially universal. However, second language acquisition, particularly among adult learners, seems to be heavily influenced by a cognate/non-cognate factor. Thus, one must critically evaluate the aforementioned methodologies on the basis of the linguistic relation between a target language and learners' native language. It seems to me that discussion in language pedagogy, especially when arguing for a particular methodology, tends to be idealistic in an attempt to make it appealing to any human language; as a result, the cognate/non-cognate factor tends to be overlooked. In this paper, while considering this factor, I will discuss pedagogy pertaining to Japanese, particularly at the college level where the students' native language is primarily English.

This article will be organized as follows. First, goals of language learning and teaching at the college level will be discussed. These goals should not be intended to be short-term which can be achieved in four years of education, but rather follow a broader guideline that is more career-oriented. The most important goal to be addressed is the attainment of *survival skills*, which I will identify with the attainment of *analytical skills*.

Second, in comparison between the Situation-Driven Approach and the Structure-Driven Approach, I will demonstrate how the analytical skills in question will be

Fujita, N. (1997). Situation-driven or structure-driven?: Teaching Japanese at the college level in the United States. In H. M. Cook, K. Hijirida, & M. Tahara (Eds.), *New trends and issues in teaching Japanese language and culture* (Technical Report #15, pp. 119–132). Honolulu: University of Hawai'i, Second Language Teaching and Curriculum Center.

best acquired. This question is synonymous with a comparison of analytical reasoning through induction to that through deduction. I argue that in a classroom setting, analytical reasoning can be better developed through a deductive process, namely through the Structure-Driven Approach, mainly due to the fact that it is more systematic for teachers to prepare materials and for students to understand them.

Third, putting aside the conceptual preference for the Structure-Driven Approach over the Situation-Driven Approach, an examination of a language-particular issue will be discussed. The main concern here is whether there is a cognate relation between a target language and students' native language. I will argue that this issue plays a very crucial role in determining which approach, situation-driven or structure-driven, language teachers should adopt for maximal results. I will support the Structure-Driven Approach by providing some examples of Japanese grammatical constructions.

Fourth, I will emphasize that the Structure-Driven Approach is by no means denying situational exercises. Rather, appropriate use of situational exercises will enable students to develop their analytical skills more effectively.

GOALS OF LANGUAGE LEARNING AT THE COLLEGE LEVEL

Needless to say, our ultimate goal of language learning at the college level is acquisition of a high level of proficiency in all four areas: speaking, listening, writing and reading. Practically speaking, many students who take language courses at the college level hope to utilize the language in their careers after they graduate. It seems to me that this tendency is much more salient in languages of which fluent speakers are scarce in the job market. As far as the United States is concerned, such a circumstance is evident in relation to Japanese: there is high demand but low supply in the job market. The job market seeks qualified Japanese speakers, who have a high level of command especially in writing and reading, not to mention speaking and listening. For this practical reason, Japanese language programs concerning such students' needs ought to include certain aspects of vocational training in their curricula.

Note that I refer to "vocational training" in a specific sense. This is not necessarily to mean that Japanese teachers should teach students technology-oriented language, and so forth. Rather, Japanese teachers should teach their students how to utilize their language skills in various "real-life" situations. In other words, students must acquire survival skills. "Acquisition of survival skills" here denotes an ability to handle any discourse situations which students have never encountered in a classroom setting.

As we know, even though a native speaker of language X has a finite linguistic knowledge of that language, that speaker is able to utter an infinite number of sentences based on his/her finite knowledge. Of course, first language acquisition and second language acquisition (especially by adults) are arguably different. Fromkin and Rodman (1993, pp. 423–424) point out that there are two possible reasons that adult learners find acquiring a second language difficult:

(1) Principles of universal grammar ("competence" applicable to first language acquisition) do not hold after the critical period; or

(2) Principles of universal grammar that govern first language acquisition do hold for second language acquisition even after the critical period; therefore, the knowledge of the first language interferes with the complete acquisition of the second language.

Whichever the reason may be, it seems to be the case that adult learners acquire a second language by employing a process cognitively different from that of children. If second language acquisition by adults has no such competence-performance relation as child language acquisition, as described in (1) above, then language teachers must introduce their students to principles of language-particular grammar and teach them how to make a connection between competence that they acquire and linguistic performance. On the other hand, if knowledge of the learners' first language interferes with the acquisition of a second language, as described in (2) above, then language teachers must provide their students with, in a sense, a "conscious" (non-intuitive) way of connecting their innate linguistic competence to linguistic performance via a language-particular filter.

In both of the above cases, for better understanding and learning a second language, it is necessary for learners to be conscious of what they are learning and how they are using the language. I argue that such a conscious (non-intuitive) process is "analytical skill". Recall that I pointed out above that students at the college level must acquire survival skills. Taking competence-performance relation in second language acquisition by adults, what I mean by "acquisition of survival skills" is equivalent to "acquisition of analytical skills". In other words, language learners must be able to consciously or subconsciously analyze what they know about the target language and consequently utilize the language successfully. In this way, language learners can handle any real-life discourse situations to which they have not been exposed in a classroom setting.

Then, a relevant question to address is how one can acquire the analytical skills in a classroom setting. In the next section let us discuss this issue by examining the Situation-Driven Approach and the Structure-Driven Approach in comparison.

INDUCTIVE LEARNING VERSUS DEDUCTIVE LEARNING

Let us first examine the Situation-Driven Approach. This approach is so designed to enhance students' spontaneous communicative skills. That is to say, the pedagogical aim of this approach is that through communication students spontaneously acquire grammatical knowledge. Under this approach, students make linguistic generalizations based on various data, namely, *situations* or *themes*. Thus, the

Situation-Driven Approach is characteristically inductive. Let us look at this approach schematically. Suppose that a teacher introduces six communicatively significant situations or themes, as illustrated in (3):

(3)

G1
G3
S1 S2 G4 S3
G2 G5 S6 G9
G10
S4 G6 S5
G7 G8

S=situations (themes); G=grammatical items

It is usually the case that each situational exercise (such as S1 ~ S6 in (3)) includes grammatical patterns (such as G1 ~ G10 in (3)). In order for students to induce a grammatical concept, they must have a logically sufficient set of data available. If the situations that the teacher provides do not constitute linguistically adequate data, in other words, if G1 to G10 in (3) are not closely connected among one another, it is difficult for students to obtain linguistic generalization. Thus, it is difficult for them to acquire analytical skills. The condition for acquiring analytical skills through induction is described as follows:

(4) **Acquiring Analytical Skills Through Induction:**
There must be solid connection among G1...GX across Ss, where G denotes "grammatical item" and S denotes "situation".

Effective language teachers who use an inductive approach are those who can make solid connections among grammatical items associated with each situation. But as language teachers know by experience, this is not an easy task to achieve.

Let us now examine the Structure-Driven Approach. Under this approach, a teacher provides students with a grammatical concept based on a previously acquired set of structural patterns which is pedagogically adequate. Students are then expected to understand each pattern by logical reasoning using their linguistic knowledge acquired from previously learned patterns. Thus, the Structure-Driven Approach is characteristically deductive. The most notable difference between this approach and the Situation-Driven Approach is that a teacher can present various patterns in a sequential manner in the Structure-Driven Approach. This is illustrated in (5).

(5)

S1   S5   S7

S3 [G1] → [G2] → [G3] →

S2   S4 S6   S8

S=situations (themes); G=grammatical items

Teachers are encouraged to provide students with as many situations as possible that can be generated by each grammatical pattern. Under this approach, effective teachers are those who can make a situation connected with other situations among various grammatical patterns. For example, in introducing G2 in (5), S4, S5 and S6 are concurrently introduced, and these situations can be connected to other situations learned through other grammatical items such as G1 or G3. The condition for acquiring analytical skills through deduction is described as follows:

(6) **Acquiring Analytical Skills Through Deduction:**
    There must be solid connection among S1...SX across Gs, where S denotes "situation" and G denotes "grammatical item".

Empirically speaking, in language education, it is easier for both teachers and students to make connections among situations across various grammatical patterns as in (6), namely the deductive or the Structure-Driven Approach, rather than to make connections among grammatical patterns across various situations as in (4), namely the inductive or the Situation-Driven Approach. The advantage of the Structure-Driven Approach is that students are introduced to a systematic flow of grammatical patterns; therefore, they can develop analytical skills relatively easily.

Note that the Situation-Driven Approach generally assumes that second language learning is characterized as "performance before competence". However, it should be noted that adult second language learners are equipped with the grammar of their first language. No matter how hard they try to concentrate on the target language, the knowledge of the first language always intervenes. The Situation-Driven Approach, which is often represented by the *communicative* method, tends to put much less emphasis on grammatical accuracy, since the pedagogical priority of this method is to achieve communicative proficiency. But we are aware that less emphasis on grammatical accuracy tends to lead to fossilization among adult learners. I mentioned earlier that the job market wanting Japanese speakers expects them to perform at a high level of proficiency, especially in writing and reading. Thus, fossilization should be avoided as much as possible and accuracy of language use should be taken into consideration.[1]

---

[1] Fossilization can be observed in both first and second language acquisition, but why is fossilization in a second language more prevalent than in first language acquisition? This may be another indication that learning a second language by adults is at least cognitively

COGNATE/NON-COGNATE FACTORS

Thus far, I have examined the Situation-Driven Approach and the Structure-Driven Approach and argued in favor of the Structure-Driven Approach. It is my observation, however, that the Situation-Driven Approach seems to be successful in teaching European languages in the United States. However, as for teaching Japanese in the United States, the Situation-Driven Approach seems to be less successful than the same approach used in teaching European languages in terms of teachers' course preparation and students' understanding the materials, putting aside this approach's shortcoming such as fossilization and lack of grammatical accuracy discussed in the preceding section. In this section, this crosslinguistic issue will be discussed in terms of cognate/non-cognate factors between a native language and a target language.

Let us consider the Situation-Driven Approach first. Recall that this approach is characteristically inductive. Induction in this case is synonymous with generalization based on adequate linguistic data. Especially, induction in language learning is facilitated by students' previous linguistic knowledge, that is, the linguistic knowledge of English in the present case. Therefore, for instruction of European languages such as Spanish, French, and German, which are cognate to English, students can easily induce (make generalization of) new grammatical concepts based on the given situations particularly due to their native language intuition, that is, knowledge of English. Hence, inductive learning can be smoothly incorporated into teaching of languages which are cognate to students' native language.

As noted above, one of the disadvantages of the Situation-Driven Approach is the difficulty of connecting grammatical items across situations (cf. (4)). In teaching European languages, this disadvantage is apparently overcome by the cognate factor, namely facilitation of induction by the students' previous linguistic knowledge, that is, knowledge of English.

Naturally, the induction process can be easily interfered with if students' previous linguistic knowledge is not applicable to a generalization of grammatical concepts of the target language. This case is exemplified in the learning of Japanese by English speakers, where there is no cognate relation between the languages. Let us examine a specific example to illustrate this point.

In Japanese, *topic* which is marked by particle *-wa* is one of the most difficult concepts for English speakers to comprehend since this notion is syntactically not realized in English. Typical topic sentence structures are illustrated in (7) and (8a):

---

different from learning a first language by children. This is an interesting issue, but it is not my intention to investigate it in this article.

---

(7) 魚は　　　　　鯛が　　　　　　　　　うまい。

Sakana-*wa*　tai-ga　　　　　　　　umai.

fish-TOPIC　　red snapper-NOMINATIVE　delicious

"(As for) fish, red snapper is delicious."

(8) a. 太郎は　　　　本を　　　　　　買った。

Taro- *wa*　　hon-o　　　　　　kat-ta.

Taro-TOPIC　　book-ACCUSATIVE　buy-PAST

"(Speaking of Taro), he bought a book."

b. 太郎が　　　　本を　　　　　　買った。

Taro-*ga*　　　hon-o　　　　　　kat-ta.

Taro-NOMINATIVE　book-ACCUSATIVE　buy-PAST

"Taro bought a book. (Lit. It is Taro who bought a book.)"

The semantic distinction between *topic* and *subject*, as shown in (7a) and (7b), respectively is particularly confusing to English-speaking students. Under the Situation-Driven Approach, the concept of topic, and consequently the distinction between topic and subject is apparently difficult to teach. Exposure to various situation- or theme-based communicative exercises does not necessarily make the students analytically generalize the concept because grammatical knowledge which is necessary for students to generalize the concept of topic has not been systematically given to them prior to introducing the concept of topic. In other words, students cannot induce the concept of topic just by being exposed to various situations. At a proficiency level where accuracy of writing and reading abilities as well as speaking is highly demanded, this is problematic since as mentioned in the preceding section, there is a risk of causing fossilization.

Such a problem can be avoided or at least minimized if students understand the concept of topic at a very early stage of learning the language, ideally at the very beginning of an elementary level course. Hence, the deductive approach, namely the Structure-Driven Approach can be employed for maximal results. Fujita and Nemoto (1995) argue that it is essential to introduce, at the very beginning of instruction, the canonical sentence structure of Japanese which includes syntactic topic position in the sentence-initial position. Crucially, they argue that introduction of topic should precede that of subject in order to avoid confusion between the two concepts.

The topic-subject dichotomy illustrated above suggests it is more effective to introduce a grammatical item/concept as the base of instruction and have students deduce the concept by means of various exercises including even situational exercises. By being exposed to as many discourse situations as possible which can be created by a given grammatical concept — in this case, topic — students can deduce the concept. Regarding this point, recall (6), restated below:

(6) **Acquiring Analytical Skills through Deduction**
There must be solid connection among S1...SX across Gs, where S denotes "situation" and G denotes "grammatical item".

It is not difficult for teachers to provide a number of situations on the basis of a grammatical concept. For example, even at a very beginning level, it is possible to introduce many situations that contain the notion of topic. Some of the examples are illustrated in (9):

(9) a. locating a place (bookstore)

本屋は　　　　どこに　　　　ありますか？

Honya-*wa*　　doko-ni　　　arimasu-ka.

bookstore-TOPIC where-LOCATIVE　exist-Q

"Where is the bookstore?"

b. asking what is in Tokyo

東京には　　　　　　何が　　　　　　ありますか？

Tokyo-**ni**-*wa*　　　nani-ga　　　　arimasu-ka.

Tokyo-LOCATIVE-TOPIC　what-NOMINATIVE　exist-Q

"What is in Tokyo? (Lit. In Tokyo, what exists?)"

c. introducing oneself

私の　　　名前は　　田中です。　　お名前は？

Watashi-no　namae-*wa*　Tanaka-desu.　Onamae-*wa*?

I-GENITIVE　name-TOPIC　Tanaka-COPULA　name-TOPIC

"My name is Tanaka. (What is) your name?"

d. buying X

この　　本は　　　いくらですか？

Kono　　hon-*wa*　ikura-desu-ka.

this　　book-TOPIC　how much-COPULA-Q

"How much is this book?"

Thus, through a variety of situational exercises, students are able to analyze the concept of topic at a very early stage.

Those who learn Japanese through this approach seem to have much less trouble understanding language-particular concepts; hence, they suffer much less from fossilization when they advance to a higher level of learning, particularly in the areas of writing and reading.

Let us consider the Situation-Driven Approach. Development of analytical skills under this approach was described in (4), repeated below:

(4) **Acquiring Analytical Skills through Induction**
There must be solid connection among G1...GX across Ss, where G denotes "grammatical item" and S denotes "situation".

In comparison, let us consider the topic phrases in Japanese under the Situation-Driven Approach. As described in (4), if teachers who adopt the Situation-Driven Approach want their students to understand the notion of topic, they must arrange themes so that the students can induce the grammatical notion. However, the students whose native language is not cognate to Japanese have no concept of topic to begin with. Then, how can they induce the concept? In order to overcome this problem, teachers must make their teaching plan innovative so that their students somehow understand the concept of topic through a variety of theme-oriented practices.

Summarizing thus far, as far as teaching of a non-cognate language is concerned, the Situation-Driven Approach apparently requires that teachers put a tremendous amount of effort onto teaching material development in order for their students to successfully induce grammatical concepts. If teachers merely introduce various situation- or theme-oriented exercises, these exercises may help the students understand what these exercises are, but do not help them to develop analytical skills which are essential to acquire "survival skills." On the other hand, the Structure-Driven Approach allows teachers to prepare materials in a logically sequential manner. In addition, since students are introduced to grammatical concepts first for the purpose of deduction, they know what they are getting at, and acquisition of grammatical concepts can be achieved without guess work.

Before closing this section, let us add a couple more examples which show that the deductive approach is more effective in language teaching and learning, especially when there is no cognate relation between a target language and students' native language.

Japanese numeral classifiers are grammatical items which are conceptually much simpler than grammatical items such as topic -wa phrases. However, students are often discouraged by the fact that there are a number of classifiers such as -mai for thin flat objects, -satsu for bound objects, and -hon for long cylindrical objects. What makes classifiers even more difficult is the somewhat irregular pronunciation for almost all classifiers. Many students become discouraged because they believe there are a hundreds of idiosyncratic classifiers.

Again, this problem can be minimized if the phonological concept of classifiers is introduced at an early stage of instruction, instead of introducing them at random along with various exercises. Teachers can tell them that there are only three basic pronunciation patterns for classifiers and each classifier falls into one of the patterns. This is illustrated as follows. Note that irregular pronunciation is indicated by bold italic.

(10)

	-tsu type	-hon type	-satsu type	-mai type
1	ひとつ *hitotsu*	いっぽん *ippon*	いっさつ *issatsu*	いちまい ichimai
2	ふたつ *hutatsu*	にほん nihon	にさつ nisatsu	にまい nimai
3	みっつ *mittsu*	さんぼん *sanbon*	さんさつ sansatsu	さんまい sanmai
4	よっつ *yottsu*	よんほん yonhon	よんさつ yonsatsu	よんまい yonmai
5	いつつ *itsutsu*	ごほん gohon	ごさつ gosatsu	ごまい gomai
6	むっつ *muttsu*	ろっぽん *roppon*	ろくさつ rokusatsu	ろくまい rokumai
7	ななつ *nanatsu*	ななほん nanahon	ななさつ nanasatsu	ななまい nanamai
8	やっつ *yattsu*	はっぽん *happon*	はっさつ *hassatsu*	はちまい hachimai
9	ここのつ *kokonotsu*	きゅうほん kyuuhon	きゅうさつ kyuusatsu	きゅうまい kyuumai
10	とお *too*	じゅっぽん *juppon*	じゅっさつ *jussatsu*	じゅうまい juumai

The following are some examples that fall into each of the above types.

(11)

a.　*-tsu* type

　　～人　（～り）　　　~ri: people (1 and 2)

　　～日　（～か）　　　~ka: date (2 to 10)

b.　*-hon* type

　　～杯　（～はい）　　~hai: cups

　　～泊　（～はく）　　~haku: nights, etc.

c.　*-satsu* type

　　～頭　（～とう）　　~tou: animals

　　～着　（～ちゃく）　~chaku: clothes, etc.

b.　*-mai* type

　　～台　（～だい）　　~dai: machines

　　～番　（～ばん）　　~ban: number/place, etc.

Once a teacher introduces the chart (10) and tells students that each newly introduced classifier falls into one of the above types, it becomes much easier for students to confront a number of otherwise confusing classifiers. In other words, based on the knowledge as illustrated in (10), students can analyze the phonological patterns of the newly introduced classifiers. On the other hand, if one attempts to achieve the same success under the inductive approach, it requires students to invest much more effort and patience since students do not have a numerical classifier system in their native language.

Just like numeral classifiers, students often believe that there are too many grammatical constructions to learn in Japanese. This statement may be true: there are indeed many grammatical patterns and mere memorization of them can be painful and discouraging. However, introduction of these patterns in a deductive manner can reduce the burden.

Again, at a very early stage of language instruction, teachers are encouraged to inform their students that there are only three canonical predicate patterns: (a) dictionary forms (a.k.a. citation forms, *-ru/-u* forms, etc.), (b) stem forms, and (c) *-te* forms (a.k.a. gerunds). Each newly introduced pattern can fall into one of these canonical predicate patterns. In the following chart, I use たべる (食べる　*taberu* 'eat') for verbs, たかい (高い　*takai* 'expensive') for adjectives, しずかだ (静かだ　*shizuka* 'quiet') for な-adjectives, and がくせいだ (学生だ　*gakusei* 'student') for nouns.

(12)

	dictionary	stem	-te
verbal	たべる taberu	たべ tabe	たべて tabete
adjectival	たかい takai	たか taka	たかくて takakute
な-adjectival	しずかだ shizukada	しずか shizuka	しずかで shizukade
nominal	がくせいだ gakuseida	がくせい gakusei	がくせいで gakuseide

Some of the patterns that fall into each canonical pattern are as follows:

(13)   Example patterns with dictionary form:

     dictionary form ＋つもりだ   (~*tsumori da*) 'intend to do X'

     dictionary form ＋と思う   (~*to omou*) 'think that X'

(14)   Example patterns with stem:

     stem ＋に行く   (~*ni iku*) 'go for the purpose of doing X'

     stem ＋そうだ   (~*soo da*) 'appear to do X; be about to do X'

(15)   Example patterns with te-form:

     te-form ＋しまう   (~*shimau*) 'end up doing X'

     te-form ＋おく   (~*oku*) 'do X in advance'

Once a teacher introduces the chart (12) and tells students that each newly introduced grammatical construction falls into one of the above types, it becomes much easier for students to confront a number of otherwise discouraging grammatical constructions. In other words, based on the knowledge as illustrated in (12), students can analyze the syntactic structures of the newly introduced constructions.

There is also a psychological advantage for the deductive approach, namely the Structure-Driven Approach. As students are given a grammatical pattern (concept) and asked to practice it, they can be encouraged to use the pattern in totally new situations that either the teacher or students create. Furthermore, after a substantial amount of such exercises, the teacher can give the students comprehensive questions (oral or written) which contain the concept. Through such exercises, students can gain confidence and as the result become more motivated in learning the language.

In this section, I argued that as far as teaching of a non-cognate language is concerned, the Structure-Driven Approach, which is deductive in nature, is pedagogically more effective than the inductive approach, namely the Situation-Driven Approach. The three specific examples, (a) topic construction, (b) numeral classifiers, and (c) grammatical conjugation show that the Situation-Driven Approach apparently requires that teachers put a tremendous amount of effort onto teaching material development in order for their students to successfully induce grammatical concepts. If teachers merely introduce various situation- or theme-oriented exercises, these exercises may help the students understand what these exercises are, but do not help them to develop analytical skills which are essential to acquire "survival skills."

On the other hand, the Structure-Driven Approach allows teachers to prepare materials in a logically sequential manner so that students can easily analyze the structure of Japanese and furthermore can develop survival skills which I mentioned in the beginning of this article.

CONCLUDING REMARKS

In this article I have argued for the Structure-Driven Approach as far as teaching Japanese in the United States is concerned. It should be emphasized, however, that I by no means categorically deny the value of situational exercises. As a matter of fact, it is even imperative to incorporate situational exercises into the Structure-Driven Approach. However, the purposes are is quite different in the two approaches. In the Structure-Driven Approach, the purpose is to enhance understanding of patterns and to facilitate the students' analytical skills, whereas in the Situation-Driven Approach, the purpose is to manipulate language to communicate thoughts.

If the ultimate goal of language learning is to develop survival skills and if the survival skills are synonymous with analytical skills by which the students can understand any linguistic situations they have never learned or encountered in a classroom setting, the Structure-Driven Approach with appropriate situational exercises can be a real communicative approach.

Acknowledgments

I am grateful to the participants at the 1996 Association of Teachers of Japanese (ATJ) Conference for their valuable input. I would especially like to thank Brad Maxfield for proofreading and for his helpful suggestions and comments. Of course, responsibility for any limitations of the work presented here rests entirely with me. Comments may be directed to: fujitan@pacificu.edu.

REFERENCES

Fromkin, V., & Rodman, R. (1993). *An introduction to language*. Fort Worth: Harcourt Brace Jovanovich.

Fujita, N., & Nemoto, N. (1995). WA: Pedagogical implications. In H. Nara & M. Noda (Eds.), *Proceedings of the 1995 ATJ conference on literature, language and pedagogy* (pp. 101–110). Middlebury: Association of Teachers of Japanese.

Shrum, J., & Glisan, E. (1994). *Teacher's handbook: Contextualized language instruction*. Boston: Heinle & Heinle.

Andrew D. Cohen
University of Minnesota

DEVELOPING PRAGMATIC ABILITY: INSIGHTS FROM THE ACCELERATED STUDY OF JAPANESE

INTRODUCTION

The case study of a single adult learner reported on in this paper began exclusively as an effort to describe the development of *pragmatic ability*, that is, the ability to deal with "meaning as communicated by a speaker (or writer) and interpreted by a listener (or reader)...[and to interpret] people's intended meanings, their assumptions, their purposes or goals, and the kinds of actions (for example, requests) that they are performing when they speak" (Yule, 1996 pp. 3–4). The narrow focus of the study was meant to distinguish it from, say, that by Schmidt and Frota (1986) which looked more broadly at numerous aspects of Schmidt's learning of Portuguese in and out of the classroom. It was also intended to help gather information on pragmatic development over time, an under-investigated area in second language acquisition research (cf. Kasper & Schmidt, 1996; Cohen, 1996a).

In the field of foreign language teaching and learning, there is a growing concern to include a systematic focus on form within even the most communicative, socially-contextualized of methods (Leeman, Arteagoitia, Fridman, and Doughty, 1995). At the same time, there has been and continues to be empirical evidence that a mastery-oriented emphasis on identifying and correcting learner errors may not be as effective as teachers would like it to be (see, for example, Chaudron, 1988; Cohen and Robbins, 1976; and most recently, Roberts, 1996). So as in many areas of endeavor, the word is "moderation." While there may be an increased interest in a systemaric focus on structure in language teaching, there is an admonition of sorts in a recent paper by Tarone (in press):

> ...there is mounting evidence that an adequate theory of SLA should model a second-language learner not solely as a decontextualized information-processor, but rather combine the work of researchers like Labov, Schumann, Giles, Allwright, Lantolf and Swain to view the learner in social context as an evaluating, converging or diverging interactor, whose cognitive capacities are significantly impacted by social interaction.

Having just gone through a four-month experience of sometimes identifying with the "decontextualized information-processor," in my case hard at work developing an interlanguage grammar in Japanese, I felt it would be beneficial to describe that experience for the sake of other learners, teachers, curriculum planners, and

Cohen, A. D. (1997). Developing pragmatic ability: Insights from the accelerated study of Japanese. In H. M. Cook, K. Hijirida, & M. Tahara (Eds.), *New trends and issues in teaching Japanese language and culture* (Technical Report #15, pp. 133–159). Honolulu: University of Hawai'i, Second Language Teaching and Curriculum Center.

administrators. The focus of this paper, then, is on a *foreign-* and not a second-language learning situation[1], in which the context for learning was almost exclusively that of a classroom in an academic setting. In addition, over half of the instructional focus was on the learning of structure, and to a large extent on more formal language rather than on plain or vernacular Japanese.

If college students are studying a foreign language in order to major in the literature of the language, then a classroom experience characterized in part by somewhat decontextualized and linguistically-focused language learning may be exactly what they want and need. Experience has shown that such study will undoubtedly provide them the solid basis in structure and literacy upon which to build upon later. If on the other hand, learners take a language course for, say, two years in order to pass a language requirement, they may be looking to acquire an ability to understand and communicate in the everday or *vernacular* form of the target language. The students might wish to study a range of structures from the more formal ones used with associates and acquaintances to the more informal ones to be used with close friends and family. In addition, they may wish for more of an emphasis on spoken language than on literacy skills.

A language program in an academic setting where the focus is on the development of literacy skills is likely to serve the development of reading and writing skills better than it serves the development of communicative ability. The following are four principles or working hypotheses regarding language learning set in the academic classroom, and the nature of the social context likely to be created as a result of this (E. Tarone, personal communication, November, 1996):

1. If the classroom is reserved for the teaching and use of the more formal register (the superordinate norm), then learners will not have sufficient exposure to the more informal or vernacular to be able to use it effectively when called upon to do so. Native-speaking teachers, like other native speakers, may assume that everyone already knows the vernacular norm, that everyone picks it up, because that is what they did and what people do in the outside world (Tarone and Swain, 1995).

2. In the best of classroom situations, learners are still in a rarefied world, a world of language usage rather than use (see Widdowson, 1978, on use and usage). In such an environment, the best performers may indeed be those who monitor their language behavior for accuracy to a lesser or greater extent. This may not be so much the case in the real world where fluency of speech may be more important than accuracy.

3. In the social context of a classroom, the teacher is in charge, always to be performed for, always correcting and grading the learners on form and accuracy, and not necessarily paying attention to or interested in the content that the learners transmit or want to transmit. Since for the most

---

[1] That is, not in a country where the language is the official or dominant language of the society.

part, the teacher is not really engaged in what the learners did yesterday, they could make it up and the teacher would be perfectly happy, as long as the output were grammatical, used the expected structures, and had appropriate vocabulary.

4. When their vernacular (or automatized) rule system is small, learners have to produce everything by paying attention to form, memorizing, monitoring, using retrieval strategies such as mnemonic devices, and so forth. This need to access linguistic forms takes longer than the rapid accessing of an automatized rule system and can fall apart under pressure.

The current case study, while intending to focus just on the development of pragmatic ability, broadened its focus somewhat to view pragmatic development again the backdrop of the interaction between the given instructional method and the language learning experience. The following were the research questions:

1. How might the learner's in-class and out-of-class experience of learning Japanese in an academic setting be characterized?

2. What are the perceptions of the learner about the development of his ability to use pragmatic rules? Specifically, to what extent would the learner assess himself as being able to

   a. recognize the sociocultural strategies needed in order to perform the given speech act?

   b. use the appropriate sociolinguistic expression?

   c. use the appropriate amount of speech and of information?

   d. use the appropriate levels of formality (e.g., through word choice, phrasing, use of titles, and choice of verb forms)?

   e. use the appropriate degree of directness (e.g., through verb form or strategy choice)?

   f. use the appropriate degree of politeness through politeness markers (e.g., "thank you," "please," "if you don't mind") as well as through appropriate levels of formality and directness? (adapted from Hudson, Detmer, and Brown, 1995, and as operationalized by Yamashita, 1996)

3. What is the role that explicit information about pragmatic facts plays in language learning? To what extent do the teacher, the textbook, other students, natives in the environment, or others provide this information?

4. To what extent does the social context of the classroom contribute to pragmatic success?

5. How does the learner's motivation, learning style, and learning strategy preferences relate to the acquisition of pragmatic ability?

DESIGN OF THE STUDY

SUBJECT

The 52-year-old author of the paper served as his own subject in this case study of pragmatic development in Japanese. This was my eleventh foreign language, after Latin, French, Italian, Spanish, Bolivian Quechua, Bolivian Aymara, Portuguese, Hebrew, German, and Arabic. I lived for sixteen years in a Hebrew and Arabic-speaking city (Jerusalem), two years in an Aymara-speaking community within the Spanish-speaking world (the High Plains of Bolivia), a year and a half in a Portuguese-speaking city (São Paulo, Brazil), and five months in French-speaking cities (Bordeaux and Grenoble). The foreign languages that I can currently read, write, and give academic talks in are Hebrew, Spanish, Portuguese, and French. I have a masters degree in descriptive linguistics and a doctorate in international development education. My professional interests have included the application of language learning and language use strategies to the study of second and foreign languages.

At the time I started my study of Japanese for this study I would classify myself as a *false beginner* because I had audited parts of a beginning Japanese course at the University of Minnesota (1994–95), during which time I had had some private tutoring sessions as well. I was learning to read *hiragana* and *katakana*[2], but had done no writing. Prior to these studies, I had spent about two months in Japan on three separate trips, the longest for a month, when I taught a summer course on second language acquisition in Tokyo.

During the Japanese learning project at the University of Hawai'i, I took a series of cognitive style measures to see how these might relate to my language learning. On the Myers-Briggs Type Indicator (Myers & Briggs, 1976) I came out very much as being *extroverted* as opposed to *introverted*, more *intuiting* than *sensing*, more *thinking* than *feeling*, and far more *judging* than *perceiving*. On the Measurement of Ambiguity Tolerance (MAT–50) (Norton, 1975), I came out at 170 (lowest ambiguity=64, highest=434) which meant that according to the results of this administration of the MAT, I am slightly more intolerant of ambiguity than I am tolerant.[3] I also took the Group Embedded Figures Test, a measure of cognitive restructuring of visually presented geometric figures (Oltman, Raskin, & Witkin, 1971). This test of visual disembedding is intended to reflect the kind of cognitive restructuring of verbal material required in language learning. While there is question as to whether it does this (Ehrman, 1996. p. 89), I am aware that I do my best not to be distracted by material in the field when I am working with certain targeted material. I got a

---

[2] *Hiragana* is a phonetic syllabary used for Japanese words for which *kanji* — Chinese characters — cannot be easily provided (e.g., conjugating ends of verbs and adjectives, grammatical particles, and auxiliary verbs), and *katakana* is another phonetic syllabary used for transcribing foreign loan words (other than Chinese).

[3] The categories on the measure dealt with personal philosophy, interpersonal communication, public image, relationship toward one's job, problem-solving, social behavior, importance of first impressions for the individual, habits, and art forms.

---

perfect 18 out of 18 correct, suggesting that I am not distracted by material in the field when I am focusing on particular material.

COURSE STRUCTURE, THE TEACHER, AND THE STUDENTS

The first-year Japanese course that I took (Japanese 105) was referred to in the time schedule as "accelerated," as it covered two semesters in one at the University of Hawai'i during Fall 1996. It ran for four months, one hour and forty-five minutes each morning or 140 hours in total, plus lab time (12 tapes covering model conversations, listening tasks, and conversational drills for each lesson[4]). The social setting for this case study in foreign-language learning was for the subject almost exclusively the academic setting of a classroom, and the instructional approach, while eclectic in nature, favored the following:

1. rote mastery of structure (a "spiraling structure approach"),

2. the use of native language for cuing language tasks,

3. the use of translation between Japanese and English for some of the oral exchanges and for the completion of literacy tasks, and

4. a concern for correcting non-native-like forms whenever possible.

One quarter of the class time (35 hours) was devoted to instruction in speaking, given all the other instructional needs. This setting provided somewhat limited exposure to the form of communicative language that promotes rapid development of pragmatic ability. Tasks were for the most part cued in the students' native language (English), students were asked to translate reading texts into English and to prepare responses in English, and spoken utterances were translated as well (depending on the task).

The textbooks were from a series developed in Tokyo by the Tsukuba Language Group (1991, 1994). Lessons 1 through 12 were included in the accelerated first-year course. The books were supplemented by departmental handouts on vocabulary, functional expressions, structure-focused tasks, and reading and writing exercises. For the most part, the teacher followed the textbooks closely, covering all of the grammatical structures, most of the vocabulary, and doing many of the drills. The syllabus was essentially predetermined by the Japanese teaching unit and major tests were constructed by the unit as a whole. This meant that on any given day, the teachers of a given level of Japanese would all be teaching the same portion of the same unit more or less. The instructor was free, however, to design her own materials and pair work in order for students to apply the structures, vocabulary, and phrases in context. She also had the students view a videotaped model conversation along with each lesson, and showed several culturally-oriented videotapes of life in Japan.

---

[4] A number of the drills were modified by the Department so that they would be more comprehensive and more intelligible as well.

The teacher of the course was a senior teacher in the department with years of teaching experience. The accelerated nature of the course put her under considerable pressure to teach *hiragana*, *katakana*, and 140 *kanji*, as well as a large vocabulary list and numerous grammar rules all in four months. She was committed to teaching all these aspects of the course, and requested that we get as much exposure as possible to the spoken language through the language lab tapes and through contact with Japanese speakers outside of class. She was impressively energetic, diligent, thorough, and always of good cheer. The very next day after homework assignments were handed in, she would return them with feedback. When students were engaged in paired drills from the textbook and in the activities that she had designed and distributed in advance of the class sessions, she would circulate around the room enough to catch and correct as many non-native-like utterances as she could at the moment in which they were produced. She was responsive to feedback from students as well.

The course began with seven registered students and myself as a sit-in audit, who was generously afforded by the teacher an opportunity to participate fully in the class. The students were all expected to have had some exposure to Japanese before the course, ideally including some familiarity with the writing system. Consequently, we are were required to take a Japanese placement test before being placed in the intensive course, and had to have demonstrated some basic familiarity with the Japanese language.[5] Toward the end of the four-month semester, there were five students, three undergraduates who had taken the equivalent of this course before, a fourth who had made numerous trips to Japan, and a graduate student who had lived in Japan for a few years. None of them were of Japanese background ethnically.

DATA COLLECTION PROCEDURES

The means of data collection included a tape-recorded journaling of insights as they occurred, plus a series of written notes, also recorded as the insights occurred. I made 25 audio-taped journal entries in all — one or two per week. I had intended to collect journal data more often, but since I was already spending almost two hours per day in class plus up to eight hours on homework before the next class, I found myself an unwilling subject when it came to a more extensive collection of data regarding my learning experiences. Every two weeks or so, I reviewed the research questions and determined what my responses to them were at that point in time.

Another rich source of data was the continual flow of quizzes and tests that I took and on which I received immediate and thorough feedback regarding my non-native-like forms. I recorded all of these corrections both in terms of vocabulary, structure, and spelling; and with regards to the *kanji* strokes. I reviewed these items

---

[5]   I took the grammar portion in a version of the placement test that used the Latin alphabet, or *romaji*. I opted out of the second portion which involved reading comprehension because although I had a some grammatical background in Japanese, I was not literate at the beginning of the course.

repeatedly as a means of eradicating them, perhaps determined to show that careful, systematic attention to teacher feedback on written work could, in fact, have an impact on learning, contrary to what research evidence has tended to show (cf., for example, Truscott, 1996).

DATA ANALYSIS PROCEDURES

The Hudson, Detmer, and Brown (1995) scales served as a means for me to self-assess my development in pragmatic ability. I considered each scale in turn from a qualitative standpoint at approximately three stages during the semester, and then after the course had ended. The pragmatic assessment scales were actually intended to be rated by native speakers of Japanese on the basis of their intuitions as to the meaning of *native-like*. But for the purposes of this research, it was not an issue of having me rated on each of the scales, but rather of studying my perceptions as a learner as to the cognitive structuring and restructuring of language material that I was doing and my sense of achievement (cf. McLaughlin, 1990, concerning *restructuring*). In addition, the audio-taped journal entries were transcribed and served as another source of qualitative data.

RESULTS

It is likely that many of the experiences I will recount here are not unique to my learning experience with Japanese. Undoubtedly other learners have encountered some of the same kinds of experiences, first, in part because the challenges that I faced are shared by English-speaking learners as a group. Second, it was because others have learned languages in accelerated courses in an academic setting. Third, it is because others have taken a course looking for a focus on communication and have found that concerns for grammatical structure and literacy have been given somewhat more emphasis.

There is no intention to be critical of the instructional method, nor of my own teacher's instructional practices. The focus is intended to be exclusively on my experience as a learner in the given accelerated program of instruction in this academic setting. Undoubtedly, this experience is largely an individual one. What I intend to contribute through the report that follows is a linking of personal language learning experience with theoretical principles regarding language learning. Ideally, the recounting of these experiences will be useful to curriculum planners, teachers, and other learners.

IN-CLASS EXPERIENCE

Let me preface my characterization of classroom results by noting that I completed all of the classroom and homework assignments, usually spending over seven hours on homework each day. (My wife, Sabina, is a witness to that.) I received grades in the A range for most of my work and a grade of over 90% (A) on the two-hour final exam that was given to all students completing a year of Japanese. In the case of the final exam, I used every test-taking strategy I could muster, especially when there was only one-half hour left (out of two) and I still had a long text to read, nine open-ended questions to answer about it, sixteen items relating to the *kanji* in the text to do, and a letter to write to a friend giving advice about the island to visit and hotel at which to stay. In the last few weeks of the course, although the teacher continued to correct my work, she did not grade it since I was an audit. (In fact, I was very fortunate to have had her grading my work up to that point because she was not obliged to do so.)

My performance in the course overall ranked me first in the class of six students, but it needs to be remembered that this was the only course that I was taking, unlike the other students in the class who had either two or even three other classes that they were taking simultaneously. In addition, I was using a host of language learning and language use strategies in a systematic way and other learners were doing less of this. The instructional program did not provide guidance in how to learn Japanese; the emphasis was on the teaching of it.

Looking back over the course as a whole, it is probably fair to say that I was spending a fair amount of class time learning about the Japanese language, being engaged in a meta-conversation with myself in my mind about the way the language worked, rather than just sitting there letting myself acquire the language that the teacher was using and wanted us to use. In addition, the teacher requested that the students come to class with the functional phrases for conversational drills already memorized, along with some sense of how to use them in the appropriate sociocultural contexts. Given the other demands of the course (learning the different writing systems, learning long vocabulary lists, learning numerous grammatical patterns, and completing a number of worksheets), I could not get sufficiently motivated to memorize those expressions as well, nor was there much time to do so. In addition, I found it difficult to do so, although I did succeed in learning several of the important phrases from flash cards — for example, the Japanese for "Could you please tell me what this means in English?" and "What is the meaning of this word?" so that I could perform the communicative drills that called for these patterns. Thus, what should have been rather effortless oral drills of communicative expressions often became a belabored reading of the exchanges in the Drills textbook. What made the reading more laborious was that the textbook often used *kanji* that we had not been expected to have learned, in order to familiarize us with them in advance, and consequently there appeared tiny *hiragana* equivalents over these *kanji* (referred to as *yomigana*), intended to facilitate recognition of the words.

Classroom talk was focused primarily on completing a series of planned transactions, such as making introductions, buying stamps or postcards at a post office, buying clothes in a department store, telling the doctor about our illness, and the like. There was little non-transactional social conversation in class, other than asides in English. In addition, spoken language tended to be focused on structures that we were to learn, often by rote memory — the strategy recommended by the instructor. Toward the end of the second month, we would start the class off with teacher-directed questions and answers, usually inquiring about what we had done the previous day or weekend, or what we intended to do — usually with the purpose of practicing some structure or other. The drills were partly mechanical (i.e., calling for the provision of a word or phrase from a set of choices), and partly meaningful (i.e., focusing on language form, using meaningful language material).[6] Communicative drills (i.e., the transmission of information that was unknown to the receiver of the message and not in the textbook or worksheet) usually were orchestrated by the teacher and not prompted by the students. In fact, students did not initiate interactions with each other in Japanese except in paired activities, and then according to prompts in the worksheets or textbook. It is not clear the extent to which students were actually listening to their peers while the peers were responding to a question posed by the teacher, except in several cases where the teacher quizzed the rest of the students as to what their peer had said.

In one or two lessons we were called upon to drill with the plain form of the verb. While I had been drilled on this form to some extent, my exposure to it had not been adequate to make it automatic. At the point where we needed the plain form to use in certain more complex constructions, the teacher seemed somewhat surprised that we did not have control over it. This lack on our part was perhaps due to a lack of sufficient practice with the form in meaningful and, especially, communicative contexts. The problem that I encountered here was consistent with Tarone's Principle #1, as listed above: if learners are not exposed to the vernacular forms, they will not be able to use them regardless of how common they are in the vernacular as spoken by natives.

Partly because we were covering *two* semesters in one in this accelerated course, the material came so fast that grammatical and discourse patterns that I was being exposed to simply did not "stick." In order to at least reference a growing list of connectors and their accompanying verb forms (e.g., ~*ndesu* [used to explain, make an excuse, react to suspicion, or indicate surprise], *toki* 'when,' ~*node* 'because,' ~*tara* 'when, if, after,' ~*to* 'if, when, whenever,' ~*atode* 'after,' ~*tekara* 'after,' etc.), I began filling a notebook with relevant rules. The problem was transferring what was in the notebook into my head. My notebook became quite knowledgeable, which was fine for homework assignments but less useful for class performance and the occasional out-of-class speech event.

My speaking repertoire seemed limited to a modest set of forms over which I had varying degrees of control in my *learner's grammar* and *mental lexicon* (i.e., the interlanguage grammar and dictionary that I created in my own mind, however non-native-like they were). In the case of verb forms, for example, I was not sure whether to use the formal or plain form with an interlocutor. So, for example, I

---

[6] A potential problem with mechanical drills is that learners can essentially put their minds "in neutral" and complete the drills effectively without engaging their black box or learning center. I was acutely aware when I would complete worksheets for homework in this manner (e.g., filling in verb forms), knowing full well that I had not retained anything for all my efforts.

would drill (through class sessions, homework, and work with a tandem partner[7]) in the use of the conditional structure ~tara 'when, if, after' with a verb such as mitsukeru 'to find' (e.g., "What would you do if you found $100?"). Yet, I never reached a point where I could produce the form in an unmonitored, natural way.

In addition, I was very aware of the restructuring (McLaughlin, 1990) going on in my learner's grammar and mental lexicon, while often *not* being in control of the situation. Rather, I frequently lapsed into overload, where just as I was achieving some control of one structure, the use of the structure would be combined with some other which would throw my mind once again into confusion. Here is a relevant entry from the journal:

> We are not just getting every structure alone. We're getting them compounded — we're not only getting comparison and superlative, as in "Where is the best place for...?" [doko ga ichi ban...], but also in reported speech [to omoimasu 'think that...']. So we are combining "where is the best place?" with our opinion ["Where do you think the best place is for..."]. (12/17/96)

Most of the class sessions were conducted in a teacher-fronted manner with every error corrected. Even when we worked in dyads, practicing discourse structures, the teacher would circulate from pair to pair, listening in and correcting our non-native-like forms as often as she could. On the homework and worksheets I handed in for checking (and I completed all that were assigned), all non-native structures of substance and mechanics were corrected in red. As indicated above, I poured over each of these corrections and dutifully recorded them, either in the grammar or the spelling section.

We learned vocabulary in long, decontextualized lists and were usually tested on a fair number of those words, sometimes without our having had much contact with the words in a meaningful context. In other words, when I would attempt to draw on my mental lexicon in order to verify the semantic range for a given Japanese word, I would often come up short, not knowing the contexts that were truly appropriate for the word. This happened to me with some verbs, like *wakaru* 'understand' and *shitte iru* 'know,' as well as with numerous other words, especially with adjectives such as *hidoi* 'terrible,' *omoshiroi* 'interesting, fun,' and *muzukashii* 'difficult,' to name just a few. Here is a journal entry on this issue of decontextualized vocabulary:

> In class we get vocabulary words in lists without being given the appropriate context. For example we are given *hidoi* 'terrible' or *shimpai* 'worrisome,' and I just will not have a good sense of what it can be used with. I found myself in class today testing the teacher out — throwing out adjectives until I got some that worked for describing her. [This was in response to her request that we do so, and the adjective I ended up using for her was *majime* 'hard-working. I also wanted to know if I could refer to a person as *shimpai*.] (11/7/96)

---

[7] Six weeks into the course, I found three Japanese graduate students with whom I met once a week, spending thirty minutes on Japanese and thirty minutes on their work.

We were quizzed regularly on structure, vocabulary, literacy skills from symbol recognition, and production (in *hiragana*, *katakana*, and *kanji*) to memo writing, according to a written weekly schedule. The frequent quizzes in the course tended to test my knowledge about the language. In part, since some if not many of the teacher's metalinguistic comments about the Japanese language were provided in English, we learners became to some extent linguists engaged in meta-talk about Japanese. Then, we were offered data about Japanese and were tested on our knowledge about Japanese. Tarone's Principle #1 above would suggest that there may be a somewhat tenuous link between knowledge about a language that was consciously learned and efforts at operationalizing that knowledge in a controlled manner in meaningful contexts. While students such as I might be able to perform well on quizzes and tests (especially if we crammed for these tests), our language base was susceptible to substantial attrition, given that only some of the material was unconsciously acquired and made automatic. (My attrition rate was high during the month after the course ended when I had virtually no contact with Japanese, and remained high even after renewed contact with my tandem partners.)

If students nominated a topic in class, it was almost invariably to ask a question about Japanese. We were to raise our hands and ask permission to ask the question. If we wanted to do so in English (which was almost always the case), then we were to ask permission. This format tended to reinforce the pragmatic norms for use of language by a subordinate to a superior: students were not to ask a question directly, but to precede it by making another formulaic request. This ritual put those several question askers amongst us in the role of linguistic field workers, attempting to analyze Japanese and to learn about its linguistic forms. The instructor would even comment from time to time that I should not analyze so much but just memorize the structures. I analyzed in order to find patterns so as to reduce the amount that my 52-year-old mind had to learn by rote memory. Unfortunately, it was not only a matter of memorizing the preferred phrases for different situations. We were also supposed to know when it was appropriate according to pragmatic norms to use each of them. The textbook usually provided this information as well, but this was simply more information to be memorized.

Furthermore, much of my language processing as a learner involved translation. In a discussion with the instructor out of class, she indicated several reasons for this use of the native language of the learners. One was that having cues for tasks (i.e., the instructions and the prompts) entirely in Japanese would be too difficult for the students and would take them too much time.[8] Another was that having learners provide native-language responses to reading passages helped to determine if the learners accurately understood the sentence structure, and such understanding was deemed essential in successful incremental learning. A third reason was to see if the learners really understood the meaning of the material since they could not simply

---

[8]   According to my instructor, the direct method of teaching Japanese to English speakers has not worked well at the university level in Japan in the early stages of instruction, and is generally not practiced there. Her view was that it would not work at the University of Hawai'i either.

lift material directly from the prompt or from the text in composing their response. Having some of the oral tasks and most of the writing tasks cued in English meant that initial processing of these tasks was substantially in English, and then answering the reading comprehension tasks in English meant that the texts were translated into English for the purpose of preparing responses. In addition, the teacher requested literal translation of the texts to check if we fully understood the structure.

This native-language cuing and response approach may possibly have had some effect on the nature of my language processing. I noticed then that when someone spoke Japanese to me, I needed to translate what they were saying into English in order to understand it, and when I spoke I needed to think it out in English first and then translate it into Japanese. This was also my experience in reading and writing, where I came to rely on translation almost exclusively. In other words, there may have been some causal link between the emphasis on translation equivalents in the course and my need to translate when in language use situations. On the other hand, there were other forces at work as well, such as my generally analytic style, plus a generally low level of automatized language. In fact, studies on adult second language learners are beginning to document the extent of mental translation in performing second-language tasks (Kern, 1994).

Studies have found, for example, that even the most advanced learners may use translation to help accomplish reading tasks, and that the less proficient learners use translation more often than the more advanced ones, with poorer results as well (Hawras, 1996; Cohen & Hawras, 1996). The literature notes the benefits accruing from mental translation such as helping the reader to chunk material into semantic clusters, to keep the train of thought, to create a network of associations, to clarify grammatical roles, and to make the input more familiar and consequently more user-friendly. On the other hand, extensive mental translation may inhibit the development of an independently functioning second language system in that the reader who employs a heavy dose or even an overdose of mental translation in order to comprehend a given text successfully may not learn much of the second language in the process.

While translation was a source of security for me — knowing what everything meant all the time, I found it slowed down my receptive and productive language processing and took me out of the Japanese context into the world of English. So in effect, it seemed to me as if my Japanese was being "laundered" by English and by American culture. The original Japanese would lose some of its authenticity since each time I would lapse into English, I would take from American sociocultural norms for communication and most likely transfer those norms when attempting to perform speech acts in Japanese. Thus, in this case, the instructional method may have inadvertently been reinforcing my "foreignness" in efforts to communicate. In addition, while one goal of Japanese instruction was to produce learners who were knowledgeable about Japanese sociocultural norms, few sociocultural rules were explicitly taught and reviewed because of lack of time. Much was left for learners to master on their own.

Consistent with Tarone's Principles #2 and #3 listed above, the Japanese classroom in which I spent approximately 140 hours was, in fact, a somewhat rarefied world of language usage rather than language use. Nonetheless, I found the classroom and the teacher's corrections and positive feedback (e.g., "excellent," "very good," "good") reassuring. In the classroom, I could always plead ignorance since no one expected me to be anything but a learner. I found myself preferring to render my attempts at Japanese in the classroom, where an always-patient teacher was likely to correct me for form whenever I made an error, than to try it on the "outside" where I was not sure how Japanese speakers (mostly well-dressed, package-laden tourists on the busses) would respond. For example, one time I was called upon to read my handwritten response (in Japanese) to a reading comprehension text, and much to my chagrin, spent a minute just staring at my answer on a worksheet, not able to decipher what I had written in Japanese. When I finally replied, it was out of only semi-comprehension of what I had written and with the emission of what proved to be a foolish answer. Since I found it difficult enough to recite printed texts, I found it all the more difficult to read my own handwritten responses.[9] In any case, my goof was only shared by the small group of peers who could emphathize with what I was going through and the patient teacher.

Here is a journal entry regarding my problems with response time in reading:

> We have *kanji* with several different representations depending on the context. So I have to decide which context it is in. I can't just go ahead and sound it out. So that slows me down while I check the context and then I back up and say, "Oh, if it's that context, then it's ~*kata* 'the way to' [as opposed to *ho* 'side, option']." (12/16/96)

Given that my oral recitation skills were limited and that the teacher frequently had us read aloud for much of the course, I found myself engaging in a language use cover strategy[10] of keeping track of which students had already read (since the teacher would have every student read before having students read a second time) and practicing my item in advance so that I would be ready to read it when called upon — a strategy identified many years ago by Hosenfeld (1976). This strategy for covering oneself by looking good in class is one that I as a conscientious language learner would wish to avoid because it means that it removes the learner from exposure to other classroom language data while engaged in it.

---

[9] A study of the reading comprehension strategies of six high-school seniors reading in Chinese as a foreign language found certain effective strategies for reading in Chinese different from those used in English as a first language. The investigator suggested that readers be taught such strategies (Pavlidis, 1990).

[10] Cover strategies (term supplied by T. McNamara, personal communication, July 3, 1996) are those strategies that learners use to create the impression that they have control over material when they do not. They are a special type of compensatory or coping strategy which involves creating an appearance of language ability so as not to look unprepared, foolish, or even stupid.

I was usually aware of why I had produced the non-native-like forms that I was corrected for in class and was able to identify the source of my deviation from the native norm in all the homework assignments, either on my own or with the assistance of the teacher or a tandem partner. In this respect, the correction that I received differed in part from that which Schmidt often reported receiving, which in his case was frequently in a more naturalistic language environment where he was not necessarily aware that he was being corrected (Schmidt & Frota, 1986). I was almost always aware that I was being corrected. Yet in retrospect the effect of correction, even with my rigorous record keeping, was short-lived. I could prepare for these problem areas on the next quiz or test much to my benefit, but did not necessarily internalize those items so that I would avoid non-native-like use of them subsequently.

My personal configuration of cognitive style preferences and adaptability, along with my active use of strategies were successful in getting me through the classroom experience with relative success. I was aware that at times my learning style preferences were not fully in sync with the teaching style of the instructor so I shifted to accommodate to her style, such as when she adopted an analytic approach to teaching structure with an emphasis on accuracy and I accommodated to that mode, engaging in all homework tasks dutifully though certainly not without difficulty. For example, even in the areas in which I was relatively strong on the cognitive measures, such as field independence, I found myself challenged repeatedly and made careless mistakes that were a function of the myriad of demands being placed upon me. The following is a journal entry referring to the field dependence issue:

> I made a field-dependent error on a writing task: "Write a note to a co-worker, Eichi. Start by explaining that you borrowed a video called, 'Tokyo Love Story,' and invite him to watch it at your house." So I had *tokyo labu stori toiu video Eichi ni karitandesu*. I was so worried about the *ni* particle that I didn't put the *-san* [politeness suffix] after *Eichi*, and I didn't put the *o* particle after *video* [to indicate its role as direct object]. I think that's being distracted by the stuff in the immediate context. (11/30/96)

In addition, I made it seem as if I borrowed the video from Eichi, also a careless mistake since I knew how to write a request for Eichi to see the video with me.

OUT-OF-CLASS EXPERIENCE

I found that I learned a good deal of Japanese during the four months, but did not appear to learn a lot at the automatized level. Until I started sessions with *tandem partners* (Japanese grad students in the ESL M.A. program) in mid-October, I was not speaking Japanese out of class at all. Meeting once a week with each of the three students definitely improved my willingness to speak Japanese, both in and out of the classroom, although I found it difficult to resist the temptation even with them to lapse into meta-discussions about Japanese in English, rather than listening to them speak in Japanese and responding to them as best I could. Furthermore, since they did not know just what vocabulary and structures I knew at least receptively, they would invariably use structures that I could not recognize. In addition, I found my ability to infer meaning from context in Japanese was far weaker than it had been at a similar level of development in the other languages that I had studied. I realize, of course, that this lack of similar progress in Japanese was due in no small part to the inherent difficulty of the language, rather than to the instructional method and its interface with my learning styles and strategies.

Furthermore, my encounters with other Japanese speakers out of class remained rare during those four months and after the course as well. I found that I did not feel comfortable initiating a conversation with the host of Japanese tourists that I come in contact with every day — on the busses, in the streets, in shops and restaurants, and so forth. What worked was when two women tourists from Kyoto were waiting for a bus to the University at the same stop I was, noticed me studying Japanese, and started talking with me. We had a 20-minute conversation, en route to campus. I even escorted them to a campus cafeteria for their lunch. But that only happened once.

Even after the four-month accelerated course, I had a residual feeling of insecurity about what I did not know (given all my non-native-like utterances), about my slowness of speech (and need to perform constant mental translation), and about my inability to understand what they might say back. Also, my pronunciation was apparently accurate enough in Japanese so that it worked to my detriment in that those Japanese speakers that I did interact with might have thought that I knew more than I did. Furthermore, I felt insecure about my knowledge of the social rules for how to begin a conversation, what to talk about, and how to talk about it. I learned the phrase to say when I saw a Japanese tourist struggling with a map, not sure where to go (Do shimashitaka? 'What happened?'). The problem was that the tourists all seemed so much at ease with the maps and explanation booklets (printed in Japanese and readily available) that they certainly did not need my assistance.

Furthermore, whereas I felt unsure as to how to "break in" with Japanese tourists, this has not the case when I overhear someone speaking French, Spanish, Portuguese, or Hebrew. I feel more at ease with those cultures and with the kinds of remarks that may be looked upon by the members of those cultures as appropriate to say to strangers. While English is seen as a language of international communication, as are Spanish and French as well, observers of Japanese society have suggested that Japanese is in some ways a "private" language, and that the Japanese are not used to having outsiders use it and may not welcome its use or mastery by nonnatives (Lew, 1996; Stronach, 1995, pp. 73–74). So, this perception of Japanese culture, however accurate, has contributed to limiting my "out-of-class encounters" considerably.[11]

---

[11] Perhaps in areas of he US where there are numerous Japanese tourists, it would be beneficial to include in the first-year instructional materials a unit (perhaps optional) with suggestions on how American learners of Japanese might start and conduct

Let us now move from the first research question regarding the overall in-class and out-of-class experience to the other four research questions which relate more specifically to pragmatic ability.

LEARNER'S PERCEPTIONS ABOUT
THE DEVELOPMENT OF HIS ABILITY TO USE PRAGMATIC RULES

As a way of summing up the perceptions I had of my development of pragmatic ability over the accelerated course, below I provide my own personal responses to the self-assessment questions presented as research questions and based on the Hudson, et al. (1995) scales.

Recognizing the sociocultural strategies needed in order to perform a given speech act

Over the semester, I developed some ability to perform speech acts, such as requesting, thanking, and apologizing. At times, however, the sociocultural patterns from other languages that I speak interfered with my performance in Japanese. For example, during paired drills in Lesson 2, the teacher was playing the role of a friend who found out that I was going to the post office and asked whether she could come along. The appropriate response would have been simply, "*Ee*" 'yes.' Instead, I said, "*Ee*" followed by "*ja*" 'well,' indicating that I was somewhat unwilling to have her go with me. When I said, "*Ee ja*," the class laughed because of the infraction both in meaning and in level of formality, so the teacher said her line again. Once again, as if on automatic, I repeated, "*Ee ja*," and again everyone laughed, this time a bit more. I actually had several non-native-like features in the same utterance. I was seemingly informal and a bit reluctant to have her accompany me. The vernacular expression for "OK, let's go" would most likely be "*Un, ja iko*," an expression that I did not know. In this drill, the textbook did not include an alternative form apart from *ee* 'yes,' as the signal for her to come along, such as *ikimasho* (*Ee, ikimasho* 'OK, let's go'). Then the *ja* was interference from several of my stronger foreign languages, where Spanish *ya* 'now, already' and Arabic/Hebrew *ya'ala* 'let's go' would be the next appropriate thing to say to indicating that we should get going. The interference was so strong that I did it a second time after public correction. It just came out automatically. It was not clear to me at that moment what I needed to say, and I certainly did not think that a simple "yes" was enough.

Another example involved an apology in a task where I was to supply a written version of what I would say in the given situation:

---

conversations with Japanese tourists in a way that is cross-culturally acceptable to the tourists. For example, students could conduct a mini-survey where each is given an official name tag, a survey-team title, and a clip board and sent out to collect data from tourists (D. Yoshimi, personal communication, February 19, 1997).

You have received a letter in Japanese. Interrupt your friend, and explain that because this has a lot of kanji, *you don't understand. Apologetically request that he or she read it to you.*

My reaction to this was that I did not have enough Japanese to do this properly. All I could think of for this situation was *sumimasen* 'excuse me' without any softeners except perhaps *chotto* 'just a little.' When I raised my hand and inquired, the teacher indicated that *sumimasen* was all that was expected. Thus, in this instance the Japanese speech act strategy actually paralleled that used in various other foreign languages that I speak. So in this case, I was avoiding transfer of the response strategy from another language out of a fear that I would probably be committing negative transfer if I did. My problem here was that I never really sorted out the difference in register between the language used in written tasks and oral tasks. Most of the tasks for homework were written memos to people rather than spoken requests. In cases where a written task was meant to simulate an oral one, the use of the written mode ruled out the use of facial expression mitigators, intonation mitigators (i.e., the way I said *sumimasen*), and silence/space mitigators.

Using the appropriate sociolinguistic expression

In completing the many worksheets assigned as homework (often involving the writing of memos to specified recipients), at times I had the uneasy feeling that the expressions which I was selecting were not the appropriate ones. When I spoke in class, if I simply mimicked the phrases appearing in the text, I could get by in a paired task but rarely felt that I had full control over choice of the appropriate phrase. For example, if I greeted my drill partner with *ogenki desuka?* (literally, 'how is your health?' but meaning 'how are you?'), I was not sure whether it was an acceptable utterance. My mind would question whether it was accurate enough in terms of content (i.e., whether it can be used on a daily basis or only if I haven't seen the person for some time) and level of formality (*ogenki* vs. *genki*) to be appropriate for use with a peer in an academic setting, as opposed to using a "safer" greeting relating to time of day, such as *ohayoo* 'good morning' or *ohayoo gozaimazu*, if I chose to be more formal.

Because I was operating from my rule base of Japanese usage rather than from any automatized or vernacular source, I did much better when I had plenty of time to sit and think about what to write than when I had to say the utterance rapidly under pressure in class, consistent with Tarone's Principle #4 as stated above. The notebook that I filled with handy grammar rules provided me relatively quick access at home to the rules so that I could, for instance, furnish the appropriate verb forms to go with clauses using connectors such as ~*node* 'because,' and ~*tara* 'when, if, after.'

With regard to the sequence for introducing myself or someone else to others of same status, lower status, or higher status (Lesson 1), I knew cognitively that these differences existed between Japanese and English. I did not foresee that the socially crucial speech act situation of making introductions would confuse and even intimidate me somewhat, especially when I was called upon to introduce a friend to a higher-status professor and to do it in a way that did not exalt the fellow student nor downgrade the professor. The following is a portion of my tape-recorded journal on the matter of introductions:

> In many cases, they seem to be the same after *hajimemashite* 'how do you do?' — *doozo yoroshiku* 'nice to meet you' and *kohen to mooshimasu* 'I'm Cohen.' But I guess there is a point at which the more elevated person says *doomo* 'hello,' thanking A for introducing B to him. So it's a bit complex. (9/4/96)

During the course, I found myself likely to be too formal with the equal status person and perhaps a bit too informal with the senior one. After the course was completed, I found that I had some of the vocabulary for introductions but that since it was some four months since the material had started, I had forgotten which forms to use with whom. It had become a hodgepodge in my mind.

Using the appropriate amount of speech and of information

I wanted to use more speech than Japanese do. It was not just the amount of speech but also the level of specificity. I wanted to be more specific, and reveal more about myself, my emotions, my desires, where it would appear that in Japanese culture more is left to be inferred or intuited. The Japanese language, however, had one built-in check against my being too verbose in conversation. I needed to think out my entire utterance in advance because since I was translating everything from English, I had to change the word and phrase order considerably. If I tried using an "on-line" approach to speaking Japanese (as I do with my other languages), rather than thinking out my utterance in advance, I would find that I frequently came to a place where I wanted to use an adverbial phrase or a clause (e.g., a clause using ~*node* or ~*kara* 'because') but by then it was too late to insert it. I soon learned why Japanese listeners would be unlikely to cut me off when I spoke, and would in fact give me extra time to finish my utterance — because they would often need to hear the end of the utterance to understand what I intended to say, especially since the verbs are placed at the end in most clauses.

Using the appropriate levels of formality (e.g., through word choice, phrasing, honorifics, and choice of verb forms)

We were introduced to irregular honorific (*keigo*) forms of the verb in Lesson 9 and regular ones in Lesson 10 (i.e., in the last month of the course). In the case of the irregular forms, there were totally different verbs for the same concepts — for example, *taberu* 'eat' became *meshiagaru* and *miru* 'look at' became *goran ni naru*. Once we learned these honorific forms, I expected that we would start to use them regularly in addressing the teacher. On several occasions we performed drills where we had to use the honorific form in asking her a series of questions. However, aside from those drills, we were not asked to do so. Although I achieved some control over the irregular and regular honorific verb forms, I did not acquire a good sense of when to use them, partly due to their limited use in the course. Although the teacher explicitly taught the rules for the use of honorific verb forms, I must admit that I did not learn to use these forms when speaking about a higher status person to an equal or lower status person, even when that higher status person was not present. I suppose that I was resisting this rule, since it seemed illogical to me. It also underscores the point that what is taught is not necessarily learned — that input is not necessarily converted automatically by the learner into intake. There may well be a screening out of some of the material, as in this case.

In the process of learning verb forms, I needed to learn the plain form, so I developed fairly reasonable control over the structure in isolation. However, I still did not have any real sense of when and how to use it other than some limited control of its required use in certain subordinate clauses such as with ~to 'if, when, whenever' and ~node 'because' clauses. Adding to my confusion was an interaction with the teacher which I recorded as follows in my journal:

> The professor pointed out that ohayoo 'good morning' was appropriate when talking down to a person of lower status. I asked him [my drill partner] where he was going and I said, Doko e ikimasuka? And then again it seemed simple [i.e., informal] to me but the teacher pointed out that the ~masu part in doko e ikimasuka? makes it more formal; iku no would be more informal. (9/11/96)

It was at this point that I became even more confused because I had thought the plain form of the verb would stand alone, and now saw that it was, in fact, modified through the use of some tag, whether no, ~nda, ~yo, or some other structure.

As of the middle of the course, the Drills book had examples that I noticed which contrasted the use of the formal and the plain forms of the verb. Here is a journal entry regarding contrasts of this type, where the use of the formal ~masu verb form wakarimasuka 'do you understand' was contrasted with the plain form, wakaru:

> ...a clear contrast in the textbook between more formal and less formal speech — asking a very close acquaintance as opposed to a friend for their phone number. Also, there's a contrast between formal and informal thanks. So one is pitted against the other. So whether I will remember to do this remains to be seen. (10/24/96)

In truth, I did not remember to make this specific contrast subsequently, perhaps in part due to the fact that I did not create opportunities for myself to use the plain form in contexts where it would be appropriate to do so.

Aside from some familiarity with levels of formality in the verb system, I also acquired some notion of terms to describe my own as opposed to someone else's family. However, much of what I was taught was not really learned and consequently has not been accessible. Given all the other material that I needed to learn, I found it burdensome to have to learn two forms of the same word — one to use when describing myself or my own family and another one in asking about someone else's family.

Using the appropriate degree of directness
(e.g., through verb forms or strategy choice)

I acquired some sense of how to address people without being too direct. By not using a pronoun but rather their name plus the polite suffix ~*san*, this already reminded me not to be direct, but my language skills at being indirect were limited. A good example of that came up during the oral midterm exam that I was permitted to take. Although I was supposed to be referring to the teacher in the role play as *Yamadasan* 'Ms. Yamada,' I kept avoiding doing so. I wanted to use *anata* 'you' a number of times, even though I was informed by the teacher and by the textbook that it was inappropriate in many contexts to use the direct pronominal form in Japanese. So, instead of saying *anata* and in place of what seemed to be the overly indirect form, *Yamadasan*, I ended up not saying anything, which must have seemed a bit peculiar to the teacher. This was a case of my avoiding negative transfer with the cost being that my already slow speech got slower and the gaps in my speaking became more pronounced.

Using the appropriate degree of politeness through politeness markers
(e.g., "thank you," "please," "if you don't mind")
as well as through appropriate levels of formality and directness

I learned a few politeness markers and mitigators but came away from the course unsure when to use one or the other. For example, whereas there are two forms of "please," *onegai shimasu* and ~*kudasai*, I was not able to arrive at a working distinction between them, partly because at times there is no distinction. Several times when I used ~*kudasai* in class or on worksheets, however, I was corrected and informed that I needed to use *onegai shimasu* instead. I never pursued this point to determine what rule governed the differential use. The teacher later informed me that *onegai shimasu* would be more appropriate if the addressee were of higher status.

THE ROLE THAT EXPLICIT INFORMATION ABOUT PRAGMATIC FACTS PLAYED IN MY LANGUAGE LEARNING — THE EXTENT TO WHICH THE TEACHER, THE TEXTBOOK, OTHER STUDENTS, NATIVES IN THE ENVIRONMENT, OR OTHERS PROVIDED THIS INFORMATION

The teacher provided numerous pragmatic facts, as did the textbook. From time to time, I also elicited from her other facts or fine tuning regarding the ones we had been given. For example, I once asked in class about the extent to which Japanese speakers actually use all of the foreign words that we were being drilled on through *katakana*, since there exists amongst speakers of other languages (such as Hebrew) a desire to resist using the foreign loanword if at all possible. The teacher's response was that the Japanese do, in fact, use these loanwords a good deal. I also received several pieces of corrective feedback from one of the students who had already taken a first-year course at a community college and had been in a sales position where she had used Japanese with customers. For example, I referred to "my family" as *watashi no kazoku* and my fellow student corrected me that since *kazoku* was only used by the speaker in referring to his or her family, it was redundant to say *watashi no kazoku*, that just *kazoku* was enough.

THE EXTENT TO WHICH THE SOCIAL CONTEXT CONTRIBUTES TO PRAGMATIC SUCCESS

Since my social context was restricted primarily to the language classroom, it was the teacher who created it for me. She had her hands full with our intensive course. She was speeding through a curriculum that was prescribed by the department, and she needed to move through it in one semester rather than two. For each lesson we saw an accompanying videotaped segment on the dialogue from that lesson.[12] Several times we saw other videotapes in Japanese, English, or both, with the focus on cultural content. But for the most part, the social context was that of a language lesson with the teacher in charge, running down a list of language teaching activities, and orchestrating what we said, when, to whom, and why. Since my exposure to naturalistic data (through native speakers, TV shows, and so forth) was limited, I did not perceive that I had any "feel" for what sounded good in the language to fall back on when I wanted to check if my pragmatic choices were correct. I was largely limited to the phrases that I had either memorized from the textbook or handouts in advance, or read out from the Drills book.

THE RELATIONSHIP BETWEEN THE LEARNER'S MOTIVATION, LEARNING STYLE, AND LEARNING STRATEGY PREFERENCES AND THE ACQUISITION OF PRAGMATIC ABILITY

I was clearly motivated to learn Japanese and to learn the appropriate pragmatic structures. I did all the homework assigned, so this included the tasks which provided pragmatic information. The instructional program had built-in limits with regard to my pragmatic development in that it was offered in an academic setting where Japanese was taught as a foreign language, removed from direct contact with native speakers and their culture. One of the areas in which I fell short was in not getting the maximum out of the audiotapes that accompanied each of the twelve lessons. My sense was that while the speakers on the tapes delivered their lines authentically, the pace was sometimes too rapid for my untrained ear. For most tasks, I had to listen repeatedly to the same utterances and then check what was written in the Drills textbook as well. Consequently, as mentioned above, the tasks would lapse more into exercises in reading comprehension than in listening comprehension, as intended, so that unfortunately I began to rely more on my eyes than on my ears. The effect was that the exercises did not work to benefit my listening comprehension and the reading of the structures, especially if I had to recite them aloud,[13] did not fix them in my memory.

---

[12] While it may have been helpful to have had ready access to a copy of those videotapes and to have been able to play them over a few times, there were apparently copyright restrictions on making the videotapes available to students.

[13] After an initial recoding phase where the teacher is checking for sound-symbol correspondence, oral recitation of reading comprehension texts is likely to serve less as an

When the teacher would give presentations about Japanese structure, discuss course logistics, or provide instructions about current or future tasks, these interventions were partly or totally in English. Thus, somewhat to my surprise, I found myself not making an effort to understand the Japanese that she might use in these situations because I knew that she would most likely repeat what she had said a second time in English. Consequently, I was behaving in a way similar to the native English speakers in the concurrent bilingual education classrooms in Redwood City, California (Cohen, 1975) who used to (and perhaps still do) wait for the teacher's message to come along again in their dominant language rather than making the effort to understand it in their weaker language. There was a week or so in which the teacher used primarily Japanese in class, in response to a discussion that the two of us had. In reality, I was not listening in a way that enabled me to follow much of what she said, so her return to alternating between Japanese and English improved my sense of security in class, although it provided me less exposure to teacher talk, which would at times include the vernacular (e.g., if the teacher was recounting an anecdote).

With regard to learning styles, I was willing to be flexible in my learning style choices in order to conform with the method. Hence, I embraced an analytical style in order to cope with the numerous grammatical structures that I encountered. I also used a host of language learning and use strategies. Among the vocabulary learning strategies, I used the *mnemonic keyword technique* repeatedly, that is, linking a native-language or other-language word or phrase similar in sound to part or all of the target-language word, as well as an image of the keyword "interacting" with the native-language word or phrase. I would not have survived without using the mnemonic keyword device. For example, in order to learn *jidohanbaiki* 'vending machine,' I thought of using judo to get my money back from the vending machine, and if that did not work then using my hand by means of a key. This keyword phrase worked both in helping me identify the meaning of *jidohanbaiki* when I encountered it orally or in writing, and also in production when I had to say or write it. As another example, I learned *shukudai* 'homework' by means of a Hebrew mnemonic keyword phrase using *shuk* 'market' and *dai* 'enough.' I thought of being assigned enough (i.e., so much) homework that I did not have time to go to the shuk.

DISCUSSION AND CONCLUSIONS

It can be seen that the social context in which I, as an older adult language learner, found myself, namely, an academic setting, was conducive to the successful learning of grammatical structures, some grammar rules, literacy skills, vocabulary, and the

---

exercise in comprehension and more as an oral performance where at times little of the text may be understood by the reader and where other learners may tune out, especially if it is read poorly. Such exercises use up class time and may be counter-productive. Oral reading by the teacher with the students just listening may be a more effective instructional tool.

ability to engage in basic conversation. According to the standards set by the Japanese instructional unit, I succeeded at learning the material in their course. In effect, I had become socialized into the culture of rote mastery learning well enough to succeed at it (cf. Lim, 1996, for an empirical study on this form of instruction). The question that needs to be raised concerns the depth and durability of that learning. Let me return to the four principles now, relating them to my own language experience in summary fashion.

Consistent with Principle #1, I learned a lot of linguistic information about Japanese but did not perceive myself as acquiring much language at an automatized level, which inhibited me in my limited efforts to have conversations with Japanese tourists in Waikiki. Consistent with Principle #2, I did find myself constantly monitoring my language behavior in the classroom over the 140 hours of instruction, and it was tiring at times. In addition, the payoff for so much effort may have been short-lived. With regard to Principle #3, I found the focus on the transmission of short segments primarily in order to practice structures did not give me much practice communicating information in full. Without this practice, I was not comfortable enough in communicative situations to be motivated to try out my language knowledge in such contexts. In addition, the focus on form made me self-conscious about the non-native-like forms that I was bound to use in attempting to speak. Although it is perfectly normal to have interlanguage grammar and lexicon, in this type of structure-oriented classroom I found myself feeling guilty about the fact that I had an interlanguage grammar and not a target-language one.

Consistent with Principle #4, not only was my vernacular or automatized rule system small at the end of the course, but given the considerable attrition that I experienced over the semester break, it became even smaller. In addition, efforts at using Japanese required me to access specific linguistic structures, which in turn called for a good deal of attention to form, memorization, and monitoring. This material attrited even more quickly — that is, the material that I had, in fact, stored in long-term memory. For example, we were taught in Lesson 8 how to warn people about doing things that were prohibited. At the beginning of February, I was at the top of the Haleakala volcano in Maui and wanted to tell a Japanese tourist that it was against park rules for his two friends to hike off the trail. There were signs in English posted everywhere. I could not remember how to convey the notion of "prohibited," and kept saying *iie* 'no' and *michi dake* 'only the road' (intending to say that his friends had to stay on the designated trails). What I said was clearly incomprehensible to him, given his response. So my experience in this, and in other situations, was consistent with the principles posited by Tarone. I wonder how many other learners going through the type of instructional program described above have a somewhat or largely similar experience.

As with any qualitative study, there is a need to mention a series of limitations. First and foremost, this was the experience of a single adult learner, going through an intensive as opposed to a regular course, and experiencing the instructional approach of only one teacher from the instructional staff. In addition, the language was a very difficult one for an English speaker to learn, and one that was distinct from any others that the learner had encountered.

With regard to other limitations, although the unit had a series of standard operating principles, there were undoubtedly differences in interpretation of these principles, depending on the individual teacher. Hence, my experience in this one accelerated course offering by the Japanese teaching unit may not be similar to that of learners in other classes in the same teaching unit or even to other learners in the same class. Furthermore, it would be unrealistic to have expected my classroom teacher to have expended greater effort in providing me more exposure to the vernacular. Just as Tarone and Swain (1995, p. 174) concluded with respect to the teaching of the vernacular in French immersion classrooms, it would be highly unrealistic to expect extended coverage of vernacular structures even in the most intensive of classroom contexts.

With regard to other limitations with the study, it needs to be stressed that the course was not intended as a single, terminal Japanese learning experience, but rather as the first in at least a two-year sequence. Students were expected to be aiming at fulfilling the two-year obligatory language requirement by starting with this course and then continuing on afterwards. Hence, the next two semesters of Japanese would be intended to help solidify the vocabulary and structures that they were exposed to in the accelerated first-year course. Unfortunately I was not able to continue studying in the program in order to determine the extent to which subsequent instruction provided that type of reinforcement, as opposed to being more of the same type of instruction as described above.

In retrospect, I did not attain adequate pragmatic control to be able to investigate at a more finely-tuned level the degree of control that I had over a number of, for example, speech acts such as requesting, apologizing, and even complaining, as I have been able to do with other languages, such as Hebrew. All the same, I took on the study of Japanese expressly because I knew from time spent in Japan and from the literature that speakers of Japanese might vary greatly both socioculturally and sociolinguistically from English or Hebrew speakers in their pragmatic behavior. For example, it may be that a Japanese speaker would avoid performing the speech act of complaining in a given sociocultural situation (e.g., discontentment with a given policy at a public bath house), but even if they did perform the same speech act as Westerners would (e.g., acknowledging their hosts at the end of a home-cooked meal), they might use sociolinguistic forms that are different from those used by English or Hebrew speakers (e.g., seemingly apologizing to their hosts at the end of a meal) (Cohen, 1996b).

In closing, the field of second language acquisition can benefit from more learner descriptions of their classroom and concurrent out-of-class experiences, such as that by Schmidt and Frota (1986), and those with a more narrow focus, such as the study reported here. It would be beneficial if more learners were to do case studies of themselves as learners in different social situations in the classroom since this is a social context — however rarefied — and one that many foreign language learners find themselves in most of the time while in high school and even in college (except in the case of study abroad programs; see Freed, 1995. There are probably numerous learners like myself, who although having the possibility of contact with unlimited numbers of native speakers of the language that they are learning, rarely venture out of the classroom in order to use the language that they are learning and provide themselves with only limited exposure to the vernacular for the duration of the course or courses.

Acknowledgments

I would like to thank the faculty of the Department of East Asian Languages & Literatures at the University of Hawai'i at Mānoa for allowing me to study Japanese in their program. I would especially like to thank the teacher, Kathy Kitsutani, for permitting me to be a sit-in audit and for treating me just like a regular student. I would also like to thank the students in the course for allowing me to be in their midst. It was a most stimulating and rewarding experience. In addition, I wish to acknowledge the Department of English as a Second Language at the University of Hawai'i for accepting me as a visiting scholar during the 1996–97 academic year, enabling me to be a full-time audit in the Japanese language class. I would also like to acknowledge the input that I received on earlier drafts of this paper from Elaine Tarone, Dina Yoshimi, Haruko M. Cook, Leslie Beebe, Dick Schmidt, Mika Kirimura, Megumi Matsuoka, and Midori Furukawa. A special debt of gratitude goes to Kathy Kitsutani for discussing the paper with me at length.

REFERENCES

Chaudron, C. (1988). *Second language classrooms: Research on teaching and learning.* Cambridge: Cambridge University Press.

Cohen, A. D. (1975). *A sociolinguistic approach to bilingual education: Experiments in the American Southwest.* Rowley, MA: Newbury House.

Cohen, A. D. (1996a). Developing the ability to perform speech acts. *Studies in Second Language Acquisition, 18,* 253–267.

Cohen, A. D. (1996b). Speech acts. In S. L. McKay & N. H. Hornberger (Eds.), *Sociolinguistics and language teaching* (pp. 383–420). Cambridge: Cambridge University Press.

Cohen, A. D., & Hawras, S. (1996). Mental translation into the first language during foreign-language reading. *The Language Teacher, 20,* 6–12.

Cohen, A. D., & Robbins, M. (1976). Toward assessing interlanguage performance: The relationship between selected errors, learners' characteristics, and the learners' explanations. *Language Learning, 26,* 45- 66.

Ehrman, M. E. (1996). *Understanding second language learning difficulties.* Thousand Oaks, CA: Sage Publications.

Freed, B. (Ed.) (1995). *Second language acquisition in a study abroad context.* Amsterdam/Philadelphia: John Benjamins.

Hawras, S. (1996). *Towards describing bilingual and multilingual behavior: Implications for ESL instruction.* Minneapolis: Double Plan B Paper, English as a Second Language Department, University of Minnesota.

Hosenfeld, C. (1976). Learning about learning: Discovering our students' strategies. *Foreign Language Annals, 9*, 117–129.

Hudson, T., Detmer, E., & Brown, J. D. (1995). *Developing prototypic measures of cross-cultural pragmatics.* Technical Report 7. Honolulu, HI: Second Language Teaching & Curriculum Center, University of Hawai'i.

Kasper, G., & Schmidt, R. (1996). Developmental issues in interlanguage pragmatics. *Studies in Second Language Acquisition, 18*, 149–169.

Kern, R. G. (1994). The role of mental translation in second language reading. *Studies in Second Language Acquisition, 16*, 441–461.

Leeman, J. A., Arteagoitia, J., Fridman, B., & Doughty, C. (1995). Integrating attention to form with meaning: Focus on form in content-based Spanish instruction. In Schmidt, R. (Ed.), *Attention and awareness in foreign language learning* (pp. 217–258). Technical Report 9. Honolulu, HI: Second Language Teaching & Curriculum Center, University of Hawai'i.

Lew, M. A. (1996). *In Tokyo, don't always do as they do: Foreigners' fluency in Japanese snubbed.* Chicago Tribune (November 27, 1996).

Lim, D. S. J. (1996). *Cross-cultural instruction and classroom discourse: A study of the foreign language classroom culture.* Unpublished masters of arts thesis, Department of East Asian Languages and Literature, University of Hawai'i at Mānoa.

McLaughlin, B. (1990). Restructuring. *Applied Linguistics, 11*, 113–128 .

Myers, I. B., & Briggs, K. (1976). *The Myers-Briggs Type Indicator, Form G.* Palo Alto, CA: Consulting Psychologists.

Norton, R. W. (1975). Measurement of ambiguity tolerance. *Journal of Personality Assessment, 39*, 607–619.

Oltman, P. K., Raskin, E., & Witkin, H. A. (1971). *Group Embedded Figures Test.* Palo Alto, CA: Consulting Psychologists.

Pavlidis, M. (1990). *Reading strategies of second-language learners of Chinese.* Unpublished masters of arts thesis, Department of Linguistics and Language Studies, University of Melbourne.

Roberts, M. A. (1996). Awareness and the efficacy of error correction. In Schmidt, R. (Ed.), *Attention and awareness in foreign language learning* (pp. 163- 182). Technical Report 9. Honolulu, HI: Second Language Teaching & Curriculum Center, University of Hawai'i.

Schmidt, R. W., & Frota, S. N. (1986). Developing basic conversational ability in a second language: A case study of an adult learner of Portuguese. In R. R. Day (Ed.), *Talking to learn: Conversation in second language acquisition* (pp. 237–326). Rowley, MA: Newbury House.

Stronach, B. (1995). *Beyond the rising sun: Nationalism in contemporary Japan.* Westport, CT: Praeger.

Tarone, E. (in press). Analyzing IL in natural settings: A sociolinguistic perspective on second-language acquisition. *Culture and Cognition.*

Tarone, E., & Swain, M. (1995). A sociolinguistic perspective on second-language use in immersion classrooms. *Modern Language Journal, 79*, 166–178.

Truscott, J. (1966). The case against grammar correction in L2 writing class. *Language Learning, 46*, 327–369.

Tsukuba Language Group. (1991). *Situational Functional Japanese, Volume 1, Notes and Drills* [two separate books]. Tokyo: Bonjinsha Co.

Tsukuba Language Group. (1991). *Situational Functional Japanese, Volume 2, Notes and Drills* [two separate books]. Tokyo: Bonjinsha Co.

Widdowson, H. G. (1978). *Teaching languages as communication.* Oxford: University Press.

Yamashita, S. O. (1996). *Six measures of JSL pragmatics.* Technical Report 14. Honolulu, HI: Second Language Teaching & Curriculum Center, University of Hawai'i.

Yule, G. (1996). *Pragmatics.* Oxford: Oxford University Press

ABOUT THE AUTHORS AND HOW TO CONTACT THEM

THE EDITORS

Haruko Minegishi Cook is an associate professor of Japanese at the University of Hawai'i at Mānoa. She earned her Ph.D. in Linguistics at the University of Southern California in 1988. Between 1978 and 1984, she taught Japanese at universities in Southern California. Her main research interests include language socialization, discourse analysis, and pragmatics. She has published articles on the Japanese sentence-final particles and addressee honorifics from the point of view of indexicality. Currently, she is working on indexicality and language socialization at home and in schools.

Kyoko Hijirida is a professor of Japanese at the Department of East Asian Languages and Literatures, University of Hawai'i, where she teaches Japanese, conducts a teaching practicum, and is developing a textbook for teacher training. She received her M.A. and Ed.D. from the University of Hawai'i. Her publications include articles and books on Japanese language and culture, pedagogy, and curriculum development. She has served as President of the Hawai'i Association of Language Teachers and the Hawai'i Association of Teachers of Japanese. She is a newly elected Board member of the Association of Teachers of Japanese. She has received teaching awards from both the University and the Hawai'i Association of Language Teachers.

Mildred M. Tahara, an associate professor of Japanese Literature in the East Asian Languages and Literatures Department, University of Hawai'i at Mānoa, received her Ph.D. from Columbia University in 1970. Her study and translation of *Yamato monogatari* (*Tales of Yamato*) was published by the University of Hawai'i Press in 1980. She is also the translator of *Kokotsu no hito* (*The Twilight Years*), *Kinokawa* (*The River Ki*), and *Kazunomiyasama otome* (*Her Highness Princess Kazu*) by the Japanese woman writer Ariyoshi Sawako (1931–1984). In recent years she has been focusing on the classical court poetry of the tenth through thirteenth centuries, with a special interest in imperial anthologies, and image and text.

THE AUTHORS

Yukie Aida (Ph.D., 1988, University of Texas at Austin) is a lecturer in the Department of Asian Studies, University of Texas at Austin. She teaches second-year Japanese I and II and third-year Advanced Conversation. Her interest in technology integration into the curriculum started in 1994 when she received a Project Quest award from the UT Computation Center. Two of her articles on computer activities in the classrooms appeared in *Virtual Connection* (Technical Report #8 in this series). Her research interests include a multivariate study of learner variables (motivation, anxiety, self-esteem, and attributional styles) on language learning, and the use of language learning strategies and styles among students of Japanese.

of the National Language Research Institute. She has published a textbook for Japanese and articles on applied linguistics and Japanese language teaching. She

Andrew Cohen is a professor of Applied Linguistics in the Institute of Linguistics and Asian and Slavic Languages and Literatures, and the director of the National Language Resource Center, University of Minnesota, Minneapolis. He is also Secretary General of the International Association of Applied Linguistics (AILA). Professor Cohen has published books and articles on bilingual and immersion education, language learning strategies, and language testing.

Naoya Fujita is an assistant professor of Japanese and Linguistics at Pacific University, Oregon. He has published a number of articles on Japanese syntax and language teaching. He received his Ph.D. in Linguistics from the University of Rochester, New York. His current research interests are Japanese syntax and morphology, and integration of theoretical Japanese linguistics into language teaching.

Elaine Gerbert received her Ph.D. in Japanese Literature from Yale University in 1990 and is currently an associate professor in the Department of East Asian Languages and Cultures at the University of Kansas. Her interests lie in the intersection between literary and anthropological studies and in the literary and artistic aspects of Japanese modernism. Recent articles include "The Suwa Pillar Festival Revisited" (*Harvard Journal of Asiatic Studies*, December 1996) and an introductory essay on Satō Haruo in *Beautiful Town, Stories and Essays by Satō Haruo*, translated by Frances Tenny (University of Hawai'i Press, 1996) She has translated works by Uno Koji ("Love of Mountains," University of Hawai'i Press, 1997) and is currently working on a book on Uno.

Yukiko Abe Hatasa is a senior lecturer of Japanese at Monash University and an assistant professor and coordinator of Japanese at the University of Iowa. She received her Ph.D. in Linguistics at the University of Illinois at Urbana-Champaign in 1992. Her resech involves language processing, second language acquisition of Japanese, and Japanese pedagogy. She has published articles in various journals and books including "Investigating the validity and reliability of native speaker and L2 learner judgments about sentences" in *Research Methodology in Second Language Acquisition* (Gass, S., Cohen, A., and Tarone, E. [Eds.]). She co-authored with S. Makino and K. Hatasa the beginning level Japanese textbook *Nakama: Communication, Culture, Context* (Volume 1; forthcoming) as well as an intermediate reader, *Dokkai: Kakudai Bunsetsu no Ninchi*, with S. Makino.

Nobuko Miyama Ochner (Ph.D. 1984, University of Hawai'i) is currently an associate professor of Japanese at the Department of East Asian Languages and Literatures, University of Hawai'i at Mānoa. Her area of specialization is modern Japanese literature, particularly fiction of the first half of the twentieth century. With Jean Yamasaki Toyama she has co-edited a volume entitled *Literary Relations East and West: Selected Essays* (1990), published by the College of Languages, Linguistics and Literature, University of Hawai'i, and the such collections as, *Contact Between Cultures, Vol. 3: Eastern Asia: Literature and Humanities* (1992, B. H. Luk and B. D. Steben [Eds.]), *Translations/Transformations: Gender and Culture in Film and Literature East and West* (1993, V. Wayne and C. Moore [Eds.]), and *Self as Image in Asian Theory and Practice* (1996, W. Dissanayake et al. [Eds.]).

Yoko Okita is a lecturer in Japanese in the Department of Asian Studies at the University of Texas at Austin. She received her Ph.D. in East Asian Languages and Literatures (Japanese) from the University of Hawai'i. Her interests include psycho- and neurolinguistic aspects of reading and learning Japanese, and computer-assisted language learning. Her current research and publications focus on individual differences in *kanji* learning processes.

Hideko Shimizu is a native of Japan who studied literature at Keio University before going on to earn her baccalaureate in psychology from the University of Colorado at Denver in 1983. She then returned to Japan as a graduate research student at Keio University where she studied socio- and psycholinguistics under Dr. Takao Suzuki (author of *Japanese and the Japanese: Words in Culture*, 1978, Tokyo: Kodansha International) and Dr. Takaaki Koyazu, a professor of cognitive psychology specializing in psycholinguistics and memory. She has collaborated on several cross-cultural research studies which examined American, Japanese, and German perspectives on success, responsibility, and interpersonal relations. Her dual interest in literature and gender issues took her to the Tokyo campus of Philadelphia's Temple University to study the role and perspective of women in Japanese literature of the Heian era. She earned her M.A. in Curriculum and Supervision from the University of Colorado at Denver in 1994. She is currently completing her doctoral studies in multicultural education and second language acquisition at the University of Denver. Professionally, she has taught a variety of courses in Japanese language and culture and English as a foreign language at Teikyo University (Tokyo), University College (Denver) the University of Denver and in public school systems in Colorado.

Yasu-Hiko Tohsaku is an associate professor at the Graduate School of International Relations and Pacific Studies, University of California, San Diego, where he is the director of the school's Language Program and Japanese Studies Language Program. He has published *Yookoso!: An Invitation to Contemporary Japanese* and *Yookoso!: Continuing with Contemporary Japanese* (both from McGraw-Hill) as well as papers on language pedagogy and language acquisition. He is currently the chair of the California Japanese Framework Project. He received his Ph.D. in Linguistics from University of California, San Diego. His areas of research are language pedagogy, second language reading, and the effect of instruction on Japanese language acquisition.

Sayoko Okada Yamashita is currently teaching Japanese as a second language in the Division of Languages at International Christian University and the teaching practicum for the Labo International Foundation. She has also been developing audiovisual materials for language teaching as a committee member

East-West Center. Her articles on Nakajima Atsushi and Satō Haruo appeared in the academic journals *Monumenta Nipponica* and *Journal of the Association of Teachers of Japanese*. Her publications also include articles on Akutagawa Ryūnosuke, Kawabata Yasunari, Nakajima Atsushi, and Tanizaki Jun'ichirō in received her Ed.D. from Temple University. Her current research interest is in the testing of pragmatics.

SLTCC

TECHNICAL REPORTS

The Technical Reports of the Second Language Teaching and Curriculum Center
at the University of Hawai'i (SLTCC) report on ongoing curriculum projects,
provide the results of research related to second language learning and teaching,
and also include extensive related bibliographies. SLTCC Technical Reports are available
through University of Hawai'i Press.

RESEARCH METHODS IN INTERLANGUAGE PRAGMATICS

GABRIELE KASPER
MERETE DAHL

This technical report reviews the methods of data collection employed in 39 studies of interlanguage pragmatics, defined narrowly as the investigation of nonnative speakers' comprehension and production of speech acts, and the acquisition of L2-related speech act knowledge. Data collection instruments are distinguished according to the degree to which they constrain informants' responses, and whether they tap speech act perception/comprehension or production. A main focus of discussion is the validity of different types of data, in particular their adequacy to approximate authentic performance of linguistic action. 51 pp.

(SLTCC Technical Report #1) ISBN 0–8248–1419–3 $10.

A FRAMEWORK FOR TESTING CROSS-CULTURAL PRAGMATICS

THOM HUDSON
EMILY DETMER
J. D. BROWN

This technical report presents a framework for developing methods that assess cross-cultural pragmatic ability. Although the framework has been designed for Japanese and American cross-cultural contrasts, it can serve as a generic approach that can be applied to other language contrasts. The focus is on the variables of social distance, relative power, and the degree of imposition within the speech acts of requests, refusals, and apologies. Evaluation of performance is based on recognition of the speech act, amount of speech, forms or formulæ used, directness, formality, and politeness. 51 pp.

(SLTCC Technical Report #2) ISBN 0–8248–1463–0 $10.

PRAGMATICS OF JAPANESE AS NATIVE AND TARGET LANGUAGE

GABRIELE KASPER
(*Editor*)

This technical report includes three contributions to the study of the pragmatics of Japanese:

- A bibliography on speech act performance, discourse management, and other pragmatic and sociolinguistic features of Japanese;
- A study on introspective methods in examining Japanese learners' performance of refusals;
- A longitudinal investigation of the acquisition of the particle *ne* by nonnative speakers of Japanese.

125 pp.

(SLTCC Technical Report #3) ISBN 0–8248–1462–2 $10.

A BIBLIOGRAPHY OF PEDAGOGY & RESEARCH IN INTERPRETATION & TRANSLATION

ETILVIA ARJONA

This technical report includes four types of bibliographic information on translation and interpretation studies:

- Research efforts across disciplinary boundaries: cognitive psychology, neurolinguistics, psycholinguistics, sociolinguistics, computational linguistics, measurement, aptitude testing, language policy, decision-making, theses, dissertations;
- Training information covering: program design, curriculum studies, instruction, school administration;
- Instruction information detailing: course syllabi, methodology, models, available textbooks;
- Testing information about aptitude, selection, diagnostic tests.

115 pp.

(SLTCC Technical Report #4) ISBN 0–8248–1572–6 $10.

PRAGMATICS OF CHINESE AS NATIVE AND TARGET LANGUAGE

GABRIELE KASPER
(*Editor*)

This technical report includes six contributions to the study of the pragmatics of Mandarin Chinese:

- A report of an interview study conducted with nonnative speakers of Chinese;
- Five data-based studies on the performance of different speech acts by native speakers of Mandarin: requesting, refusing, complaining, giving bad news, disagreeing, and complimenting.

312 pp.

(SLTCC Technical Report #5) ISBN 0–8248–1733–8 $15.

THE ROLE OF PHONOLOGICAL CODING IN READING *KANJI*

SACHIKO MATSUNAGA

In this technical report the author reports the results of a study that she conducted on phonological coding in reading *kanji* using an eye-movement monitor and draws some pedagogical implications. In addition, she reviews current literature on the different schools of thought regarding instruction in reading *kanji* and its role in the teaching of non-alphabetic written languages like Japanese. 64 pp.

(SLTCC Technical Report #6) ISBN 0–8248–1734–6 $10.

DEVELOPING PROTOTYPIC MEASURES OF CROSS-CULTURAL PRAGMATICS

THOM HUDSON
EMILY DETMER
J. D. BROWN

Although the study of cross-cultural pragmatics has gained importance in applied linguistics, there are no standard forms of assessment that might make research comparable across studies and languages. The present volume describes the process through which six forms of cross-cultural assessment were developed for second language learners of English. The models may be used for second language learners of other languages. The six forms of assessment involve two forms each of indirect discourse completion tests, oral language production, and self assessment. The procedures involve the assessment of requests, apologies, and refusals. 198 pp.

(SLTCC Technical Report #7) ISBN 0–8248–1763–X $15.

VIRTUAL CONNECTIONS: ONLINE ACTIVITIES & PROJECTS FOR NETWORKING LANGUAGE LEARNERS

MARK WARSCHAUER
(Editor)

Computer networking has created dramatic new possibilities for connecting language learners in a single classroom or across the globe. This collection of activities and projects makes use of e-mail, the World Wide Web, computer conferencing, and other forms of computer-mediated communication for the foreign and second language classroom at any level of instruction. Teachers from around the world submitted the activities compiled in this volume — activities that they have used successfully in their own classrooms. 417 pp.

(SLTCC Technical Report #8) ISBN 0–8248–1793–1 $30.

ATTENTION & AWARENESS IN FOREIGN LANGUAGE LEARNING

RICHARD SCHMIDT
(Editor)

Issues related to the role of attention and awareness in learning lie at the heart of many theoretical and practical controversies in the foreign language field. This collection of papers presents research into the learning of Spanish, Japanese, Finnish, Hawaiian, and English as a second language (with additional comments and examples from French, German, and miniature artificial languages) that bear on these crucial questions for foreign language pedagogy. 394 pp.

(SLTCC Technical Report #9) ISBN 0–8248–1794–X $20.

LINGUISTICS AND LANGUAGE TEACHING: PROCEEDINGS OF THE SIXTH JOINT LSH-HATESL CONFERENCE

C. REVES,
C. STEELE,
C. S. P. WONG
(Editors)

Technical Report #10 contains 18 articles revolving around the following three topics:

- Linguistic issues: These six papers discuss various linguistics issues: ideophones, syllabic nasals, linguistic areas, computation, tonal melody classification, and *wh*-words.
- Sociolinguistics: Sociolinguistic phenomena in Swahili, signing, Hawaiian, and Japanese are discussed in four of the papers.
- Language teaching and learning: These eight papers cover prosodic modification, note taking, planning in oral production, oral testing, language policy, L2 essay organization, access to dative alternation rules, and child noun phrase structure development.

364 pp.

(SLTCC Technical Report #10) ISBN 0–8248–1851–2 $20.

LANGUAGE LEARNING MOTIVATION: PATHWAYS TO THE NEW CENTURY

REBECCA L. OXFORD
(Editor)

This volume chronicles a revolution in our thinking about what makes students want to learn languages and what causes them to persist in that difficult and rewarding adventure. Topics in this book include the internal structures of and external connections with foreign language motivation; exploring adult language learning motivation, self-efficacy, and anxiety; comparing the motivations and learning strategies of students of Japanese and Spanish; and enhancing the theory of language learning motivation from many psychological and social perspectives. 218 pp.

(SLTCC Technical Report #11) ISBN 0–8248–1849–0 $20.

TELECOLLABORATION IN FOREIGN LANGUAGE LEARNING: PROCEEDINGS OF THE HAWAI'I SYMPOSIUM

MARK WARSCHAUER
(Editor)

The Symposium on Local & Global Electronic Networking in Foreign Language Learning & Research, part of the National Foreign Language Resource Center's *1995 Summer Institute on Technology & the Human Factor in Foreign Language Education* included presentations of papers and hands-on workshops conducted by Symposium participants to facilitate the sharing of resources, ideas, and information about all aspects of electronic networking for foreign language teaching and research, including electronic discussion and conferencing, international cultural exchanges, real-time communication and simulations, research and resource retrieval via the Internet, and research using networks. This collection presents a sampling of those presentations. 252 p.

(SLTCC Technical Report #12) ISBN 0–8248–1867–9 $20.

LANGUAGE LEARNING STRATEGIES AROUND THE WORLD: CROSS-CULTURAL PERSPECTIVES

REBECCA L. OXFORD
(Editor)

Language learning strategies are the specific steps students take to improve their progress in learning a second or foreign language. Optimizing learning strategies improves language performance. This ground-breaking book presents new information about cultural influences on the use of language learning strategies. It also shows innovative ways to assess students' strategy use and remarkable techniques for helping students improve their choice of strategies, with the goal of peak language learning. 166 pp.

(SLTCC Technical Report #13) ISBN 0–8248–1910–1 $20.

SIX MEASURES OF JSL PRAGMATICS

SAYOKO OKADA YAMASHITA

This book investigates differences among tests that can be used to measure the cross-cultural pragmatic ability of English speaking learners of Japanese. Building on the work of Hudson, Detmer, and Brown (Technical Reports #2 and #7 in this series), the author modified six test types which she used to gather data from North American learners of Japanese. She found numerous problems with the multiple-choice discourse completion test but reported that the other five tests all proved highly reliable and reasonably valid. Practical issues involved in creating and using such language tests are discussed from a variety of perspectives. 213 pp.

(SLTCC Technical Report #14) ISBN 0–8248–1914–4 $15.

NEW TRENDS & ISSUES IN TEACHING JAPANESE LANGUAGE & CULTURE

HARUKO M. COOK,
KYOKO HIJIRIDA,
& MILDRED TAHARA
(Editors)

In recent years, Japanese has become the fourth most commonly taught foreign language at the college level in the United States. As the number of students who study Japanese has increased, the teaching of Japanese as a foreign language has been established as an important academic field of study. This technical report includes nine contributions to the advancement of this field, encompassing the following five important issues:

- Literature and literature teaching
- Technology in language classroom
- Orthography
- Testing
- Grammatical vs. pragmatic approaches to language teaching

(SLTCC Technical Report #15) ISBN 0–8248–2067–3 $15.